National Curriculum Assessment

RY

)

National Curriculum Assessment
A Review of Policy 1987–1994

Richard Daugherty

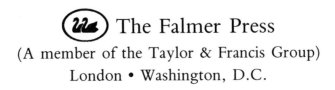 The Falmer Press
(A member of the Taylor & Francis Group)
London • Washington, D.C.

UK	The Falmer Press, 4 John Street, London WC1N 2ET
USA	The Falmer Press, Taylor & Francis Inc., 1900 Frost Road, Suite 101, Bristol, PA 19007

First published in 1995

A catalogue record for this book is available from the British Library

Library of Congress Cataloging-in-Publication Data are available on request

ISBN 0 7507 0254 0 cased
ISBN 0 7507 0255 9 paper

Jacket design by Caroline Archer

Typeset in 10/11.5pt Bembo
Graphicraft Typesetters Ltd., Hong Kong.

Printed in Great Britain by Burgess Science Press, Basingstoke on paper which has a specified pH value on final paper manufacture of not less than 7.5 and is therefore 'acid free'.

Contents

Abbreviations

ACAC	Curriculum and Assessment Authority for Wales (from April 1994)
AMMA	Assistant Masters and Mistresses Association (to December 1992)
APU	Assessment of Performance Unit
ASE	Association for Science Education
AT	attainment target
ATL	Association of Teachers and Lecturers (from January 1993)
ATM	Association of Teachers of Mathematics
CCW	Curriculum Council for Wales (to March 1994)
CPS	Centre for Policy Studies
CSE	Certificate of Secondary Education
DES	Department of Education and Science (to April 1992)
DFE	Department for Education (from April 1992)
ERA	Education Reform Act 1988
GCE	General Certificate of Education (at Ordinary and Advanced levels)
GCSE	General Certificate of Secondary Education
GSA	Girls' Schools Association
KS (1 etc.)	Key Stage (1 to 4)
LEA	local education authority
NAHT	National Association of Headteachers
NAS/UWT	National Association of Schoolmasters/Union of Women Teachers
NATE	National Association for the Teaching of English
NCC	National Curriculum Council (England) (to September 1993)
NFER	National Foundation for Educational Research
NFER/BGC	National Foundation for Educational Research/Bishop Grosseteste College (a test development agency)
NRA	National Record of Achievement
NUT	National Union of Teachers
PC	profile component
PoS	programme of study
PTA	Parent Teacher Association
RANSC	Records of Achievement National Steering Committee
RoA	record of achievement

Abbreviations

SAT	standard assessment task
SCAA	School Curriculum and Assessment Authority (England) (from October 1993)
SEAC	School Examinations and Assessment Council (England and Wales) (to September 1993)
SoA	statement of attainment
TA	teacher assessment
TES	*The Times Educational Supplement*
TGAT	Task Group on Assessment and Testing
UCLES	University of Cambridge Local Examinations Syndicate (a test development agency)
WO	Welsh Office
Y (1 etc.)	school years (1 to 13)

Glossary of terms

Assessment arrangements: Arrangements, made through regulations issued by the Secretaries of State (for Education and for Wales), for assessing pupils' attainment in each National Curriculum subject.

Attainment target: A term used in the Education Reform Act to refer to the 'knowledge, skills and understanding which pupils of different abilities and maturities are expected to have by the end of each Key Stage'. In practice it has come to be used to refer to the sub-sets of attainment identified within most National Curriculum subjects (some have a single attainment target). Attainment targets are defined in most subjects in terms of statements of attainment grouped at each of ten levels, i.e. *not* separately defined for each Key Stage.

Core subjects: Certain of the foundation subjects named in the Education Reform Act to which particular emphasis has been given in curriculum planning and assessment arrangements, viz. mathematics, science, English and, for Welsh-speaking schools in Wales, Welsh.

End of Key Stage statements: Statements defined in the National Curriculum Orders in art, music and physical education which describe the knowledge, skills and understanding pupils are expected to achieve at the end of a Key Stage.

Foundation subjects: The subjects of the National Curriculum as set out in the Education Reform Act: mathematics, science, English, Welsh (in Wales only), technology, history, geography, a modern foreign language (Key Stages 3 and 4 only), art, music, physical education.

Key Stages: The periods in each pupil's schooling to which the National Curriculum requirements apply. There are four Key Stages, related to the ages of the majority of pupils in a teaching group: from the beginning of compulsory education to the age of 7, from 7 to 11, from 11 to 14, from 14 to the end of compulsory education.

Level descriptors: Broad descriptions of the attainments expected at each level of attainment in each attainment target, replacing the more specific statements of attainment. To be introduced from 1995, in line with the recommendations of the 1993/94 National Curriculum Review, 'to create a more integrated description of what a pupil must know, understand and be able to do' (Dearing Final Report, para. 7.29).

Levels of attainment: The ten different sets of statements of attainment, from level 1 (lowest) to level 10 (highest) defined within each attainment target of each National Curriculum subject except art, music and physical education. Developed from a model of attainment originated by the Task Group on Assessment and Testing.

Orders: The legal documents ('Statutory Instruments') which put into effect decisions of the Secretaries of State using powers given to them by Act of Parliament. In the context of the 1988 Education Reform Act, the term usually refers to the detailed specifications of attainment targets and programmes of study in each National Curriculum subject, for example, 'the English Order'.

Profile component: A term introduced by the Task Group on Assessment and Testing to refer to a small number of sub-sets of attainment within each subject which would be used for reporting a pupil's 'profile' of attainment. In practice the term 'attainment target' came to be used to describe sub-sets of attainment and, in certain subjects only, 'profile component' came to refer to a group of attainment targets in a subject, for example, 'Writing' in English, comprising the three attainment targets of Writing, Spelling and Handwriting.

Programme of study: A term used in the Education Reform Act to refer to the 'matters, skills and processes which are required to be taught to pupils of different abilities and maturities during each Key Stage'. The National Curriculum Orders for each subject set out the programmes of study for that subject alongside the attainment targets.

Standard assessment task: A term introduced by the Task Group on Assessment and Testing to refer to the many possible types of standard, externally devised, test materials which could be used in National Curriculum assessment arrangements; included optional, within-Key-Stage 'SATs' as well as statutory, end-of-Key-Stage SATs. The term has fallen out of official use partly because of ministerial dislike of educational jargon and partly because the agency responsible for Scholastic Aptitude Tests in the USA threatened legal action over the copyright of the acronym 'SAT'.

Statements of attainment: The specific attainment descriptors set out at each of ten levels in each attainment target in all National Curriculum subjects except art, music and physical education. Scheduled to be replaced by more general 'level descriptors' following the 1993/94 National Curriculum Review.

Teacher assessment: Assessments of the attainments defined in the National Curriculum Orders which are undertaken by teachers during a Key Stage as part of their normal teaching. From 1994 those teacher judgments of pupil attainment will be reported to parents alongside the pupil's test results.

Tests: Externally devised, end-of-Key-Stage assessment instruments administered and marked by teachers (though external marking of some tests is proposed from 1995).

Preface

The writing of this book has its origins in 1988. That was the year in which the most substantial piece of education legislation since 1944, bringing in radical changes affecting the education system of England and Wales, completed its passage through Parliament. It was also the year in which I found myself not only an academic lecturing and researching in the field of educational assessment, but also a bit-part player in the large supporting cast of people helping to implement a central provision of that Act, the National Curriculum with its associated assessment arrangements. I was appointed a member of one of two newly-established curriculum councils and was later to chair that body (the Curriculum Council for Wales), but it was natural that my interest should turn to policies for national assessments of pupil attainment.

For the first three years of its existence I was also a member of the third Government education quango created by the Act, the School Examinations and Assessment Council (with a remit covering both England and Wales). I must therefore take a share of the responsibility for the advice SEAC Council offered to ministers and for the actions it took. However, without disclaiming such responsibility, I have attempted to stand back from that involvement and offer an account which is not dependent on 'inside knowledge' or spiced with anecdotes and overemphasis on the personalities of the main actors in the story which has unfolded since 1988. Some of those characters have undoubtedly left their mark on the system but it is the policies themselves and the policy-making process which are at the centre of this version of events. Indeed I have made a point of drawing only on documents which are in the public domain when reporting the positions taken by influential individuals and groups.

The documents I have made use of are of three types. The major policy papers, such as the Report of the 1987 Task Group on Assessment and Testing (TGAT), are inevitably referred to frequently. More specific and ephemeral documents, such as speeches by ministers or the lengthy correspondence they and their officials engaged in with the principal advisory body, SEAC, are also used to fill in the details of the story. However, to have relied solely on such sources would have given a false impression of policy-making being conducted only through official channels, ignoring the many whose opinions, privately or publicly expressed, influence the thinking of the decision-makers within Government. To find out exactly who was actually involved in shaping policies inside Government would have required a different approach from the one I have adopted here; even someone who has chaired a quango must rely largely on hearsay and surmise for that. But, to place the policy-making in the wider context of the public debate about the National Curriculum and assessment, I have made extensive use of quotations from the popular, broadsheet and specialist press. A fourth type of source, academic studies of the National Curriculum and national assessment, has been used less frequently. Such studies are already offering a growing body of relevant evidence and interpretation but this is not a book which is written primarily for an academic audience. It is more an account of policies in the making than a review of the research into those policies and their impact on the system.

Readers interested in developments in Wales may be disappointed to find so little attention being given to that country, especially in a book written by someone who is an advocate of a more distinctive National Curriculum (not just a modified version of what is largely decided in England) for pupils in Welsh schools. The explanation lies in the fact that, while the 1988 Act has, perhaps inadvertently (Jones, 1994), been a catalyst for significant steps towards a distinctive *curriculum* for the schools of Wales, there has been no move to date to define, still less to develop, policies on *assessment* which differ from those adopted in England.

The national assessment story is different in Wales in two matters of detail within a common policy framework. One National Curriculum subject, Welsh, is a requirement only in Wales and the assessment of some pupils in other subjects takes place through the medium of Welsh (Wiliam, 1994). In fact it seems to have gone largely unnoticed in England that perhaps the biggest success story of all in the decidedly chequered history of implementing the National Curriculum is the introduction of Welsh as a school subject for all pupils and the development of generally well-received assessment methods and materials (Williams *et al.*, 1993). The story of National Curriculum and assessment in Wales is an interesting one, worth telling, but it is not the purpose of this book to do so. Rightly or wrongly, the policy framework for National Curriculum and assessment remains, for the time being at least, an England and Wales one, with Wales 'opting out' of it only when what is proposed in London proves so unpalatable to Welsh Office ministers that they are moved to go down a different route from that taken by their counterparts in the Department for Education.

The book is arranged so that the story of the period begins and ends with an overview of policy, while the main events in between are dealt with topic by topic. Thus, after a necessarily brief sketch in chapter 1 of the decade prior to 1987, chapter 2 is concerned with the foundations of the system which were erected during 1987 and 1988, in particular the TGAT Report. Chapters 3 to 6 deal in turn with the national tests, teacher assessment, moderation, reporting and publishing of results, and the largely separate story of 'Key Stage 4'. Events referred to in those chapters occurred mainly in the years from 1989 to 1992. In 1993 all aspects of the curriculum and assessment system came to be considered together as the case for fundamental review became, belatedly, unanswerable. The different strands discussed separately in the previous four chapters are therefore interwoven in the story of events from the autumn of 1992 to the summer of 1994. Since my main reason for writing the book was to provide an accessible account of how policy evolved, it is only in the conclusion, chapter 8, that I have gone beyond the role of informed commentator on events to offer a more general analysis of policy and of policy-making.

The book would not have been completed if it had not been for the encouragement and help I have received from colleagues. In particular, I am indebted to Peter Dines, Mary James and Kathleen Tattersall for their detailed comments on sections of the manuscript. Grateful though I am to them, the responsibility for any factual errors and for the opinions expressed is, of course, entirely mine.

By the time this is being read, the story of national assessment policy will have moved on. If an account of the first six years can help reinforce the case for an assessment system which seeks to enhance the learning of the individual pupil — the only point at which 'standards' have any real meaning — the telling of this story will have served some purpose.

Richard Daugherty
University of Wales, Aberystwyth
July 1994

1 The Policy Context

Introduction

A national system of assessing pupils in England and Wales throughout the eleven years of compulsory schooling was one of several radical provisions of the 1988 Education Reform Act. Central Government policy on national assessment, the specific focus of this book, must necessarily be considered alongside policy on the curriculum to which that assessment relates. A National Curriculum could have been introduced without any associated assessment arrangements at the national level, but, following re-election in June 1987, a new Conservative Government committed itself to a system in which assessment of pupil attainment would, it was argued, complement and reinforce curriculum objectives. Other writers have sought to explain and interpret the origins and outcomes of National Curriculum policy, referring in so doing to decisions on how that curriculum should be assessed (for example, Lawton, 1989; Pring, 1989; Kelly, 1989). This account reverses that emphasis, considering curriculum policy only in so far as it is necessary to explain and interpret policy on assessment.

The Education Reform Act also brought in other major changes for publicly-maintained schools in England and Wales, affecting their funding and control, as well as important provisions in respect of other sectors of education. The 1988 Act, the seventh in a series of Education Acts introduced since the election of a Conservative Government in 1979, was to be the most substantial and wide-ranging of Government initiatives to change the education system and, more particularly, the control of that system. Much has also been written since on the significance, taken together, of the diverse provisions of the 1988 Act (for example, Simon, 1988; Maclure, 1989; Bash and Coulby, 1989; Flude and Hammer, 1989).

The chapters which follow do not seek to cover the same ground as those who have analyzed policy, either on National Curriculum or, more broadly, in relation to the 1988 Act taken as a whole. Attention is focused instead on the assessment of pupil attainment as an element in the education policies of central Government. The period covered by this account runs from the consultation paper in July 1987, which preceded what was then termed *The Great Education Reform Bill* (which would in due course be enacted as the 1988 Act), through to mid-1994 when the first major review of National Curriculum and assessment policy was near to completion.

While the scope of the policy considered here in detail is limited to national assessment over that seven-year period, it would be unsatisfactory simply to start the story in mid-1987. Then, in the wake of a third successive Conservative election victory, the Secretary of State for Education and Science, Kenneth Baker, formally announced his intention to introduce legislation which would implement, for the first time in England and Wales, a national system of assessment of pupils from the age of 5 through to 16. However, the origins of that decision to centralize control of the curriculum and of assessment can be traced back at least to the early 1970s. The 1976 Ruskin College speech of the then Labour Prime Minister, James Callaghan, can be seen as the first significant stage in a process which saw the educational system in England and Wales abandon the post-war assumptions of curriculum policy being essentially matters for schools and local education authorities to determine. The Conservative Party policies which were the antecedents of those which influenced the provisions of the 1988 Act can be traced back through the internal Party debates of the 1980s to the period in the late 1970s when the Party, then in Opposition, formulated a more explicit, more radical policy for education (Knight, 1990).

An outline of the place of assessment in the policy debate inside and outside the Conservative Party in the fifteen years prior to the 1988 Act may therefore be helpful in interpreting decisions taken in 1987 and subsequently.

The 1970s Curriculum Debate

Prior to the intervention in 1976 of the Prime Minister, James Callaghan, on a wide range of education policy issues, there was already a debate about the school curriculum in progress at the national (England and Wales) level. In an era when a large and growing percentage of pupils who attended maintained schools were in primary and secondary schools, the intake of which was not selected by ability, questions were inevitably posed about the nature of the common curriculum experience those pupils should be offered. That debate was conducted on the basis that the responsibility for curriculum remained, in the terms of the 1944 Education Act, with local education authorities and schools. However, Callaghan's speech can be seen in retrospect to signal the start of a period of several years during which the Government Department responsible for Education, the DES, and the Schools Inspectorate, HMI, would take the lead in influencing the terms of the curriculum debate. In time, central Government would move from a stance of urging schools and LEAs to rethink curriculum policy to one, in the form of the 1988 Act, of requiring them to do so.

For much of the 1970s curriculum debate, assessment figured in a relatively minor, supporting role. Central Government already had, in 1974, taken steps through the Assessment of Performance Unit (APU) to obtain evidence from a 2 per cent sample of pupils in order to to monitor pupil attainment. The terms of reference of the APU included:

to identify significant differences of achievement related to the circumstances in which children learn, including the incidence of underachievement, and to make the findings available to those concerned with resource allocation within the Department (of Education and Science), local education authorities and schools.

While maintaining for the most part a relatively low profile, the APU was one means by which Government could gather evidence on what was becoming, by the mid-1970s, a major policy issue — trends in educational 'standards'.

Government statements on the curriculum of this period typically referred to the importance of raising (as yet undefined) standards and to public examinations and other forms of assessment as sources of evidence on which to base judgments about such standards. Callaghan himself edged towards a position of more direct Government action on the curriculum when he said in his Ruskin speech:

> It is not my intention to become enmeshed in such problems as whether there should be a basic curriculum with universal standards — though I am inclined to think that there should be . . . (quoted in Moon *et al.*, 1989)

He stopped short, however, of advocating that Government should give a lead in defining that 'basic curriculum' and measuring those 'universal standards'.

In the Green Paper, *Education in Schools: a Consultative Document* (July 1977), which rounded off what was termed the 'Great Debate' on education in the months following Callaghan's speech, one of the main sections was headed 'Standards and assessment'. It argued for 'a coherent and soundly-based means of assessment for the educational system, for schools, and for individual pupils' (p. 16). A further ten years would elapse before the Task Group on Assessment and Testing would be given the job of devising just such a national system of assessment.

In 1977, and in the decade which followed, the assessment of attainment was discussed, at least in official policy documents, in terms of making better use of already existing arrangements, perhaps in modified form. Thus the Green Paper, when considering standards at the national level, relied (apart from a brief reference to the APU) on the work of HM Inspectorate, 'the traditional and long established means for assessing the performance of the educational system as a whole' (p. 16). Referring to assessment of the performance of schools, the Green Paper was equally cautious in advocating improved use of existing evidence. More radical steps were not then favoured. For example:

> 'league tables' of school performance based on examination or standardized test results in isolation can be seriously misleading because they fail to take account of other important factors such as the wide differences between school catchment areas. (*ibid*, p. 17)

When turning to the assessment of individual pupils, the Green Paper tentatively reviewed the case for change in public examinations for 16- and 18-year-olds (and a possible new certificate for 17-year-olds) but was clearly not yet ready to move to a decision on any of the proposals then under consideration. As to the possibility of new national tests for other age groups:

> It has been suggested that individual pupils should at certain ages take external 'tests of basic literacy and numeracy', the implication being that those tests should be of national character and universally applied. The Government rejects this view. Because of the differing abilities and rates of development of children of school age, tests pitched at a single level could be irrelevant for some and beyond the reach of others. Moreover the temptation for schools to coach for such tests would risk distorting the curriculum and possibly lowering rather than raising average standards. (*ibid*, p. 18)

The Green Paper did signal the intention of the Secretaries of State (for Education and for Wales) to 'seek to establish a broad agreement with their partners in the education service on a framework for the curriculum' (*ibid*, p. 12). But, for all the rhetoric of 'it is not sufficient just to maintain present standards; the schools like the nation as a whole have to meet the growing and changing demands of the future', there was clearly no mood for radical change in assessment policy and practice (or indeed in curriculum policy) among the officials who drafted the Green Paper or the ministers who approved it. The agenda which would shape developments in the late 1980s was already in evidence among the possible courses of action considered, but then rejected, in the Green Paper — regular testing of all pupils in basic skills, national monitoring of standards, performance tables enabling parents and the public to compare schools. In 1977 that agenda was the agenda of voices on the Right of the Conservative Party. It had yet to reach even the stage of being adopted as official Party policy (see Knight, 1990), still less of dominating education policy-making in Government.

The Early 1980s: Concluding the Debate

The late 1970s and early 1980s saw a series of publications on the school curriculum, from the Department of Education and Science, from HM Inspectorate, and from others such as the main national advisory body on curriculum and examinations, the Schools Council. Each was written in the context of the intention to reach agreement on a national framework for the school curriculum (see Moon *et al.* (1989) for a helpful chronology of these and other landmarks along the road towards a National Curriculum). A closer look at *A View of the Curriculum* from HMI (1980) and *The School Curriculum* from the DES (1981) is instructive for what they reveal about HMI and DES thinking on assessment at that time.

The HMI paper discusses the curriculum in terms of a broad framework within which teachers and schools determine what learning experiences are appropriate:

> the broad definition of the purposes of school education is a shared responsibility, whereas the detailed means by which they may best be realized in individual schools and for individual children are a matter for professional judgment. (*A View of the Curriculum*, p. 2)

This leads HMI to a view of standards and how they should be measured which locates the individual teacher at the centre of the system:

> The successful implementation of different programmes for different pupils also puts a premium on teachers' sense of 'standards'; they need to be able to formulate appropriate expectations of what individual children should know or be able to do at a given stage. In order to feel assured that their expectations are reasonably pitched, they need bearings outside as well as inside the school: that is, they need to know how children of similar ages and broadly similar circumstances perform in comparison with their own pupils, locally and nationally. Comparative information such as the Assessment of Performance Unit is beginning to supply will be helpful to teachers in this respect; programmes of sample local testing by LEAs may give other points of reference; public examinations at 16+ already provide bench marks at the end of the period of compulsory education. (*ibid*, p. 3)

In this HMI view of things, standards grow out of the collective experiences of professional teachers. 'Bench marks' are acknowledged as necessary, though the sources of them referred to in the last sentence would not begin to do justice to the range of learning encompassed across eleven years of compulsory schooling. *A View of the Curriculum* concludes by advocating 'further defining parts of the curriculum' including 'statements identifying necessary skills and knowledge' (p. 23). The DES/Welsh Office paper, *The School Curriculum*, has even less to say about the place of assessment in any agreed curriculum framework. It recommends:

> Schools should . . . analyze and set out their aims in writing, and make it part of their work regularly to assess how far the education they provide matches those aims. Such assessments should apply not only to the school as a whole but also to each individual pupil . . . (*The School Curriculum*, p. 20)

Apart from a routine discussion of the role of public examinations at the end of compulsory schooling it would seem that nothing is envisaged beyond the use by schools and teachers of their own means of assessing attainment.

The sequence of DES and HMI curriculum policy papers can be regarded as having begun in 1977 with publication of the Green Paper and of the HMI 'working papers' *Curriculum 11–16*. It was concluded in 1985 with *Better Schools* and, from HMI, *The Curriculum from 5 to 16*. As in their predecessors, some attention is given to the role of assessment.

While HMI were by this time more strongly advocating clearer definition of expectations and improved methods of assessment, their perception of the nature and purposes of assessment remained clearly rooted in the day-to-day interaction of teachers and pupils. 'From time to time informal assessment needs to be supported by more objective forms of testing' (p. 52), for example by the 'occasional use' of standardized tests. But 'assessment is inseparable from the teaching process since its prime purpose is to improve pupils' performance' (p. 51).

In contrast the DES, in *Better Schools*, discusses assessment mainly in the context of external public examinations for secondary school students. The chapter entitled 'Examinations and assessment' is noticeably more positive than the equivalent section of the 1977 Green Paper. In addition to the established examinations for 16- and 18-year-olds it notes development work on the use of graded assessments and on records of achievement, the introduction of which was by then a Government policy commitment. In the preceding, and more substantial, chapter on curriculum policy, one of four 'strands' in moving towards agreed objectives for the curriculum is the definition of 'levels of attainment'. Defining desired levels of attainment for 16-year-olds of differing abilities is described as a 'necessary step' towards the longer-term goal of 'a more precise definition . . . of what pupils of different abilities should understand, know and be able to do' (p. 26). But 'it will be no short or easy task to move towards a more precise definition of attainment targets'. External assessment procedures, apart from public examinations for older secondary pupils, are not yet in evidence as a component in Government thinking:

> Assessment of each pupil's performance is a complex professional task, in which a wide range of evidence has to be taken into account
> . . .
> The teacher's assessment of pupil performance is also the basis of a school's evaluation of its own performance. (*Better Schools*, p. 27)

These HMI and DES policy papers are the product of an era when the main aim in education policy as it related to schools was a clearer definition, arrived at by consensus, of the aims and scope of the school curriculum. Assessment puts in an appearance in a relatively minor, supporting role. It is as if the process of definition of curriculum objectives would, in itself, result in higher standards of attainment. There is no hint, in the many pages of discussion, of schools and teachers being required, as distinct from encouraged, to assess their pupils' attainment at more regular intervals and on a more systematic basis.

Changes in Conservative Party Policy 1981–1986

However, over the period when these DES and HMI papers were published, Conservative Party policy on education was already moving towards a more interventionist view. Sir Keith Joseph, Secretary of State for Education and Science from 1981 until his resignation in 1986 had a key role in shaping as well as implementing education policy during that period. In a seminal speech to the North of England Education Conference at Sheffield in January 1984 he announced three major policy initiatives. First, he set a target of bringing 80 to 90 per cent of pupils up to the standards then attained by the average pupil. This initiative was in keeping with Joseph's longstanding view that under-achievement by the pupil of average or below average ability was a serious cause for concern. But he also stressed that his objective of higher standards of attainment applied to all students and not just those stigmatized as 'less able'. Second, he argued that the public examination system should be shifted from an emphasis on placing candidates in rank order relative to each other to describing results in terms of what candidates had demonstrated they were capable of doing. Joseph believed that employers would welcome information on the specific skills and understandings shown by pupils in the course of being examined. Third, Joseph asserted the need for clearly-defined curriculum objectives, agreed by parents and employers, as a means of ensuring that pupils aspired to, and teachers helped them reach, the highest possible standards.

If Callaghan's Ruskin College speech of October 1976 inaugurated a period of more active involvement by central Government in the debate about curriculum policy, it was Joseph's Sheffield speech which heralded significant elements in the policies which would shape the legislation of the late 1980s. Curriculum legislation was not yet foreshadowed as such but the Government was making very clear its intention to move to specifying curriculum objectives and to involving parents and employers in that process. If curriculum objectives, rather than the more broadly-stated aims which had featured in the curriculum statements of the late seventies and early eighties, were to be defined at national level, questions would inevitably arise as to the extent to which schools would be expected to plan the curriculum in those terms. Also, once curriculum objectives had been spelled out, questions about the assessment of attainment in relation to those objectives would, equally inevitably, be posed.

The main context in which Joseph was able to implement the ideas expressed in his Sheffield speech, prior to the introduction of legislation, was the new General Certificate of Secondary Education (GCSE). The GCSE replaced the General Certificate of Education (GCE) Ordinary ('O') level examination and the Certificate of Secondary Education (CSE) during the period 1986 to 1988, with the first certificates being awarded in 1988. The decision to proceed with introducing what was referred to as a 'common examination system for pupils at 16+' had been taken by his predecessor, Mark Carlisle, but it was Joseph's ideas which gave the GCSE the characteristics of a major reform of both curriculum and assessment for the 14–16 age group. For those ideas to have such an influence on that stage of schooling did not require new legislation. Examination certificates were issued by the examination boards but were countersigned by an Under Secretary in the DES; through that convention the Government had the means to shape policy even though syllabuses and examining remained the responsibility of independent examination boards.

During 1985 and 1986 the Secretary of State for Education took a close interest in plans for the new examination.

In line with the first of the policy initiatives in his Sheffield speech, Joseph announced that, unlike the examinations it replaced, the GCSE would be designed for all pupils who could benefit from it. 'O' level and CSE had, taken together, been intended to cater for the top 60 per cent of the assumed 'ability range', though in practice a larger proportion of the age cohort actually entered for those examinations (with the numbers entered varying both regionally and from subject to subject). Additionally, he announced that candidates would be awarded grades, however modest they might be in absolute terms, which were based on the 'positive achievement' they had demonstrated (as distinct from the lowest grades being based on having picked up a handful of marks on questions which were very largely beyond the candidates' reach). One of Joseph's favourite concepts across the whole field of social policy, that of 'differentiation', was also to be a guiding principle for GCSE. All syllabuses and examination schemes were required to specify the methods which would be used to differentiate the curriculum and its associated assessment arrangements so that they were appropriate across the wide ability range of students taking GCSE courses.

The second and third of Joseph's Sheffield initiatives were taken forward in the context of GCSE through the concept of 'grade criteria' (see chapter 6). For each aspect of each subject examined, specific curriculum objectives would be defined; the curriculum, the way student attainment was assessed and the way it was reported would all, it was hoped, be explicitly linked to pre-specified objectives.

A further defining feature of the GCSE was the contribution which work assessed by the students' own teachers during the course ('coursework') would make to the overall grade awarded at the end of the examination. Such assessment had typically been more prominent in the lower-status CSE than in the high-status GCE 'O' level but in Joseph's view such activities as practical work in the sciences or oral competence in languages were vital parts of the new GCSE curriculum. Through a combination of coursework assessment and end-of-course examinations the procedures leading to the award of GCSE grades would, it was argued, ensure a valid assessment of that new curriculum.

Thus during the period 1984 to 1986, curriculum and assessment policy for the 14–16 age group was being determined by ministers in the Department of Education and Science and guided by policy parameters which would be carried forward into the design of a national assessment system. Through GCSE there would be, from 1986, a common curriculum and assessment framework set out in 'General Criteria' and subject-specific 'National Criteria' in each of the main subjects examined. Both general and subject-specific criteria were, though matters for extensive consultation, ultimately for the Secretary of State to approve. The curriculum and assessment framework was couched in terms which implicitly accepted the virtues of a model which described attainment in terms of a series of specific, assessable curriculum objectives. Moreover, when it came to certificating attainment, not only was it expected that 'grade criteria' would guide the design and marking of assessed tasks, but the results would be reported in those terms. In other words, the new curriculum and its assessment would be 'criterion-referenced'.

The Mid 1980s: National Assessment Takes Shape

Yet, however firmly the Conservative Government seems to have been set on a course of taking responsibility for decisions on curriculum and assessment policy, it was far from clear at the time of Joseph's 1984 speech and the GCSE developments which followed that a similar intervention would follow in respect of the curriculum for younger pupils and the assessment of pupils before the age of 16.

Much attention in the general literature on Conservative education policy has been given to identifying several, often conflicting, strands of thinking among those who were active in party policy-making (see Ball, 1990; Lawton, 1992). Ball, for example, in his analysis of 'New Right' ideas on education within the Conservative Party, argues that thinking about the role of assessment:

> bridges between a neo-liberal, free-market concern, for the making of comparisons between schools and teachers in order to facilitate informed parental choice, and the neo-conservative distrust both of teachers and of new teacher-based forms of assessment. (Ball, 1990, p. 52)

At times 'neo-liberals' and 'neo-conservatives' were united in opposition to the education policies actually implemented by the Conservative Government. The GCSE, for example, with too much Government involvement for the former group and too much reliance on teachers' own assessments for the latter, was viewed with suspicion by all shades of opinion on the Right of the Conservative Party.

The interviews conducted by Ball with some of the key participants, politicians and officials, in the policy decisions leading up to the decision to legislate for a National Curriculum and assessment system, reveal some of the influences at work in policy-making. One of these was the trend in vocational education, mainly in the further education sector rather than in schools, to define and measure basic skills and competences.

By the mid-1980s, employers' organizations were increasingly expressing discontent with conventional means of grading attainment and arguing for receiving from schools information which revealed what had been attained and went beyond the familiar lists of grades in academic subject examinations. The Director of Education at the Confederation of British Industries was enthusiastic about the advantages of an assessed National Curriculum:

> there are some immeasurable benefits that will arise from the National Curriculum and the associated bits of it, the GCSE exams. Because it will set standards, and it will provide the testing, and the

> testing will not only provide for pupils but it will also, by implication, be testing the teachers as well. (Webb, quoted in Ball, 1990, p. 111)

Developments in other countries, notably the USA and the Federal Republic of Germany, were also drawn into the discussions about curriculum and assessment policy. Indeed, Ball argues that the final linking of National Curriculum and National Testing seems to have been firmed up in this way.

It was clear that, by 1986, there was 'indirect evidence of the DES interest in an assessment-led mode of curriculum change and control' (*ibid*, p. 164) though a DES Under-Secretary, recalling the events of the period, remembers the question of whether to legislate not being 'at all settled' by the autumn of 1986 (*ibid*, p. 182). In the view of the same official 'the relationship between assessment and a prescribed curriculum were the clear objectives' though 'the curriculum push did come from a separate place from the original assessment and testing push'. Pressed to say where these policy positions were fought out, he added:

> it wasn't just within the DES, it was within the DES and within the Centre for Policy Studies, No. 10 Policy Unit and Cabinet, and all the usual people that are involved in policy formulation . . . which is nothing unusual, nothing different from normal policy formulation. (quoted in *ibid*, p. 183)

A picture thus emerges of a policy debate within Government and the Conservative Party about the potential shape of legislation in which there would be a statutory National Curriculum and also a requirement on schools and teachers to assess pupil attainment at regular intervals throughout their compulsory schooling. Such legislation would not only be directed towards specifying and raising standards of attainment by making them clearer to pupils, teachers and schools. Also, in the words of the same DES official, 'by having a National Curriculum and assessment you provide a basis for information to be given to parents about what is happening' (*ibid*, p. 183), information which parents could use when making decisions about their own child's future and when, acting collectively, they were deciding whether a school should 'opt out' of LEA control. A national system for assessing attainment thus became not only integral to the curriculum debate, it was also to be a vital source of evidence for empowering the parent in the process of redistributing powers within the education system.

The identities of 'all the usual people' involved in policy formulation are not entirely clear, though the members of one Right-wing 'think tank', the Centre for Policy Studies, seem to have been especially close to the process of shaping the policies enacted in 1988 Education Act, both in the period leading up to it and in subsequent years as its provisions were implemented. But it would be a mistake to see the influence of the Conservative Right as taking Government policy on assessment in a particular direction. Even as the debate moved to the point of decisions on policy, contrasting views on the virtues of a centrally-defined, Government-controlled, policy on curriculum and assessment were still very much in evidence within the Conservative Party. This can be illustrated by reference to two policy statements, both of them from right-wing sources and both published in 1987. Stuart Sexton, in *Our Schools — A Radical Policy*, takes a stance on issues such as central control and the role of examinations and assessment, markedly different from that of The Hillgate Group in *The Reform of British Education*.

On control, Sexton argued that:

> . . . the wisdom of parents separately and individually exercised, but taken together becoming their 'collective wisdom', is more likely to achieve higher standards more quickly, and more acceptably to the public, than the collective wisdom of the present bureaucrats, no matter how well meaning those bureaucrats may be. (Sexton 1987, p. 9)

> Regardless of which Government is in power, centralization of education becomes, in practice, bureaucratic control by the civil servants at the centre . . .
> More central government control over education would be disastrous, and is the least likely way of raising standards or of spending the money more efficiently. (*ibid*, p. 7)

In contrast, for the Hillgate Group:

> The eventual liberation of schools raises the important question as to what controls are exercised over what goes on in them. The eternal vigilance of parents is neither to be expected nor desired. Sensible parents are usually too busy to ruminate on the niceties of the curriculum . . .
> We therefore sympathise with the Government's call for a National Curriculum, and for continuous assessment of standards . . . (Hillgate Group 1987, p. 5)

On assessment and examinations, Sexton (1987) suggests:

> that the Department of Education and the Secretary of State should pull out completely from the examinations scene . . . It is far better for the examinations to be run by bodies which are independent of Government. (p. 26)

But for the Hillgate Group (1987):

> Priority should be given to establishing a statutory framework for national attainment targets and tests, and for the publication of information. (p. 17)

They go on to dismiss in turn each of the counter arguments that 'teachers will concentrate on the tests and neglect the rest of their tasks', that 'the publication of so much information will be misleading and harmful' and that 'information about attainment will be used to make unfair comparisons'.

Conclusion

By the time the crucial decisions were taken to legislate for a National Curriculum and for a national assessment system, the interventionist 'paternalist' element in Conservative Party thinking, much closer to the Hillgate Group than to Sexton and the Institute of Economic Affairs, had clearly gained the upper hand on this aspect of policy. Ironically both the Prime Minister, Margaret Thatcher (see p. 31) and the former Secretary of State, by now Lord Joseph, who had done more than any other individual to change the course of Conservative policy, were clearly unhappy about the degree of central control which the 1988 Act would vest in the Secretary of State.

However, as is so often the case with a major policy initiative, neither the 1988 Act in general, nor the national assessment system in particular, can be interpreted in terms of a single clearly-stated set of ideas informing every aspect of it. In reviewing the policy debate leading up to it and the policy decisions which followed in the course of implementing its provisions:

> it is a mistake to look for ideological coherence in the Act as a whole. It is a messy set of compromises between neo-liberal and neo-conservative policies. (Lawton, 1992, p. 49)

2   Designing and Planning the System

Introduction

1987 saw the culmination of the debate about the desirability of a National Curriculum and the first steps towards designing and implementing one. Within that one year, the issues rehearsed so often in the course of the preceding decade had begun to crystallize as Government policy took shape. In the course of a major speech in January, the Secretary of State for Education and Science, Kenneth Baker, signalled the Government's intention to legislate. In June, a sweeping election victory gave the new Conservative Government a firm base on which to design and implement the educational reforms outlined in its manifesto. By December the Bill to enact an assessed National Curriculum in England and Wales had completed its second reading in the House of Commons. In the same month, the recommendations of a group established to lay the foundations for national assessment were submitted to the Secretaries of State for Education and for Wales.

Though the intention to legislate for a National Curriculum became clear during the early part of 1987 (Kenneth Baker had aired the possibility in the course of a *Weekend World* television interview towards the end of the previous year), the place which assessment would have in the new scheme of things remained vague. In January, at the North of England Education Conference, Kenneth Baker referred to the 'need to be much clearer about the school curriculum'. He proposed 'establishing a National Curriculum which works through national criteria for each subject area of the National Curriculum'. Progress had been made, he claimed, in defining criteria for GCSE but 'we are a long way from similar targets for the end of the primary phase'. Such targets would serve several purposes including:

- explicit goals for the education system;
- teachers (having) bearings outside the classroom;
- customers (knowing) what they are entitled to expect from the education system.

The first formal announcement of intended legislation came in April with a statement by Kenneth Baker to the House of Commons Select Committee on Education which included, *inter alia*:

For each subject within the foundation curriculum it will be necessary to determine clear and challenging attainment targets for the key ages of 7, 11 and 14. These targets should allow for variations in ability. They should not result in an unduly narrow approach to teaching and learning.

Having decided the core of what should be learnt we need to assess pupils' performance in relation to the attainment targets. Those attainments which can be tested will be tested at the key ages.

But we do not want teachers to teach only what is testable, so it will be essential also to assess work done in the class at the Key Stage. The tests and the assessments would fall to the teachers but each would be externally moderated.

With this carefully worded outline of a possible assessment system Baker was not just setting out his intentions; he was at the same time countering some of the criticisms already being levelled at the proposals for assessment. His approach to national testing would acknowledge differences in the abilities of pupils, would be based on a broad definition of attainment, would discourage 'teaching to the test' and would place the judgment of teachers at the centre of the assessment process.

The Consultation Document

The next step on the path to legislation, after the re-election of a Conservative Government in June 1987, was publication of *The National Curriculum 5–16: A Consultation Document* the following month. It set out the reasons why 'a National Curriculum backed by clear assessment standards' would be introduced and it described in general terms what would be contained in a Bill to be introduced that autumn. An assessed National Curriculum would, it was argued, ensure that all pupils studied a broad and balanced range of subjects, set clear objectives, make possible the checking of pupils' progress and enable schools to be more accountable. More detail about the kind of assessment and reporting system which would be needed to achieve these aims would await the recommendations of a Task Group on Assessment and Testing but the broad lines of policy were explained in a section of the document on 'Assessment and examinations'.

The 'main purpose' of assessment would be 'to show what a pupil has learnt and mastered and to enable teachers and parents to ensure that he or she is making adequate progress' (p. 11). It is thus the benefits of assessment for the individual learner which are being highlighted at this early stage in the evolution of policy. The use of aggregate assessment data as an indicator of performance was, for the moment at least, taking second place to assessment's function as a direct contributor, through feedback to teacher and pupil, to effective learning.

The assessment procedures indicated by the consultation document reflect the priority given to assessment as a day-to-day aspect of work in schools.

'The Secretaries of State envisage that much of the assessment . . . will be done by teachers as an integral part of normal classroom work' (p. 11). However, 'to supplement individual teachers' assessments', there would be nationally prescribed tests. The tests, though supplementary, were also described as being 'at the heart of the assessment process' (*ibid*).

In addition to such assessment procedures, a national system would have to resolve how attainment would be recorded and reported. In this context, the consultation document reiterated the Government's commitment to introducing records of achievement which would be broader in scope than simple summaries of attainment in the proposed foundation subjects. 'Such records . . . will have an important role in recording performance and profiling a pupil's achievements across and beyond the National Curriculum' (p. 12).

On a fourth aspect of policy it was made clear that, for assessment at the age of 16, rather than replacing the recently introduced General Certificate of Secondary Education, the Government envisaged a coming together of the new approach to national assessment and the existing system of public examinations for 16-year-olds. 'GCSE and other qualifications at equivalent level will provide the main means of assessment through examinations' (p. 12).

Thus, in six short paragraphs of the consultation document (paras 28–33), the main items on the agenda for debate and development were identified: the purposes of national assessment, the techniques and procedures, how attainment would be recorded and reported, adjusting the existing GCSE examination to take account of the new system. Within each item on that agenda, many of the sources of tension and conflict in what was to follow are already in evidence in the document's wording. On purposes, the tension between using assessment to help the individual learn and relying on aggregate data to evaluate the work of teachers and schools. On procedures, the relative significance, on the one hand, of methods of assessment flexible enough to be integral to teaching in each teacher's classroom and, on the other, standard national tests. On recording and reporting, the use of records of achievement as end-of-key-stage summaries of National Curriculum attainment levels and their role as a means of monitoring, supporting and reporting educational achievement. On GCSE, the uneasy marriage of an examination system in which the grades were still largely dependent on where a candidate came in a rank order drawn up on the basis of marks awarded to a new system in which assessment and reporting were to be in terms of pre-specified criteria spelled out as 'attainment targets'.

Responses to the Consultation

Though the shortage of time available for consultation was a common complaint of many who responded to the proposals, there were numerous submissions made in the course of the following two months. Referring back to a sample of those responses — '100,000 words chosen from several million' — compiled by Haviland (1988) in *Take Care, Mr. Baker*, it is interesting to note how many of the dimensions of the policy debate which was to ensue were already being defined by one or more of the organisations commenting on what was proposed.

A minority of respondents challenged the propositions which underpinned the policy. The Royal Society of Arts Examinations Board was 'not convinced of the practicability or desirability of "established national standards" at ages 7, 11 and 14'. Others questioned the proposals for testing at those ages, especially at 7, and the use which would be made of test results. As the RSA Board put it (p. 77):

> The document suggests that 'nationally prescribed tests' are in some way to be preferred to other forms of assessment. No justification is advanced for this view . . .

Others argued for a National Curriculum supported by assessment but against national tests:

> The proposed national tests . . . will not help meet most of the aims outlined in the consultation document and will make it more difficult for other forms of assessment to do so. (p. 78) (Godfrey Thomson Unit for Educational Research)

Opposition to the use of test results as performance indicators was expressed bluntly by the teacher unions:

> (The National Union of Teachers) rejects the view that tests can be used as a competitive stimulus between pupils or between schools. (p. 88)

A joint submission from three subject associations representing teachers of mathematics, English and science was not just unconvinced of the value of national testing but expressed 'grave doubts concerning the number of different purposes which the tests are expected to serve' (p. 73). The conflicts and tensions associated with potentially incompatible purposes, later to become a major feature of policy implementation, were also foreshadowed in a single sentence from the Godfrey Thomson Unit:

> Problems will arise . . . where tests which are too narrow in scope or content are used to assess the important results of learning, and interpreted too broadly as evidence of educational outcomes. (p. 78)

A similar theme is developed in this submission from a primary assessment project based at the University of Southampton:

> The purpose of tests at 7, 11 and 14 (is described as) being for both diagnosis at the level of the learning of individual pupils and for monitoring the education system nationally. We are convinced that it won't be possible to achieve such diverse aims with a single system of assessments. (p. 80)

It was not only in respect of the plans for national testing that the underlying assumptions were questioned. The more perceptive respondents were already pointing to an ambiguity at the heart of the proposals — whether the national system could serve both the interests of the individual learner and the demands of those whose priority was to define national standards and to measure performance in relation to them:

> The problem with the document's approach is that it tries to relate the individual child's potential ('each child to develop his or her potential', 'each child, according to his or her ability') to a general (average or very broad?) standard for a year group ('setting clear objectives for what children over the full range of ability should be able to achieve'). (p. 91) (Hertfordshire Country Council)

Others however, rather than challenge head-on what were understood to be the fundamentals of Government policy (the setting of national standards and the introduction of national tests), chose to question the feasibility of what was proposed. The cost, the time and the training required if such elaborate and ambitious curriculum and assessment arrangements were to be implemented successfully were natural targets both for the more pragmatic among the critics and for those who, while supporting the principles, were anxious about the preconditions for success.

A submission from the Secondary Examinations Council pointed to some of the internal contradictions in the proposals and highlighted the need for training and for 'quality control mechanisms'. The practicability of national assessments and their associated arrangements for training and moderation was also questioned by others:

> The moderation of national tests, sat by every single pupil in the land four times during their school careers in most foundation subjects and marked by their own teachers, is an undertaking on a scale which is barely imaginable. It is also bound to be very expensive and it is not clear who is to meet the additional cost. (p. 92) (Hertfordshire County Council)

Other respondents aired concerns about the design brief, whether explicit or implicit in the consultation document, for a national assessment system spanning the eleven years of compulsory schooling and achieving acceptable levels of validity and reliability. Was it a realistic proposition given our understanding of children's learning and the measurement of it?

> Children acquire expertise in different areas in different orders, at uneven rates and often in response to different experiences. Valid assessment of achievements of this kind requires sensitivity and subtlety. A written test designed to be taken by every child of a particular age cannot pinpoint the child's position on the complicated and idiosyncratic route towards understanding and competence. (p. 76) (ASE/ATM/NATE)

The doubts being expressed in such submissions focus on the technical feasibility as well as the educational desirability of a system of national assessment. An alternative approach, providing 'collections of questions, tests and other exercises for schools. . . . to use for their own assessment purposes' (p. 79) (Godfrey Thomson Unit), was among the suggestions put forward for overcoming doubts among many assessment specialists that a workable and cost-effective system could be designed on the basis outlined in the consultation paper.

In drawing attention to what are argued as unacknowledged or under-emphasized possibilities within a national assessment system, other respondents offered variants on, or alternatives to, what the consultation paper seemed to envisage. The need to think through more carefully the implications of the new system for pupils with special educational needs, the place of records of achievement in the new arrangements for reporting attainment, and the importance of judging a school's performance in context are all themes running through several of Haviland's sample of responses.

However, even more pervasive is a fundamental scepticism, expressed in various ways by different organizations, about the ways in which national assessment would influence the curriculum, the learning of individual pupils and thus the performance of teachers and schools. Doubts and anxieties are not confined to the teacher associations. For example:

> A programme of testing on four occasions during a pupil's school career may have the unintended effect of placing emphasis on factual content and memory, which are more easily tested, than other aspects of achievement such as the capacity to solve problems, to apply knowledge and to develop concepts and skills. (p. 83) (School Curriculum Development Committee)
>
> . . . we are concerned that the proposals about testing and the publication of test results could have the effect not of raising standards but of distorting the teaching in order to produce apparently good test results. (p. 99) (National Association of Governors and Managers)

In a characteristically diplomatic and deadpan way, the Government's own specialist advisers on examinations and assessment may have come closest to identifying the largely unacknowledged issue to be faced in designing and implementing a national assessment system:

> It is not clear who is to act on the information generated, how and with what kinds of guidance and accountability. Who is responsible for ensuring that appropriate action is taken in classrooms in the light of the evidence arising from assessment within the national curriculum? (p. 82) (Secondary Examinations Council)

As in any informed discussion of assessment in education, the central question is not what to assess or how but, having obtained evidence of the attainment of individuals and/or groups, how can that information be used to have a beneficial effect on the learner, the teacher and the school.

From GERBIL to ERA

Following the consultation process, the first stage towards enacting the required legislation came with the publication of a Parliamentary Bill in November 1987. Dubbed the 'Great Education Reform Bill' or GERBIL, the Bill was to be extensively debated in both Houses of Parliament before emerging largely unchanged. Much of the discussion focused not on the proposals for assessment but rather on the extent of the prescription involved in requiring the teaching of ten foundation subjects (eleven in Wales) plus religious education (already a requirement from the 1944 Act).

The Act stipulated three ways in which each of the National Curriculum subjects would be defined:

(a) the knowledge, skills and understanding which pupils of different abilities and maturities are expected to have by the end of each Key Stage (in this chapter referred to as 'attainment targets');

(b) the matters, skills and processes which are required to be taught to pupils of different abilities and maturities during each Key Stage (in this chapter referred to as 'programmes of study'); and

(c) the arrangements for assessing pupils at or near the end of each Key Stage for the purpose of ascertaining what they have achieved in relation to the attainment targets for that stage (in this chapter referred to as 'assessment arrangements'). (*Education Reform Act*, chapter 1, 2(2))

It goes no further than that towards clarifying how these novel terms should be interpreted. What an attainment target, programme of study or assessment arrangement would look like would have to await secondary legislation, in the form of Orders to be laid before Parliament in due course. Some of the central concepts associated with national assessment which were later to loom large as the system evolved, notably that of a 'statement of attainment', do not figure at all in the wording of the Act. As Margaret Brown (1991) has argued, the Act set out some of, but by no means all, the defining features of national assessment policy. Certain things — regular assessment by teachers as part of normal classroom work, tests at 7, 11, 14 and 16, moderation to ensure comparability of results — had already been signalled in the consultation document. The Education Reform Bill, and the Act which followed it, ensured that four significant characteristics were enshrined in the primary legislation on which the system would be built:

— the assessment should be criterion-referenced, since its function is to ascertain achievement in relation to ATs;

— the assessment should be differentiated, since the definition of ATs

    makes them differentiated in relation to pupils of different abilities and
    maturities;

— reporting should indicate attainment in terms of separate ATs;

— the assessment should be summative, taking place at or near the end
    of each Key Stage. (*ibid*, p. 215)

But, if these were the defining features of national assessment, how were they
to be assembled into a coherent design? While the Bill was going through
Parliament, steps were being taken to develop a design brief for national
assessment, taking account of such features but linking them into a model on
which planning and implementation could be based.

The Task Group on Assessment and Testing: Remit

In July 1987, with the skeleton of an assessment system barely discernible and
already subject to widespread criticism, the Secretary of State for Education,
Kenneth Baker, had turned to a specially convened 'Task Group on Assessment and Testing'. It is perhaps surprising that a Government which was
uneasy about the hold which what it saw as an 'educational establishment' was
exercising on the education policy agenda as well as on practice in schools
should turn for advice to a group whose membership was drawn almost
entirely from within the education system. However, it may well be that
Baker was more receptive to professional advice, for example from HM Inspectorate, than some of his successors were to be in subsequent years.

    The Task Group (known as 'TGAT'), under the chairmanship of Professor
Paul Black of King's College, London, was initially given a very general
formal brief. Its establishment was accompanied only by a brief listing of the
'practical considerations' on which it was asked to advise the Secretary of
State (see DES/WO, 1988a, appendix A). The announcement of the Group,
during the first week of August, was a relatively low-key affair, exciting little
press comment. The *Times Educational Supplement* Editorial of 7 August 1987
greeted the Group with a strong note of scepticism:

    Professor Black and his colleagues will have to break the news to Mr.
    Baker that it is impossible to meet his prescription as it stands. All
    they can do is suggest the least bad line of approach.

Two of the four paragraphs in the Group's terms of reference related to
questions about the phasing of implementation and about 'the need not to
increase calls on teachers' and pupils' time for activities which do not directly
promote learning, and to limit costs'. The rest of the Group's brief was com-
pressed into one sentence stretching to 132 words:

    To advise the Secretary of State on the practical considerations which
    should govern all assessment including testing of attainment at age

(approximately) 7, 11, 14 and 16, within a National Curriculum; including the marking scale or scales and kinds of assessment including
testing to be used, the need to differentiate so that the assessment can
promote learning across a range of abilities, the relative roles of informative and of diagnostic assessment, the uses to which the results
of assessment should be put, the moderation requirements needed to
secure credibility for assessments, and the publication and other services
needed to support the system — with a view to securing assessment
arrangements which are simple to administer, understandable by all
in and outside the education service, cost-effective, and supportive of
learning in schools. (DES/WO, 1988a, appendix A)

There are few signs in that wording of the Group being steered by politicians
or officials to emphasize either a particular approach to assessment or one of
the several purposes to which assessment could be put. Though the curious
DES neologism 'informative assessment' appears for the first time (is not all
assessment intended to inform action of one kind or another?), it is set against
the evidently alternative 'role' of using assessment to diagnose learning difficulty. Indeed assessment as a source of evidence to help children learn looms
large in the Group's brief, with assessment which 'can promote learning' and
is 'supportive of learning in schools' also rating a mention. The purpose which
was in due course to dominate the evolution of the system originated by
TGAT — using published aggregate data to evaluate the performance of
teachers and schools — is nowhere to be seen in the way the Secretary of State
first explained what was required of the Task Group.

The Task Group's chairman, Professor Paul Black, has given an account
(in Ball, 1990) of how the Group worked in which he makes it clear that,
perhaps surprisingly in view of the political sensitivity of national assessment,
the Group was allowed to develop its thinking with very little direction from
politicians or officials as to what was expected of them. On the basis of
Black's account, Ball concludes there was:

> . . . no evidence of pressure or interference from Secretary of State
> or DES officials, nor of fixed constraints. Given that some form of
> national testing was required, the determination of its form, in the
> first instance at least, was given over to a group primarily drawn
> from the educational establishment. (*ibid*, p. 190)

When the Group was less than two months away from the deadline for completing its report, it did receive an elaboration of its brief in the form of a
letter from the Secretary of State dated 30 October 1987 (DES/WO, 1988a,
appendix B). That letter is in effect the first full statement of Government
intentions on national assessment and it clarifies some, at least, of the policy
issues alluded to in the Task Group's terms of reference.

On the purposes of assessment, the four which the Task Group was soon
to set out as the purposes its system was designed to serve — formative,
diagnostic, summative and evaluative — are stipulated, with Baker adding: 'I

attach importance to all of these, and I expect your recommendations to cover all'. The evaluative purpose, 'mainly concerned with publicizing and evaluating the work of the education service', is thus now firmly in the frame.

Yet no clear picture emerges at this stage of the methods of assessment preferred by the Government. 'Simply-administered tests' are mentioned but so is 'a range of approaches including written, practical and oral tests'. Formal testing is expected to play some part but, even when the focus of the letter is on what should be done at the 'age points' of 7, 11, 14 and 16, the Group is asked to advise 'what forms of assessment, *including* testing' (my emphasis) would be appropriate.

The October letter thus explores more fully the ground ministers expected the Group's report to cover but contained few pointers to ministerial preferences. Unlike the situations in which some subsequent letters from Secretaries of State were received by their advisers — letters of the 'I will be expecting you to advise me to do this' type — the initiative remained with the Task Group.

The TGAT Report: Four Principles

The Group's Report was delivered to ministers on Christmas Eve, 1987, and published the following month. After a brief preamble, covering such sentiments as assessment's contribution to effective learning and its being 'the servant, not the master, of the curriculum', the Group spelled out the criteria which should, in its view, govern the design of a national system:

— the assessment results should give direct information about pupils' achievements in relation to objectives: they should be criterion-referenced;
— the results should provide a basis for decisions about pupils' further learning needs: they should be formative;
— the scales or grades should be capable of comparison across classes and schools, if teachers, pupils and parents are to share a common language and common standards: so the assessments should be calibrated or moderated;
— the ways in which criteria and scales are set up and used should relate to expected routes of educational development, giving some continuity to a pupil's assessment at different ages: the assessments should relate to progression. (TGAT Report, para. 5)

In these four criteria the Group was in effect setting out the principles on which what followed was to be based. In respect of moderation, it was giving a high priority to ways of ensuring that results would be comparable, with the calibration or moderation of assessments having the status of a fundamental criterion rather than being seen as a technical matter to be explored as part of the operation of the proposed system. For the Task Group, moderation was a central feature of the design.

Similarly, the placing of the formative purpose of assessment as one of its four criteria represents an expression of the Group's belief in the value of assessment which influences directly the individual pupil's learning, whatever else it is also required to do. This was a deliberate counter to the most common use of assessment in schools, to summarize what had been achieved rather than to help pupils progress further. But, as the Group put it, unless this and the other three criteria were met 'the potential value of national assessment in assisting learning and supporting the professional development of teachers is unlikely to be realized'.

The remaining two criteria involved more than elevating part of the Group's brief to the status of a basic principle. In placing progression at the centre of its design the Group was stressing the importance of tracing pupils' learning development as they moved through their experience of schooling. In a later section of the Report (paras. 96–101) the Group reviewed and rejected the case for age-specific scaling — the comparing of a pupil's performance with that of others in the same age group.

The thinking leading to advocacy of the first of the Group's stated criteria — a criterion-referenced approach to assessment — is closely related to the case for a scale defined in terms of progressively more demanding levels of attainment. If attainment is not to be described in terms of expectations of an age group, expressed as performance above or below a norm for the group, a set of explicit criteria would be needed to define what would count as 'progress'. Where it had been tried, the use of criterion-referencing for defining and measuring achievement of objectives had proved problematic (see for example Sally Brown's international review of criterion referenced assessment — Brown, 1981). But the Task Group argued that it was the only approach which made sense:

> The overall national purpose is for achievement of the attainment targets of the curriculum. Assessment, whether for feedback to pupils or overall reporting and monitoring, should therefore be related to this attainment i.e. it should be criterion-referenced. (TGAT Report, para. 99)

The first and last of the Group's four criteria or principles — criterion-referencing and the use of assessment to support progression in learning — embodied an approach at odds with pre-National Curriculum practice in the schools of England and Wales. Most of the existing testing arrangements, whether standardized tests in primary schools, selection tests for 11-year-olds or public examinations at 16, were grounded in the norm-referenced traditions of psychometric testing. The testing methods were designed to spread pupils across a grading scale which reported how well pupils had done relative to each other but told the recipient of the report nothing about specific attainments. Even where explicit objectives for assessment were set out, as was increasingly the case in the new style public examinations of the 1980s, those objectives were used only as a guide to the award of marks or grades not as a basis for reporting the attainments candidates had demonstrated. Though some commentators misleadingly referred to that use of assessment object-ives as being a 'half way house' towards criterion-referenced assessment, in practice it represented no more than a sophistication of the way in which an essentially norm-referenced system operated.

Taken together, the Group's four principles were a remarkably ambitious basis on which to build the new system. Even where the principles themselves were unsurprising — in stressing formative assessment and moderation — the Group was spelling out a formidable challenge to the profession to turn those ideals into a workable system on a national scale. But, in going further and pinning its colours to the mast of plotting progress in attainment on a criterion-referenced scale, the Task Group was leading national assessment into waters which were largely uncharted, not only in England and Wales but also in any other national or regional system of education.

The TGAT Report: Four Purposes

In setting out the purposes which a system designed on its principles would serve, the Task Group used a four-fold classification of types of purpose:

— *formative*, so that the positive achievements of a pupil may be recognized and discussed and the appropriate next steps may be planned;
— *diagnostic*, through which learning difficulties may be scrutinized and classified so that appropriate remedial help and guidance can be provided;
— *summative*, for the recording of the overall achievement of pupil in a systematic way;
— *evaluative*, by means of which some aspects of the work of a school, an LEA or other discrete part of the educational service can be assessed and/or reported upon. (TGAT Report, para. 23)

As with all attempts to classify purposes of assessment (each of the many authors on the subject has adopted his/her own version) it is possible to identify or infer the type of data required from the assessment process, the audience(s) for that data and the action it is anticipated that recipients of the information will take. These in turn link the stated purposes of the national assessment system envisaged by TGAT with the four criteria or principles referred to above.

For the *formative* use of assessment to be effective, individual pupils and their teachers need evidence of what has been achieved in a form and at a time when it can be used to plan further learning. It is essentially a 'private' feedback loop facilitated by a national assessment framework. The aim is for assessment to contribute in a systematic way to the way each pupil progresses. As argued by TGAT, the emphasis on progression and criterion-referencing is essential if assessment is to be formative. How can the pupil learn something useful from assessment unless s/he has a clear indication of what has been achieved and what will be required if further progress is to be made?

As with formative assessment, the audience for information which will be used *diagnostically* is the pupil and his/her teacher. Indeed, diagnostic assessment can be regarded as a more focused use of formative assessment, locating more accurately the source of any difficulty and suggesting what action the teacher and pupil might take next. Formative and diagnostic assessment are both largely to be realized in the personal interaction of each pupil with the teacher, backed up by nationally devised tests and procedures. TGAT was to argue (para. 78) that specially designed supplementary tests were required if accurate diagnosis and appropriate remedial action were to be a realistic aim in a national system. As with several of the TGAT proposals, little has been heard since of that idea as the evolving system has paid increasing attention to the third and fourth of TGAT's purposes.

With the third of the purposes listed, *summative* assessment, the focus of attention remains on the individual pupil but the audiences for assessment information are different. Reporting on a pupil from one teacher to another, from school to school, from school to parents or from school to prospective employer are all examples of summative assessment in action. What they have in common is that they are 'feed forward' processes, telling someone other than his/her teacher about a pupil's attainments. But that is about all these various channels of communication for summative information do have in common. While summative reporting to parents is potentially a way of helping them support their child's learning, summative reporting to a prospective employer is a contributor to the process of selection for employment. Covering as it does such diverse uses of information derived from assessment, 'summative' is the least clearly defined of TGAT's four purposes.

From the beginning the fourth purpose — using assessment information to *evaluate* the performance of teachers and schools — was the most contentious of the stated purposes. Many teachers and their organizations questioned the validity of aggregate data on pupil performance as an indicator of the quality of teaching and schooling. While this use of assessment evidence did not figure in the initial TGAT terms of reference, it was clear from references to it in the contemporaneous consultation document, *The National Curriculum 5–16*, that the Government saw national assessment as providing both prospective parents and those administering the system with evidence on which to base comparative judgments about the effectiveness of teachers, schools and local education authorities.

How to achieve this was to become a major point of contention in relation to the Task Group's proposals and in responses to subsequent developments. By depending on *aggregate* data being published, this purpose, unlike the other three, inevitably raised questions about how to aggregate, how to publish and how to interpret what was published. Evaluative assessment stands apart from the three other TGAT purposes in that it does not pretend to relate to the individual learner but rather, through publication of aggregated results, to affect the way teachers and schools judge their effectiveness.

The TGAT Report: Proposals

Having made explicit both the principles and the purposes of the system it was putting forward, the Task Group made a series of recommendations, forty-four in all. Though the Group itself did not choose to distinguish the main recommendations from others of lesser significance, it is helpful to highlight those proposals which were to be most central to what was to become known as 'the TGAT model'. Four in particular stand out as being especially significant:

- the description of attainment in terms of ten 'levels of attainment' in each of several 'profile components' to be defined within each national curriculum foundation subject;
- the case for a wide range of methods of assessment to be used with no marked discontinuity between teachers' own assessments in the classroom and the use of externally provided tests;
- the advocacy of moderation procedures which would be managed and controlled by groups of teachers;
- the proposition that the several purposes of national assessment could be served by a single set of procedures from which the various types of information would be derived.

Levels of Attainment

The first of these proposals represents a working through of the principle of criterion-referencing. If prespecified attainments were to govern the design, administration and reporting of assessment, how best to express those attainments? As the first step in classifying attainment the Group coined the term 'profile component':

> We recommend that an individual subject should report a small number (preferably no more than four and never more than six) (of) profile components reflecting the variety of knowledge, skills and understanding to which the subject gives rise. Wherever possible, one or more profile components should have more general application across the curriculum: for these a single common specification should be adopted in each of the subjects concerned. (TGAT Report, para. 35)

In time, the term 'attainment target' (a term used by the Task Group for the specific statements describing attainment at each level) came to be used for such subsets of subject-based attainments, though 'profile component' did have a currency in the early years of national assessment as a term referring to groups of attainment targets.

Within each profile component the Group suggested that the working groups in each National Curriculum subject should define up to ten levels of attainment:

> We shall use the word level to define one of a sequence of points on a scale to be used in describing the progress of attainment in the profile component. The sequence of levels represents the stages of progression. (TGAT Report, para. 100)

The principle of progression was thus embedded in the basic framework which subject working groups were to be required to fill out. It was a feature of the TGAT model which was to prove a continuing focus of attention, prompting lengthy debate among those willing to work pragmatically with that way of defining progress in learning but also more fundamental questioning from those who challenged the validity of such a model of attainment. When the time came to review the system, this aspect of the TGAT model came under particularly close scrutiny and a variety of alternatives was mooted (Dearing, 1993b). It is, however, a measure of the difficulty not only of defining progression in attainment across eleven years of schooling but also of assessing how each individual progresses that the issue of progression continued to prove as problematic as any in spite of (or perhaps because of) six years of experience of working to TGAT's ten level model.

What was to become a major source of difficulty as the subject groups developed their proposals — how to describe a 'level of attainment' — was not addressed directly in the Task Group's Report. At minimum, the Group's model implied one statement of assessment criteria at each of the levels of each of the categories of attainment within a subject. In practice, the first set of proposals, from the Science Working Group, contained 354 statements grouped into ten levels in each of twenty-two separate attainment targets. A well-recognized problem in any system of criterion-referencing was thus soon in evidence: how to combine an acceptable degree of precision and specificity in the assessment criteria with a manageable number of assessable statements.

Assessment Methods

The second of the Group's key proposals concerned the methods to be used to assess pupils in relation to the pre-specified levels of attainment. The Group emphasized the variety of possibilities available:

> The art of constructing good assessment tasks is to exploit a wide range (far wider than those normally envisaged for tests) of modes of presentation, operation and response, and their numerous combinations, in order to widen the range of pupils' abilities that they reflect and so to enhance educational validity. (TGAT Report, para. 48)

What is more, such 'standard assessment tasks' (another term coined by the Task Group) were not to be the only means of making judgments about attainment levels:

> We recommend that teachers' ratings of pupil performance should be used as a fundamental element of the national assessment system. Just

as with the national tests or tasks, teachers' own ratings should be derived from a variety of methods of evoking and assessing pupils' responses. (TGAT Report, para. 60)

Thus a twin track approach to assessment methods was established with reliance both on teachers' own judgments (what was to become known as 'teacher assessment') and on nationally devised standard assessment tasks (or 'SATs'). Moreover the two tracks were to be so similar in character as to be scarcely distinguishable from each other:

One aspect of this expanded range of possibilities is that the discontinuity between teachers' own assessment of normal classroom work and the use by them of externally provided tests need not be a sharp one. (TGAT Report, para 49)

The new world of diverse assessment activities closely integrated into the regular work of the classroom was thus clearly set out in the TGAT Report. The intended break with the long established tradition of formal written tests/exams for summative purposes and quite separate informal and unsystematic assessment to feed back into pupils' learning was a central, confidently argued, feature of the Group's proposals.

Group Moderation

The third of the proposals which were central to the 'TGAT model' referred to the methods to be used to realize the Group's declared priority that 'the scales or grades should be capable of comparison across classes and schools, if teachers, pupils and parents are to share a common language and common standards' (para. 5). It was in the minds of all those with an interest in developing a genuinely *national* system of assessment that some means would have to be found of calibrating or moderating the judgments of many thousands of teachers on the many millions of occasions that pupils were to demonstrate what they had attained. For the Task Group, moderation was one of its four basic criteria for designing the system. But how was this to be done?

In a substantial section of the main Report (paras. 64–80) the Group reviewed the options for 'bringing individual judgments into line with general standards'. It considered and rejected both the scaling of results against pupil performance on a reference test and the possibility of relying on inspection by visiting moderators. It advocated instead moderation by groups of teachers:

Group moderation allows examiners to clarify in discussion both the objectives of their syllabuses and the bases of their value judgments. It is the only one of the three moderation methods which would enable the professional judgments of teachers to inform the development of the National Curriculum. (TGAT Report, para. 72)

In line with its expressed belief in the centrality of the formative purpose of assessment and the use of methods which would give teachers considerable freedom to exercise their own judgments, the Task Group argued that responsibility for ensuring comparable and consistent interpretations of nationally defined attainments should also rest in the first instance with teachers at the local level. It was an approach which emphasized gradually working towards shared interpretations of the meanings of assessment criteria rather than the imposition, through inspection or through reference tests, of external controls on teacher judgments.

A Multipurpose System

In putting forward proposals concerning attainment levels, assessment methods and moderation procedures the Task Group was elaborating on its four principles, fleshing them out to the point where others could begin to put the proposals into effect. While each of the above three main proposals was to an extent contentious, the debate about them could be conducted on the basis of experience in the UK and elsewhere and in relation to the merits of the available alternatives.

But the Task Group's advocacy of using the evidence from a single set of procedures to serve the several declared purposes of national assessment was more of an expression of faith than the outcome of a detailed argument from the substantial experience upon which its members could draw. For pragmatic reasons they quickly rejected the possibility of even partially separate procedures to meet those different purposes:

> We judge that it would be impossible to keep the burden on teachers within reasonable bounds if different batteries of assessments and tests had to be created to serve each separate purpose. (TGAT Report, para. 24)

Instead, they suggested, several purposes could be served by:

> . . . combining in various ways the findings of assessments designed primarily for a different purpose. It is possible to build up a comprehensive picture of the overall achievements of a pupil by aggregating, in a structured way, the separate results of a set of assessments designed to serve formative purposes. (TGAT Report, para. 25)

It was not possible, however, the Group argued, to derive results which were useful formatively from assessments which were designed for summative or evaluative purposes. Thus, in a crucial paragraph of the Report, the Task Group was reinforcing its earlier placing of 'formative assessment' as one of its four criteria or principles by arguing that procedures should be established with that purpose in mind:

> We judge . . . that an assessment system designed for formative pur-
> poses can meet all the needs of national assessment at ages before 16.

The other three purposes could be accounted for by adaptation of that for-
matively-focused system. There would be shift to a *summative* emphasis only
at the final stage when pupils were assessed at age 16. The *evaluative* purposes
could be met by aggregating the available information on individual pupils.
Only the *diagnostic* purpose would require some supplementary assessment
and testing beyond that which would be routinely carried out by teachers
with or without the help of 'standard assessment tasks'.

Until the Task Group reported, it had been conventional wisdom among
assessment specialists that, in assessment contexts ranging from reading tests
for 7-year-olds to university degree examinations, a particular set of assessment procedures could only be expected to serve a limited range of purposes
successfully. TGAT challenged that assumption and the most fundamental
of all its propositions was established, that one system could serve purposes
as disparate as diagnosing an individual's learning difficulties and supplying
evidence of the effectiveness of schools. However, whether this support for
a multipurpose system was expressed with conviction by the Group or was
more of an acceptance by them of the political realities of national assessment
must be open to question. In an appendix to the Report the Task Group seems
to be contradicting this central plank of its argument:

> The choice of a particular test or testing technique depends on several
> factors. Primary among these is the purpose for which the results will
> be used . . . (TGAT Report, appendix E)

From TGAT Proposals to Government Policy

The Task Group's Report was published in January 1988, accompanied by a
welcome in general terms for its proposals from the Secretary of State, Kenneth
Baker. The *Times Educational Supplement* in its editorial of 15 January ('So far
so good') also gave the Report a warm but guarded welcome. Professor Black
and his colleagues had done 'a remarkable job in an incredibly short time' to
produce 'a humane report about children's learning not a bleak handbook for
monitors and measurers'. The Group's proposals were 'an approach to assessment which puts teachers and teaching at the heart of it'. However, there
was still much detail to be worked out. The ten levels of attainment had been
put forward without empirical evidence; 'they are asking Mr. Baker (and the
schools) to take it on trust'. Questions also remained about whether sufficient
resources would be available both for training and to develop suitable assessment instruments.

In March 1988 the Task Group's proposals were the subject of a sudden
surge of interest, with more press coverage than when the proposals had first
surfaced. National assessment came back into the headlines with the story of

a leaked letter on the subject from the Private Secretary to the Prime Minister, Margaret Thatcher, to his counterpart in the DES (though Professor Brian Griffiths of the Downing Street Policy Unit is believed to have played a major role in drafting the letter). The Prime Minister, he wrote, had agreed to the Secretary of State giving the Report an initial welcome but there were 'a number of aspects of the Report which she finds disturbing'. The four points which then follow reveal something of the gulf between the Prime Minister's Office and her Education Department on Government policy in this area.

First, 'the Committee seems to have designed an enormously elaborate and complex system'. 'Has the sort of approach advocated in the Report', asked the letter, 'been put into practice with the proposed degree of elaboration in any large group of schools?' Secondly, the letter queried the Task Group's position that 'the major purpose of assessment is diagnostic and formative rather than summative' and the associated reliance on teachers' judgments in assessing performance and on local education authorities in implementing the system. The other two concerns aired by Mrs Thatcher's Office were the likelihood, in their judgment, that the costs would be high and the Task Group's recommendation that the system should not be implemented in less than five years. The Prime Minister clearly favoured something simpler, quicker and cheaper, focussing on a limited range of 'basics' within the core subjects. With the policy differences between Number 10 and the Education Department thus given a public airing, it was by no means certain that, when a formal Government announcement was made on TGAT the Group's model for national assessment would come through unscathed.

Over the spring and early summer of 1988 the Education Reform Bill was completing its passage through Parliament (with its clauses on National Curriculum and assessment essentially unchanged) and the first two subject working groups, in mathematics and science, were finalizing their recommendations. Yet the Government remained silent about the TGAT proposals. It was not until June, more than six months after the TGAT Report had been received, that the long awaited decision was announced. In answer to a Parliamentary question (7 June), the Secretary of State for Education, Kenneth Baker, announced its acceptance of most of the Task Group's recommendations, identifying seven 'principles' as the basis for national assessment:

- attainment targets setting out what children should know, understand and be able to do; enabling progress to be measured against national standards;
- performance assessed and reported on at 7, 11, 14 and 16; attainment targets grouped for manageability;
- progress to be registered through the years of compulsory schooling on a 10-level scale;
- assessment by a combination of external tests and assessment by teachers; GCSE the main form of assessment at 16;
- results of tests and other assessments to be used both formatively and summatively;
- detailed results to be given in simple, clear reports to parents; aggregate

results to be published at 11, 14 and 16; schools to be 'strongly recommended' but not required to publish results for 7-year-olds;

- teachers' assessments to be compared with each other and with national tests to safeguard standards.

A majority of the Task Group's recommendations had thus become formal Government policy, the basis for designing the assessment system in each subject, at each stage and in each aspect of the expected 'assessment arrangements' referred to in the Education Reform Bill. The fate of some recommendations, such as the proposal for an explanatory text to accompany publication of a school's results, was unclear since they were not mentioned in the Secretary of State's announcement. On only one of the major features of the TGAT 'model' were clear doubts being expressed. The TGAT proposals for moderation, training and support (set out in the third of its three *Supplementary Reports*) were judged by Kenneth Baker to be 'complicated and costly'. Even there, however, the proposal was not rejected out of hand but a decision was deferred pending further discussions.

Thus, from a starting point where many teachers and other professionals in education had been fundamentally opposed to national assessment, the Government had reached something closer to a consensus on the subject than had initially seemed possible. The critics remained, attacking the policy on assessment from the political Right and Left as well as from within the teaching profession. The dimensions of the debate about purposes and practices of assessment which was to continue as the system was implemented were already apparent, not only in the formal responses to consultation (see above) but also in the many questions raised by those on the sidelines as the Government and its advisers devised an assessment model on the basis of which a system could be developed and implemented.

Planning and Implementation Begins

Following acceptance by Government of the TGAT model, the way in which policy decisions about national assessment would be taken was to change. In the months following publication of *The National Curriculum 5–16* the responsibility for initiating policy had rested with a specialist Task Group with a brief to design the whole system. Not only did TGAT, from its inception in July 1987 to Kenneth Baker's acceptance of its proposals a year later, have the formal lead role in the sense that the Secretary of State allowed it to set the policy agenda with a minimum of 'steering' from himself or his officials. It is also remarkable how few challenges there were, with the notable exception of the intervention of the Prime Minister's Office, from those who had entered the many caveats noted in the responses to *The Curriculum 5–16*. The Task Group's Report was the only worked-out view of how the bare outline given in the legislation might be turned into a fully operative national assessment system. As a report in *The Times Educational Supplement* commented *a propos* of the leaked letter:

if (Mrs Thatcher) was determined to throw the TGAT Report out of the window presumably she would already have commissioned like-minded people to devise alternative models. This does not appear to have happened. (Sue Surkes, 18 March 1988, p. 6)

However, once the Task Group had completed its short-term task, the responsibility for developing and implementing the TGAT blueprint was no longer clearly located in one part of the complex set of processes put in place by the 1988 Education Reform Act. To many observers of the way in which the National Curriculum evolved, the most obvious dispersion of responsibility, for curriculum and assessment, came with the setting up in sequence of separate working groups in each foundation subject. Even where two subject groups were working concurrently, as with mathematics and science, there seems to have been little or no sharing of ideas about the interpretation of their parallel briefs. Unsurprisingly, each group developed its own interpretation of key terms. While advisory bodies, officials and critics of the groups' proposals would point to some of the inevitable inconsistencies and anticipated problems in implementation, the overall design of each set of proposals for a foundation subject was very much a product of the thinking of a group of subject specialists. Subsequent reshaping of those groups' proposals in the course of statutory consultation and eventual ministerial decision could not disguise the fact that the Statutory Orders reflect eleven different interpretations, each distinctive in its own way, of the TGAT model on which each group had been required to base its thinking about assessment. There is no better example of this than the Orders for history and geography, the proposals for which emerged at much the same time but could hardly have been more contrasting in their interpretations of the central concepts of 'attainment target', 'statement of attainment' and 'programme of study'.

A second way in which policy-making was to be diffused was a consequence of the 1988 Act's separating of the functions of the statutory bodies advising the Government on curriculum and assessment. On any one issue, ministers could expect to receive not only the views of the many interested organizations and individuals in the system at large, but formal advice from no less than three statutory advisory bodies — the National Curriculum Council (for England), the Curriculum Council for Wales and the School Examinations and Assessment Council. While the last of these was clearly charged with a major role in relation to assessment policy, it was to have no direct responsibility for two crucial stages in the policy-making process. The subject working groups were established, administered and steered by the Government departments to which they submitted their reports, the DES and the Welsh Office. The later consultation on Government proposals, based on the work of those groups, was to be in the hands of the National Curriculum Council (or, in Wales, the Welsh Office).

A third reason for the diffusion and fragmentation of policy-making lay in the stage-by-stage, subject-by-subject, regulation-by-regulation schedule for implementing the National Curriculum and its associated assessment arrangements. A step-by-step approach to national assessment policy was inevitable given the scale of the enterprise. Neither the policy-makers at the centre nor those with responsibilities for implementation at the school or LEA level could cope with more than a few elements of the system at any one time. Since tests for Key Stage 1 were first in line to be introduced (in the summer of 1991), how to test 7-year-olds became a major concern of the policy-makers in the first months of shaping assessment policy. Since mathematics and science were the first subjects to reach the stage of Statutory Orders (to be introduced in schools from September 1989), the assessment issues in those subjects came to dominate the early debates about how to assess attainment. At no time in the often hectic schedule of decisions about the design and implementing a national assessment system was a considered evaluation of the model on which it was, at least in principle, based to be either an expectation or the reality. It was to become increasingly difficult to discern the grand design of the Task Group as each group of craftsmen and women came on the scene to construct its allotted part of the great edifice.

3   From Standard Tasks to Written Tests

Introduction

Origins in the TGAT Report

During its short shelf life the acronym 'SAT', coined in the Report of the Task Group on Assessment and Testing and abandoned officially by SEAC four years later, had a substantial impact on both the perception and the reality of national assessment. Until TGAT reported, most of those interested in assessment in education drew on a limited vocabulary to describe the methods used to make formal judgments about pupils' attainments. This vocabulary ranged from the long established usage of 'tests' and 'exams' to terms like 'projects' or 'coursework', associated with the wider range of assessment practices deployed in public examinations since the 1960s. The Task Group were well aware of the connotations of such terms:

> The meaning given to testing is often too narrow. Much of the discussion about testing seems to be based on a particular image. (para. 45)

To reinforce their insistence on the broadest possible interpretation of 'test', the Group decided to add to the already complex and confused terminology of educational assessment by referring to 'standard assessment tasks':

> Both terms (tests and standard assessment tasks) will be used interchangeably in this report, to specify externally provided tasks and procedures designed to produce performance data on a national scale. (para. 45)

They went on to explain that standard assessments need not only be in written form but should exploit a wide range of methods of presentation, operation and response so that the results from the tasks would give the fullest possible picture of pupils' abilities.

The stress on validity in this argument is significant. The Group was clearly attempting to allay the fears of many teachers about national testing by asserting that there were many ways of measuring attainment, some of them not fully exploited in conventional tests (examples are given in appendix E to the Report). National testing need not it seemed rely on pupils providing, under exam conditions, written responses to short answer or multiple choice questions. TGAT had made clear its view that assessment, whether using the externally provided tasks or carried out by the teacher in the normal course of classroom work, should be a matter for the teacher. There would be no sharp distinction between formal tests and classroom assessments; they were both contributing to maximizing validity by allowing the pupil to demonstrate attainment in a variety of contexts.

Nowhere in Section VII of the Report on 'Assessment and Testing Methods' is there any discussion of reliability, accepted among assessment specialists as the counterpart of validity, with assessment design necessarily involving a trade-off between the two. From the first paragraph — 'it is important for teachers to be aware of the levels reached by pupils, and their rate of development, in order to facilitate learning' — to the last, dealing with 'flexibility', the Group is emphasizing assessment as being integrated into the programme of teaching and learning. While the proposed national system would use, in combination, teachers' own assessments together with results from SATs, the latter would not be separate, formal procedures, set apart from classroom practice. Commonality of standard in the assessment was not to be sought through every pupil taking exactly the same test at the same time under exam conditions. Instead the Task Group put its faith in 'careful standardization' of marking and grading procedures together with moderation arrangements across teachers and schools.

The term 'standard assessment task', or SAT for short, gathered meanings as it came to be widely used. One significant variation from the intentions of the Task Group was soon apparent. In opening up a wide range of possible forms of testing, the Group had focused on the standardness of test materials, administration and marking procedures. They did not locate the SAT at any particular point in time within a Key Stage. The Working Group on National Curriculum Science had backed the idea of assessment taking place at whatever point the teacher judged appropriate. Yet the emphasis in the wording of the 1988 Education Reform Act was on 'arrangements for assessing pupils at or near the end of each Key Stage' with the explicit purpose of 'ascertaining what they have achieved in relation to the attainment targets for that stage'. In the minds of ministers, officials and their advisers, the term 'SAT' seems very early on to have come to mean end-of-key-stage test rather than standard test materials to be used at a time chosen by the teacher.

The Brief for SAT Development

Though the Government was subsequently to blame its main advisory body on assessment, SEAC, for embarking on what it came to regard as an unacceptable route in the development of SATs, the TGAT approach to designing tests was initially accepted by ministers, civil servants and SEAC. There is ample evidence in ministerial statements, development specifications and in correspondence between DES and SEAC, of largely uncritical acceptance of the TGAT vision of standard assessment tasks.

In a letter to the Secretary of State on National Curriculum assessment and testing (dated 13 July 1989) written after the Council had been in operation for nearly a year, SEAC made explicit that its advice was 'based on the assessment framework proposed by the Task Group on Assessment and Testing'. In his reply later that month, the Secretary of State (Kenneth Baker) stated firmly 'we welcome and accept the Council's advice'.

As developments at Key Stage 1 proceeded, SEAC continued to echo the thinking of TGAT with such statements as these, included in one of several letters of advice to ministers (12 December 1989)

All SATs (Key Stage 1) will be coherent cross-curricular exercises . . .

. . . each SAT will contain many varied activities to be introduced by the teacher. These activities will lead to a wide range of written, oral, graphical responses by pupils working alone and in groups.

Though there was by now a new Secretary of State for Education and Science (John MacGregor), it is not possible to detect in his responses to SEAC's advice any lessening of enthusiasm for the TGAT approach to SAT development:

(the SATs at Key Stage 1) will be administered by schools in the first half of the summer term preceding the end of the Key Stage, will transcend subject boundaries, focus on the statutory statements of attainment and contain varied activities leading to a variety of responses by pupils. The Secretary of State for Wales and I have endorsed this model. (Letter from Secretary of State to SEAC Chairman, 9 April 1990)

Thus, more than two years after publication of the Task Group's Report, though before the piloting of the first standard tasks at Key Stage 1, the Group's approach to assessing the National Curriculum was still very much to the fore in the minds of the makers of policy and those advising them.

Soon after Kenneth Baker's acceptance in June 1988 of the TGAT proposals work had begun on translating the few paragraphs on testing methods in the TGAT Report into tests which would satisfy the various demands to be made on them. That work was given to agencies following the submission of tenders prepared in response to published specifications. The timetable for development involved phasing in the assessment of subjects at the different stages over a period of six years (figure 1). The schedule for implementation called for development work initially on the core subjects of mathematics, science and English (and Welsh in Wales), with the other subjects to follow later. For each development, a sequence was envisaged of selective trialling followed in successive years by a national piloting of materials on a sample basis, a 'full unreported run' and the 'first full run' of the developed tests. That point would be reached earlier in some Key Stages than in others. The full use of SATs (or modified public exams in the case of Key Stage 4) in all maintained schools for pupils of the relevant age was thus scheduled to occur in 1992 for 7-year-olds, in 1993 for 14-year-olds, in 1994 for 16-year-olds and 1995 for 11-year-olds.

Figure 1: Timetable for National Curriculum Assessment

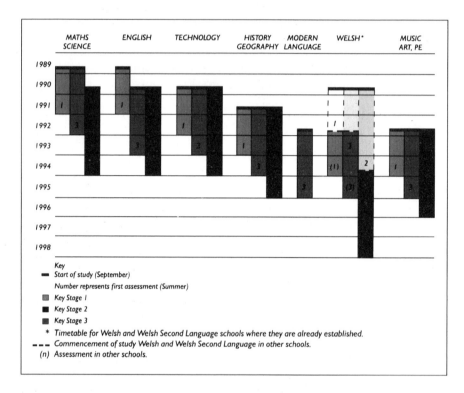

Thus by mid-1993, when the system was subjected to a full-scale review, the national assessments at Key Stages 2 and 4 were still at an early stage in their development with their ultimate character and impact far from clear. However, there had been time for the Key Stage 1 and Key Stage 3 SATs to evolve through a development phase into their full operational form affecting all pupils in the relevant age group. Much of what had been implicit or obscure in the TGAT model had been exposed to the realities of implementation and to the political and public scrutiny of the modes of assessment which emerged from the development process.

The Key Stage 1 SATs

The assessment of 7-year-olds was chosen as the first context for developing a national assessment system. The design of the end-of-stage testing arrangements could have begun at any of the Key Stages, or indeed with each being developed concurrently, and there is no clear evidence as to why officials and ministers decided that Key Stage 1 should be first in line. The formal testing of pupils at the age of 7 would be more out of line with current practice than would testing at 11 or 14 and it had met with considerable opposition from teachers. Yet, with a narrower range of attainments and greater flexibility of classroom organization, the TGAT approach of assessment activities scarcely distinguishable from routine work perhaps stood a greater chance of successful realization in year 2 classrooms.

Just as work on designing Orders for mathematics and science was well advanced before TGAT had reported, so the specification for Key Stage 1 SATs in English, mathematics and science was well in hand in the DES before the relevant advisory body, SEAC, had been established. A tight timetable, with development work to begin in January 1989, did not allow for lengthy consideration of the issues. In the event, thirty bids to undertake the work were received by SEAC, ranging from established assessment agencies through higher education institutions to individuals with an ambition to make their mark on the education system. Aside from the question of competence, substantial differences in the strategies which agencies proposed to adopt were revealed in their submissions. For example, on an important aspect of the design — whether the same tasks should be presented to pupils irrespective of their expected attainment level — two of the front runners among the agencies offered fundamentally different approaches. One agency proposed common tasks for pupils irrespective of their perceived ability level while the other favoured different tasks for pupils according to their perceived ability. In the event, the SEAC decision was to recommend allocation of funds for each of three agencies to undertake the trialling and piloting of tasks. The acceptance of this recommendation by ministers and their readiness to fund development work (the three contracts were costed at over £6m. in total) are a clear indication of their willingness to explore alternative approaches in the uncharted territory of the testing of all 7-year-olds.

The specification against which the contracts were let was the first formal attempt to turn the TGAT model into a workable scheme of assessment. It explicitly required that the SATs 'should be of the kind proposed by TGAT' and many of the Task Group's ambitions which were later to fade into the background were also prominent in the wording of the specification. The purpose of the SATs was stated as being formative — feeding back into children's learning — as well as summative. Each child would take three tasks but these would be chosen by the teacher from a bank of at least nine. Yet in spite of a firm grounding in the TGAT view of assessment there were many indications that much remained open to be determined in the light of evidence from development work. For example, 'it will be part of the task of the development agencies to assess and advise on what proportion of attainment targets should be covered'.

Whether what the agencies were being asked to do was feasible did not surface as a major concern at the time. None of the main players — ministers, officials, SEAC or (perhaps more understandably) the successful agencies — challenged the idea that valid, reliable tasks could be developed to assess pupils of very varying abilities across the full range of attainments (three or perhaps four 'levels') in the core subjects. The shape of the relevant Statutory Orders in the core subjects had by then become clear; attainment levels would be needed for each pupil across thirty-two attainment targets in the 'core subjects' of mathematics, science and English[1].

Responses to the First SATs

Glimpses of sample SAT materials were offered to the press in December 1989 and some of the cracks in the facade of the TGAT model began to show. The *Daily Mail* on the one hand, on the basis of reaction from a few able children at a school in Stoke Poges, referred to the maths tasks as 'simplicity itself'. A *Times Educational Supplement* Editorial, however, grudgingly concluded that the benefits of the original TGAT model were 'just about discernible in all this'.

As the time approached for a 2 per cent sample of schools to use the 1990 SATs with their 7-year-old pupils, DES ministers and SEAC were concerned to put across the message that lessons were being learned from the first few months of teacher assessment and trialling of SATs. Secretary of State John MacGregor, in a March 1990 speech, sought to allay the fears of teachers that 'a tremendous assessment edifice is being constructed' and assured them that the revised tests would be more manageable. Not only would the burden of assessment be reduced but the TGAT philosophy of tests scarcely distinguishable from ordinary classroom work remained, for the moment at least, intact:

> To realize the improvements in teaching and learning potentially offered by the National Curriculum, we must ensure that assessment or testing is part of normal classroom practice. (John MacGregor speech to Norfolk teachers, 10 March 1990)

However, before the end of May, *Education* was reporting: 'serious doubts over the feasibility and desirability of the Government's national arrangements emerged this week as the first pilot studies of testing for 7-year-olds came to an end'. *The Times* followed with a report headed 'New tests fail the grade' suggesting 'doubts are growing'. More signals soon followed from Education Department ministers and from SEAC to the effect that further 'slimming down' of the tests could be expected. Acknowledgment of the difficulties was welcomed by teacher union leaders as the first sign of Government admitting previous plans were 'unrealistic and over-ambitious' (Peter Smith, AMMA). The more optimistic amongst the union spokesmen, such as Nigel de Gruchy (NAS/UWT), were even able to see a prospect of the Government abandoning all formal testing until the age of 16. However, those who had always been critical of the TGAT approach to testing also took some encouragement from what was being perceived as a policy in disarray. The presentation of the issue in the tabloid press was typically uncompromising.

By the end of June it had become '7+ tears force school exam U-turn' (*Today*) and 'Betrayal of our children' (*Daily Mail*), with Dr. Sheila Lawlor of the Centre for Policy Studies commenting 'these are not real tests at all'. The image of policy-makers back-pedalling fast, already established by press response to the decision in April to limit the range of subjects to be tested at the end of each Key Stage (see below) was thus being strongly reinforced by the admission on all sides that further changes would be needed at Key Stage 1.

When the Chairman of SEAC next wrote to the Secretary of State about Key Stage 1 matters in July 1990 he stressed that 'the one clear implication of the pilot is that the 1991 SATs must demand less classroom time than the pilot SATs'. However, in his rehearsing of aspects of the pilot, it was also obvious that other things were far from clear. All the agencies had shown that assessing against all the relevant attainment targets was not feasible. But on which attainment targets should the 1991 SATs focus? Those best suited to the standard test situation? Or those most useful for making comparisons across schools? Or perhaps those judged, on criteria yet to be determined, of greatest importance to the education of 7-year-olds? And should there be any choice for teachers and schools in deciding which attainments to test in the SAT part of the assessment process? None of these were questions on which the original source book of ideas, the TGAT Report, offered much, if any, guidance.

The Assessment Council's own evaluation unit's report confirmed many of the doubts about the 1990 SATs which had been aired in the press. Indeed the unit concluded 'the pilot cannot be regarded as a reasonable trial of the effectiveness of SATs as the major lesson learned was that the SATs as piloted were unmanageable and therefore ineffective'. Clearly, at least in private if not for public consumption, something close to 'back to the drawing board' was required. Attainment would need to be assessed in sufficient depth and across a realistic range of aspects of attainment if the SAT outcomes were to reach an acceptable level of validity and reliability. The decision to revise the Key Stage 1 SAT specification and award a contract to one agency for the 1991 SATs was thus taken against a background both of critical evaluation of the pilot evidence and increasingly hostile press reaction to the 'standard task' approach to judging pupils' attainments. Though practice had already shifted some way from the TGAT vision of a sampling of attainment across a small number of profile components, concerns other than the validity of the testing procedures were beginning to dominate the debate about assessment at Key Stage 1.

The SAT Model is Modified

'Manageability' was now to the fore in much of the discussion about the future shape of SATs for 7-year-olds, obscuring the continuing need to decide how to achieve an acceptable balance between validity and reliability. As strategies for pruning the SATs were rehearsed, the major concern became whether they could be administered within a reasonable span of time in a typical infants classroom. Limiting the time spent on SATs necessarily led to restricting their coverage of the thirty-two attainment targets in the core subjects. A dilemma so familiar to test designers surfaced for the first time in the brave new world of SATs. How to sample the subject matter to be assessed in such a way that a representative picture of attainment emerges and yet the preceding teaching programme is not distorted by being focused only on what is to be assessed?

The 'Mark 2' SATs for 7-year-olds resolved this with a compromise which proved acceptable to ministers. To no-one's surprise, certain of the attainment targets in English and mathematics would remain part of the SAT for all pupils — reading, writing, handwriting and number. The assessment of pupils in the 'process' attainment targets in mathematics and science ('using and applying mathematics', 'exploration of science'), the source of much teacher anxiety and significant manageability problems, was also retained within the slimmed down SAT. In addition, teachers were to be given a constrained choice of which other attainment targets in those subjects to include in the SAT materials presented to children. In the name of 'manageability' the first steps had been taken, through the stipulation of what would be tested, to identifying a 'core within a core' — those elements of the statutory curriculum in the core subjects in which all pupils would be tested every year.

SEAC's description of the 1991 SATs continued to emphasize that the materials would take a variety of forms and, to meet the manageability concerns, much was made of the expectation that they would take about thirty hours of classroom time over a period of three weeks. Less stress was put on the fact that the 1991 SATs represented a marked shift in policy away from the original TGAT conception in three important respects. The idea of theme-based assessment activities, echoing what was thought to be (but often proved not to be!) the cross-curricular approach typically adopted in the infant classroom, was being replaced by a series of tasks each of which related to one of the three core subjects. The *Daily Mail* went so far as to describe the new SATs as 'A back-to-basics test on the three Rs', a description which owed more to the paper's hopes than to any realistic judgment of the relatively modest changes then envisaged by SEAC. In the new specification, the scope for the tasks to be scarcely distinguishable from ordinary classroom work was further limited by the restrictions on teacher choice of task. Most significant of all, however, was the first acknowledgment by policy-makers that assessing a broadly-based curriculum defined in criterion-referenced terms would necessarily entail decisions about which attainments were to be covered within the severe constraints of a time-limited assessment process. The work begun in the autumn of 1990 by the successful agency, NFER/Bishop Grosseteste College, was to prepare for the first occasion when all pupils in a particular age group would undergo the SAT experience.

In spite of the changes, and in particular the concern with manageability of the new materials, the distribution to schools of the 1991 SATs prompted renewed criticism in the press. The agency's project co-ordinator explained to *Today*:

These will be normal classroom activities for 7-year-olds. There will be no sitting in rows in silence — they are not tests in that sense. (5 April 1991)

But *The Sunday Times* headlined its report (10 March 1991) 'New classroom tests caned as too easy'. *The Daily Telegraph*, using the by now familiar tactic in several papers of contrasting experience in independent schools with that in state schools, concluded: 'clear evidence is emerging that (the national testing of 7-year-olds) is proving a costly and damaging failure' (2 May 1991).

The *Mail on Sunday* commented: 'the 272 pages of tests . . . are still based on vague and unreliable "classroom activities" which will be extremely difficult for teachers to conduct and fail to give the Government what it wants — an overall picture of national standards' (17 March 1991). For the *Mail on Sunday*, as for many other critics of Key Stage 1 standard tasks, the issue was not only one of how manageable the tests were for the teacher but also of how useful the results would be in relation to what it regarded as a central purpose of national assessment, supplying reliable evidence on 'national standards'.

Education ministers sought to distance themselves from the approach to testing approved by their predecessors. An Editorial in *The Times* (19 July 1991) referred to Kenneth Clarke being 'determined not to pay the political price for mistakes made by educational professionals. The most notable of these is the near-fiasco of the Standard Assessment Tasks for 7-year-olds . . .'. The Secretary of State himself was reported as encouraging the view that testing was a simple enough matter if only it could be taken out of the hands of specialists:

Teachers and educationalists keep telling him that there is more to reading than 'decoding' the written word. They won't devise any test which doesn't assess whether children read for meaning and enjoyment and can make sensible guesses. . . . 'It is not beyond the wit of man to devise a straightforward test of reading and I intend to persist until they do so.' (*Mail on Sunday*, 16 June 1991)

The summer of 1991 brought a series of events which were to prove significant for the direction of assessment policy at every Key Stage. The newly-appointed Chairman of SEAC, replacing former civil servant and headteacher, Philip Halsey, was Lord Griffiths who, as Brian Griffiths, had been involved in the March 1988 challenge to the TGAT Report from the Prime Minister's Policy Unit and who also chaired the influential Right wing Centre for Policy Studies. He soon made clear in interviews his preference for 'pencil and paper tests' and the priority he would give to the 'basics'. 'I'll bring back three Rs vows new exam supremo' was the *Daily Express* headline. But at the same time the Minister of State, Tim Eggar, was attempting to reassure teachers' leaders that the Key Stage 1 SATs would not be radically altered for the following year. The political balancing act thus continued. While preparing for fundamental changes to plans for testing at Key Stages 3 and 4, ministers were willing to let developments at Key Stage 1, already well advanced, to continue along the lines established in 1991.

The 1992 SATs: Further Changes

There was to be no change of agency responsible for Key Stage 1 SATs in 1992 or for 1993. Indeed, the agency in question, NFER/BGC, had been one of the three awarded the original development contracts in the autumn of 1988. However, some further adjustments were made for the next generation of SATs. Just before his sudden resignation, the outgoing SEAC Chairman, Philip Halsay, acknowledged in his advice on the Key Stage 1 SATS for 1992 the continuing problems of manageability:

> On average teachers devoted forty-four hours of classroom time to the tasks . . . The activities for the process attainment targets in mathematics and science were particularly time-consuming.

He was keen to counter suggestions that the SATs had proved not only time-consuming but of little value. Many children had enjoyed the SAT activities and, in about a third of cases, the SAT evidence had produced results which differed from those reached through teacher assessment.

In spite of SEAC's defence of the value of SATs, for pragmatic and political reasons some adjustments to the coverage and the style of SATs were made for 1992. The number of attainment targets assessed statutorily at the end of the stage was reduced still further to seven — five compulsory (four in English and one in mathematics) and two more through a constrained choice from two attainment targets in mathematics and two in science. Beyond the statutory requirements, 'SAT-type materials' were to be available to teachers to help them make their assessments in a further eight attainment targets, including speaking and listening in English, for which the material circulated in 1991 was again recommended. The aim of devising SATs which took no more than thirty hours of class time was to be realized not only by focussing on fewer attainment targets during the statutory SAT period. The pressure on classroom time was also to be eased by spreading the expected thirty hours of SAT administration over a much longer period. More significantly in relation to the original TGAT conception, the SATs were to be shorter, to be taken where possible by groups or whole classes of children at the same time and to lay greater emphasis on written modes of test.

Yet while the struggle to achieve the elusive goal of manageability was intensifying, three other steps were being taken to *extend* the scope of the standard tasks. Firstly, ministerial concern about the inability of earlier SATs to identify attainment above level 3 led to materials being devised for 1992 to show which pupils had reached level 4. Secondly, the Secretary of State had asked SEAC to commission a survey of the reading standards of 7-year-olds. Publicity surrounding the publication of the report of that survey, combined with concern about such a wide range of reading attainment covered by level 2 in the 1991 SATs (actually a built-in feature of the TGAT model and not confined to reading), led to a clear sense of 'something must be done' about the testing of reading. Ministers and DES officials pressed on SEAC the suggestion that a written test of reading comprehension be introduced in 1992, making it possible for a grade to be assigned from A to E within level 2. Thirdly, standards of spelling in schools were also the subject of ministerial concern which, in the context of marks for spelling in GCSE examinations, had been expressed to SEAC first in September 1990. The same concerns were aired in relation to Key Stage 1 and a written test of spelling was added to the SAT materials for 1992. At a time when the contrary aim of reducing the time required for SATs had appeared to be the main concern, these three initiatives showed very clearly where ministerial priorities were in the evolving process of deciding the attainments given the status of inclusion in the SAT process.

The announcement, in early December 1991, of the Key Stage 1 tests for the following year received a notably more favourable reception from most sections of the press. Most of the hoped-for political messages came through strongly: 'Bright pupils will take tougher tests' (*The Times*), 'New school tests spell out the basic values' (*Daily Mail*), 'Minister unveils "slimline" tests' (*The Times Educational Supplement*). Only from the Labour opposition and its ally in the press ('Tories botch exams for 7-year-olds—yet again' *Daily Mirror*) was the reaction still hostile. Some of the Government's fiercest critics seemed to be satisfied that the Government was now, as it embarked upon the fourth year of Key Stage 1 testing, on the right track:

> It is the end for all the experimentation. These tests will be clear, objective tests in the interests of pupils. In our grandmothers' day everyone could do sums in their heads and we want to get back to those days. (Dr. Sheila Lawlor, quoted in *The Observer*, 1 December 1991)

Though the 1992 tests would still involve teachers administering a variety of tasks in their own classrooms at times of their own choosing it would seem that even voices on the Right who had been outspokenly critical of the early Key Stage 1 developments now believed the tests to be sufficiently clear and 'objective'. It took the publication of aggregate results from the 1991 tests to raise new doubts as to whether the testing methods and procedures at this Key Stage were sufficiently consistent to provide a reliable basis for comparisons of performance across schools and local education authorities (see chapter 5).

One further, less publicized, change adopted for 1992 should be emphasized. It had from the outset been the case that teachers were expected to form their own judgments, during the Key Stage, on the levels of attainment demonstrated by their pupils. The role of what came to be referred to as 'teacher assessment' (though of course the standard tasks were also being administered and marked by teachers) is discussed more fully in the next chapter. However, it is worth noting here that, for 1992, the deadline for completing the teacher assessment record (across all attainment targets in the core subjects) was moved from before the SAT period to after that period was over. In the attainment targets where the SATs were required (four in English, two in maths and one in science), teachers would now be able to take account of the SAT evidence in finalizing their decisions on teacher assessment levels. As well as being separately recorded, the SAT levels in those targets would thus also influence the teacher assessment record. No longer would there be two distinct judgments, with the internal decision not being influenced by the external standard tasks but the latter being 'preferred' for reporting purposes where the two outcomes differed. With one simple decision, to which relatively little publicity was given, the policy-makers made a fundamental change in the model on which the whole system was based.

Steady Development?

Though the course of SAT Development at Key Stage 1 seemed now to be clearly established, the first half of 1992 saw further intermittent criticisms of the SATs for 7-year-olds (or 'tests' as they were increasingly described). Publication of the 1991 results just before Christmas 1991 reopened the question of the usefulness of the exercise as a whole and provided a fresh opportunity for the airing of critical views from teachers' organizations. According to *The Guardian* (2 January 1992) 'headteachers have criticized this year's slimmed-down tests for 7-year-olds as ambiguous, confusing and time-consuming'. In a letter to the Secretary of State, the NAHT had argued that the tests 'will fail to provide valid assessment of children's abilities in reading and other important areas' (*Daily Telegraph*, 2 January 1992). The independent evaluations of the 1991 experience, which appeared in the early months of 1992, offered an inevitably mixed bag of positive and negative features. Some pointed to the conclusion of HM Inspectors that the tests had made heavy demands on teachers and were reliably administered in only 80 per cent of classrooms and cast doubt on the future: 'Flawed tests for 7-year-olds to be published' (*The Guardian*, 22 May 1992). Others preferred to emphasize that children enjoyed the tests and, in some respects at least, they had helped improve the quality of teaching: 'Good report on the tests of 7-year-olds' (*Daily Telegraph*, 22 May 1992).

During the period when the Key Stage 1 SATs were being administered in the schools far less press comment appeared than in previous years, in part because their counterparts at Key Stage 3 had become more the focus of attention. *The Independent* did report (2 June 1992) a survey undertaken by the University of Leeds for the NUT which revealed that '96 per cent of teachers thought the level of disruption caused by the tests far outweighed any educational benefits'. However, the new Secretary of State, John Patten, was unsympathetic, preferring to blame the union itself for discontent among teachers. In a strongly-worded letter to the NUT General Secretary, Doug McAvoy, he went on to the offensive:

I have to say that I find your union's troublesome behaviour over this matter grossly irresponsible and totally at variance with what is clearly in the best interests of parents, teachers and — above all — pupils.

When more systematic evidence from the 1992 experience became available, SEAC was able to take some comfort from the fact that, on average, administration of the tasks by teachers was shown to have taken only about half the time when compared with the previous year. More minor changes were envisaged for 1993, including a further extension, to fifteen weeks (six weeks in 1991, thirteen weeks in 1992), of the period within which teachers would be expected to complete the work of testing all their year 2 pupils. The materials used in the 1993 tasks were to be further modified in the light of experience. The only significant change in coverage of attainments would be making compulsory (for pupils at level 2 and above) the specific tests of reading comprehension and spelling. As had happened when the 1992 tests had been announced, the statement by Lady Blatch (Minister of State at the renamed Department for Education) on the changes for 1993 met with a press reaction which explained rather than challenged, highlighting the new features: 'All children to have old-style spelling tests' (*Sunday Times*), 'Algebra and physics tests for 7-year-olds' (*Daily Telegraph*). Even the usually more critical *Times Educational Supplement* reported 'the shape of tests for 7-year-olds appears fixed for the foreseeable future' (23 October 1992).

Plans were indeed already in hand by mid-1992 to take a similar model of Key Stage 1 testing forward into the period 1994 to 1996. Contracts were let to an agency for each core subject. Designing entirely separate tests in each subject represented a major shift of policy from that put forward in the TGAT Report and adopted in the original Key Stage 1 pilot SATs. But in other respects — selective coverage of attainment targets, administration by teachers in their own classrooms at a time of their choosing — Key Stage 1 national assessment seemed to have settled into a pattern which would be sustained for several years. While many of those closest to the process remained unconvinced that the benefits derived from the standard tasks justified the time and expense involved, the volume of public and professionalism criticism had declined from the peaks of 1990 and 1991. Given the Conservative Government's strong commitment to formal tests at the end of each Key Stage, its re-election in April 1992 seemed to signal continuity of development.

Yet for Key Stage 1 teachers the overall problem of manageability was still very much a live issue. While the excessive demands of the original SATs had been eased, they were still required to record teacher assessment levels in all attainment targets in the core subjects. Although the number of those targets in the core subjects had been reduced with new Orders in maths and science coming into effect in September 1992, the teacher assessment workload continued to increase as other foundation subjects became statutory (figure 1).

In April 1993, problems at Key Stage 3 were to precipitate a fundamental rethink. Though not the main cause of that rethink, continuing anxiety and concern among Key Stage 1 teachers about the combined impact of teacher assessment and SATs contributed to the ultimately irresistible demand from teachers' associations for a change of direction in national assessment policy. The policy at Key Stage 1 had, however, already been modified significantly, year by year and step by step, until it bore only a very loose resemblance to the broad, varied, cross-curricular, classroom activities originally conceived. There had been a growing emphasis on written, subject-based tests administered to the whole class at the same time. And the curriculum coverage of those tests had increasingly focused on the 'three Rs'. As stated in the Government guide (*How is your child doing at school?*, May 1992) for parents on tests for 7-year-olds: 'this is when the foundations are being laid in the basics of reading, writing and arithmetic'.

The Key Stage 3 SATs

Standard assessment tasks for Key Stage 3 grew from the same roots as those for Key Stage 1. The TGAT Report argued for an approach to assessment which would be consistent across all stages with only limited adjustments to accommodate the certification of 16-year-olds. In accepting that Report ministers accepted a central tenet of the Task Group. If the system was to reinforce progression in pupils' learning from the age of 5 through to 16 it must have a common framework of attainment definitions and assessment methods across the Key Stages.

That proposition can be best viewed as an ideal, one which was always likely to be compromised by the different styles of curriculum planning and of teaching to be found in schools at the various Key Stages. It was also to be modified as the distinct purposes associated with end-of-stage reporting in each Key Stage became more apparent. The Task Group itself had recommended (para. 121) that there should be fewer, more broadly-based 'profile components' at the primary stages, linked to 'full profiles for each subject' at Key Stage 3. The Government, however, chose not to adopt that recommendation, assigning the devising of every aspect of the curriculum and assessment framework to separate subject working groups. It was for each of those working groups to define a structure of subject-based attainment targets which be the basis for teacher assessment and standard task development across all Key Stages.

Several factors combined to ensure that the form which SATs were to take at Key Stage 3 was to diverge markedly from that adopted (even in its modified 1992 and 1993 versions) at Key Stage 1. After the initial development phase of three agencies trialling SATs, the work at Key Stage 1 was in the hands of a single agency (NFER/BGC) which was thus able, steered by SEAC and the DES, to leave its imprint on the still embryo concept of a 'SAT'. At Key Stage 3, however, because separate contracts were to be let for the trialling and piloting of standard tasks in each of the subjects, thus allowing scope for the distinctive assessment philosophies and traditions of secondary subject specialisms to shape the character of the SATs in each of the five subjects in the initial phase of development (English, mathematics, science, technology, Welsh). Reinforcing this potential for divergence was the decision to award contracts in each subject separately. In the event there were seven agencies (two in English and in technology) working in parallel during 1990 and 1991 to devise SATs to be administered 'at or near the end of' Key Stage 3. In those circumstances the problems of maintaining consistency of approach to SAT design and delivery, even within Key Stage 3, were soon in evidence.

As well as that branching of the SATs concept into differing interpretations across the subjects was another factor which was ultimately to prove more influential than any other in shaping the Key Stage 3 SATs. The timetable for introducing national assessments (figure 1) meant that, while work began in some subjects at both Key Stage 1 and Key Stage 3 in September 1989, the first cohort of pupils to reach the end of a Key Stage were the year 2 pupils in the summer term of 1991. After a three-year Key Stage, the first 14-year-olds to experience pilot end-of-stage assessment tasks were those who completed year 9 in the summer of 1992. In the letting of contracts, the trialling, piloting and then the first full run of SATs with the whole age group, the earliest Key Stage 3 developments (those in mathematics and science) were thus running approximately a year behind those at Key Stage 1. Two consequences of that timescale were significant. The early impact of work at Key Stage 3, on ministers, teachers, the public and the press, was to be coloured by the climate of opinion which developed at the time of the piloting of the SATs at Key Stage 1. Secondly, at the critical decision point for the transition from pilot to first full run of Key Stage 1 SATs, the ministerial team at the DES had been led by a Secretary of State, John MacGregor, who was receptive to professional advice and looked for consensus in taking policy forward. By the time, early in 1991, that the Key Stage 3 SATs work had reached the equivalent point, he had been replaced by his more combative successor, Kenneth Clarke, who was to prove sympathetic to those who sought a more straightforward, traditional approach to testing.

Early Development Work at Key Stage 3

In the two years leading up to that point, the seven agencies had been, not surprisingly, grappling with many of the same technical problems as those being encountered by the Key Stage 1 agencies. For example, where the Statutory Orders showed more than one statement of attainment at a given level in an attainment target, was the 'pure' criterion referencing approach of requiring evidence of mastery of all of them to be adopted? The 'n minus one' rule came early on to be regarded as the preferred, though not definitive, SEAC view. In other words, a pupil's failure to demonstrate attainment in relation to one of several statements of attainment at a given level could be disregarded in the award of that level. As time went on, other more sophisticated (and more obscure) strategies emerged such as 'rolling back', allowing a pupil's attainment at a higher level to compensate for gaps in his/her performance at a lower level.

Distinct concerns relating to the Orders in the five subjects and to existing assessment practice in those subjects were also in evidence. The attainment of individual pupils in mathematics was often seen to be particularly unevenly patterned across the levels. In science as well as mathematics, the number of attainment targets and statements of attainment in the Orders (since revised), meant that only a very light sampling of the range of attainment would be possible within the time constraints of end-of-stage tasks. Should that sampling concentrate on a small number of attainment targets to give a reliable as well as valid result or should the sample be across the full range of attainments? In English and technology, the agencies exposed the difficulty of devising standard tasks which would assess adequately some of the general, loosely-worded statements of attainment in those Orders. In those subjects too there was pressure (unsuccessful at the time) to give official endorsement to the concept of 'levelness' — taking the overall features of a pupil's work into account to reach a first judgment about level attained before relating the evidence to specific statements of attainment.

More generally, and across all the subjects involved, the real meaning of the by now commonly used term 'standard assessment task' was being shaped out of the experience of development and the political response to it. Four questions were at the heart of that shaping of meaning. First, would the tasks be given to pupils by their teachers in circumstances scarcely distinguishable from a routine lesson in the subject? Secondly, would the subject content of the tasks be closely specified or would there be considerable discretion for the teacher to take a given framework and relate it to a context of his/her choosing? Thirdly, would the tasks take the form of a series of short exercises, each focused on a specific aspect of attainment, or would they be broad in scope, allowing specific attainments to be demonstrated through responses to different aspects of the task? Fourthly, within the period set aside for SATs, would pupils be attempting the tasks at times determined by their teachers or would every pupil be facing SATs at the same time in every school in the country?

All these could be considered as essentially professional questions, drawing on existing expertise in the assessing of the five subjects involved. In the early months of Key Stage 3 SAT development, the professionals in the agencies were allowed to engage in their exploration of such questions, only lightly steered by SEAC and the DES. As in the TGAT paragraphs on which the development work was loosely based, the implicit concern was more with validity and match to the subject curriculum than with the reliability of the results the tasks were to be expected to deliver. However, this relatively free rein for developmental thinking was not to survive beyond the point where the first tasks were piloted in a small sample of schools across the country. When it came to approving the form of Key Stage 3 SATs to be administered to every year 9 pupil in maintained schools, the professionals were to be left in no doubt that the 1988 Act meant that such decisions were very much in the hands of ministers and their departmental officials.

That point was, however, still two years away when the ground was being prepared for Key Stage 3 SATs early in 1989. John MacGregor was to arrive and depart as Secretary of State in the period between approval of the specification by Kenneth Baker and the critical decisions from Kenneth Clarke on Key Stage 3 in the spring of 1991. Over that period much work was done in the attempt to put the standard task model of classroom-based testing into operation for 14-year-olds.

As at Key Stage 1, the specification was drawn up by the DES in the first instance before being put to SEAC for comment and was explicit about its foundations being in TGAT. Unlike the tests for 7-year-olds, however, those for 14-year-olds would have to be able to measure attainment at all ten of the attainment levels described in the Subject Orders. Whereas the extent and character of differentiation in the tasks set for Key Stage 1 was left open to be explored, separate SATs for pupils of differing abilities were envisaged from the start at Key Stage 3. It was on such issues as these that the early development work was concentrated.

When the time came, in December 1990, for SEAC to offer ministers formal (and public) advice on Key Stage 3 assessment, there was no clear resolution of many of the dilemmas faced by the developers. The Order in technology, for example, contained many loose, generalized statements of attainment, broad programmes of study with much discretion for the individual teacher, and put the business of 'making' at the centre of its concept of the subject. How could the agencies charged with designing the SATs produce valid, reliable tasks capable of being administered over a short span of time? In mathematics, there were problems of designing coherent assessment activities which sampled adequately the diverse and disparate attainment across the fourteen attainment targets in that Order? SEAC's December letter of advice on National Curriculum assessment said nothing about such matters, promising instead further advice in July 1991 following the first national pilot of Key Stage 3 SATs in mathematics and science (the pilot exercise in the other three subjects being scheduled for 1992). SEAC's attention was focused instead on related matters such as training, moderation and the proposal to delay the completion of teacher assessment records until after the SAT period, thus changing fundamentally the relationship between the two components of the end of stage judgment of attainment. The attention of the press was largely taken up with SEAC's recommendation, also in December 1990 and based mainly on anticipated problems at Key Stage 4, that the Orders for both science and mathematics should be revised.

Written Examinations Replace SATs

It was in the first part of 1991 that the initiative on Key Stage 3 slipped away from SEAC as DES officials and their ministers mounted a direct challenge to the modes of assessment then being trialled and piloted. The Secretary of State's response to the SEAC December advice, while mainly covering the same agenda, also fired the first warning shots in a confrontation over Key Stage 3 testing which was to come to a head two months later. The SAT materials prepared for the 1991 pilot in mathematics and science were shown to Kenneth Clarke and his team on 14 March. Such meetings of ministers, officials and SEAC representatives had become a regular feature of the relationship between the Government and its advisory body, especially as major policy issues came close to the point of decision. While on previous occasions there had been polite agreement to differ, none of the earlier meetings had shown a gulf as wide as was evident this time. The Government side, with the Secretary of State (Kenneth Clarke) very much in the lead, made clear its disapproval of the pilot tests and of the style of testing they represented. The exchange of letters which followed between SEAC and the DES can be seen as a watershed in the evolution of national testing in the secondary schools of England and Wales.

'The prototype tests in their present form' wrote Kenneth Clarke to SEAC 'do not, in our view, provide an acceptable model for the future'. The first national tests (the Secretary of State had abandoned the term standard assessment tasks) would need to be 'much more straightforward and sharply focused' and 'for the most part take the form of terminal, written examinations'. 'These tests paper (sic) should be undertaken by all 14-year-olds simultaneously and under controlled conditions' and, though practical and project work were not precluded, 'the presumption should be against such testing methods except where there is no alternative'. Some of the Secretary of State's criticism was directed at the manageability of the pilot tests but the main concern of the Government, that the tests would not prove sufficiently reliable for comparisons to be made across pupils, teachers, schools and LEAs, comes through in the first official statement of the purposes of testing clearly to depart from the TGAT approach of a single testing system to serve various purposes. 'The tests must . . . be kept simple and avoid over-elaboration. Their purpose is to provide a rigorous and objective measure of pupils' attainments'.

In his earlier letter in January, Clarke had referred to the end-of-stage tests at age 14 taking the form of 'written terminal examinations', claiming that he was 'reaffirming' the Government's view, though there does not seem to be a record of any prior use of that phrase in any public statement by ministers on National Curriculum assessment (except at Key Stage 4). SEAC Chairman, Philip Halsey, was at pains to point out in his reply of 22 March that the specification on which development had been based had been agreed with Clarke's predecessor. Quoting from the specification, he referred to 'packages of tasks administered through a range of modes' and 'a plurality of other measures, using written, oral, practical and graphic work done individually or in groups'. However, whatever the rhetoric and face-saving surrounding these exchanges, they clearly mark the death, at Key Stage 3 at least, of the TGAT idea of assessment tasks scarcely distinguishable from normal classroom work. Kenneth Clarke had not only abandoned the term, 'standard assessment task'. He had for the first time introduced the concept of 'examination' into the debate about national assessment at the stages other than the one where national examinations were already in place. The tests would not be administered under classroom conditions at a time of the teacher's choosing. They would, as far as possible, be in the written mode and take the form of time-limited papers answered by pupils on the same day in every school.

During this critical period, early in 1991, Key Stage 3 issues had for the first time come into prominence in the public debate about national assessment. Announcing his decisions in a speech to the Society of Education Officers, Kenneth Clarke said:

> I am persuaded that the process will be more manageable and the results will command more confidence if the tests are mainly in the form of short written tests.

The twin planks — manageability and reliability — of the case for examinations rather than TGAT-style SATs were thus placed at the centre of the Government's testing policy at this key stage. In another speech (to the Secondary Heads Association in March), Mr. Clarke, in one of his most memorable phrases, accused SEAC of approving 'elaborate nonsense' and made abundantly clear his preference for more traditional testing methods:

> Many of my advisers insist on coming back with over-complicated proposals. We have a hang-up about examinations in this country. One reason why examinations are so attractive is precisely because they have been adopted by generations as being manageable.

From the publicity given to the new policies, teachers at Key Stage 3 became aware that they and their pupils were to be guinea-pigs in piloting, during the summer term of 1991, an approach that the Government had already decided against. Rather than suffer the embarrassment, to the DES as well as to SEAC, of abandoning the mathematics and science pilots, it was decided to proceed and present the trials as being useful since they were 'intended to try out, and gather evidence about, a variety of different approaches' (SEAC letter to DES, March 1991). However, all subsequent work on Key Stage 3 testing was geared to working out and implementing a system of timed written examinations for 14-year-olds in seven subjects (eight in Wales).

The Examinations Model Unfolds

The specifications for this new phase of development work were drawn up while the 1991 pilot was proceeding and so were, following a now familiar pattern, unable to take full account of the evidence from piloting. The development agencies and SEAC itself were in any case becoming increasingly marginal as the DES took steps to ensure that the recent changes in policy were fully incorporated in the proposals to be put to ministers. Evaluation reports of the 1991 pilot showed that manageability had not proved a significant problem in most subjects at Key Stage 3 but such evidence was conveniently ignored as the new examinations model was already into a necessarily tightly scheduled development phase.

In the core subjects of English, mathematics and science, the written examinations would be designed to assess all attainment targets except one in each subject. It was anticipated that, following the revision of the mathematics and science Orders, it would be possible to sample adequately in the course of written examinations all but the first attainment target in each — 'Using and applying mathematics' and 'Scientific investigation'. In English, the first attainment target — 'Speaking and listening' — was also 'considered not suitable for assessment through short written tests. Assessment against these attainment targets requires rather longer tasks and, in some instances, interaction between pupil and teacher which does not fit well with the timed test approach' (SEAC advice to DES, July 1991). Persevering with the terminology of TGAT, if little else from that source, SEAC envisaged that 'the three attainment targets omitted from the SATs will be assessed by teachers in the course of classroom work' (though supported by standard materials made available to schools). With ministerial approval of this proposal, it became firmly established at least at Key Stage 3, that the more complex attainments embraced by certain attainment targets should be addressed through 'teacher assessment' while the written tests dealt with the content dominated targets. This was a formula which, though challenged for its separation of 'content' from 'process' in testing, was most appropriately applied to mathematics and science, where the first of the new attainment targets in each case was concerned with the process of learning mathematically or scientifically. It did not lend itself so neatly to other subjects, including English, where other aspects of attainment were no more readily assessed through written examinations than was speaking and listening, and technology, where very little of what was in the Orders could easily be tested in a timed, unseen, written examination.

Thus ministers could be satisfied that certain requirements associated with reliability and manageability had been met in the new development contracts which would now be put out to tender. Reinforcing the break with TGAT-style SATs, three of the five development contracts were awarded to GCSE examining boards. But there were still many questions to be resolved relating to the validity of the new, more restricted, mode of testing. After all, although ministers had insisted on departing from the TGAT model at Key Stage 3, they still had to contend with the Subject Orders by then in place, the devising of which their predecessors had explicitly required should be based on the TGAT Report.

To judge from Kenneth Clarke's letter replying to SEAC's submission of the specifications for developing 1992 Key Stage 3 SATs (in effect, already scrutinized and approved by his Department), whether the new generation of national examinations for 14-year-olds would test what they were supposed to test was not a major concern. Instead, his July response to SEAC focused on three matters — the dates suggested for the examinations, whether the tests would 'promote clarity of reporting' to parents and arrangements for a 'quality audit' of the 1992 results. Such an agenda of issues illustrates very well the extent to which the debate at Key Stage 3 had shifted from the professional agenda of TGAT and the agencies engaged in initial developments to the political concerns of bureaucratic control and a growing emphasis on test results as indicators of the quality of schooling.

By January 1992, the Government was ready to announce the form and timing of the tests. There would be a 'rigorous six hours of 14+ exams for

500,000 pupils' (*Daily Telegraph*, 7 January 1992). But teachers' organizations restated their opposition to the tests on both educational and workload grounds and threats of boycott were reported, not only by teachers but also by parents ('Parents ready to boycott 14+ exams', *Today* 8 January 1992).

A New Model in Place

As the second phase of development work began late in 1991 and continued into 1992, some of the professional concerns inevitably surfaced again. Though making use of evidence from a style of testing now abandoned, the report of SEAC's Evaluation and Monitoring Unit on the 1991 experience of assessment at Key Stage 3 put forward some conclusions of continuing relevance to the debate. The 1991 SATs were judged 'in most cases . . . capable of being used in the classroom with minimal difficulty' but 'making assessments, collecting evidence, marking and recording were either difficult or onerous in most subjects'. They had achieved 'acceptable' levels of validity but the best that could be said about reliability was that 'it was probably (in most cases) as high as could be achieved under the circumstances'.

The SEAC Unit proceeded to develop an argument that, with the new type of SAT being devised for 1992, both the characteristics and potential uses of the SATs and of teacher assessment were diverging. 'It may be that SATs, because they are carefully constructed with standard interpretations laid down, enable a more accurate assessment of pupils to be made. On the other hand it may be that the teacher assessment, because it covers a much wider range of attainments over a longer period of time, is a more thorough and thus better description of the child's overall attainment'. It would seem that, as the end-of-stage test became more distinct from 'teacher assessment', the possibility of them having separate though related functions was coming more sharply into focus. The implications of this for the status and role of teacher assessment are discussed more fully in the next chapter.

The work on the new model tests proceeded now in seven subjects; agencies embarked in January 1992 on early trials in geography and history. Of those agencies appointed to undertake development in the original five subjects, three had experience in the first phase of Key Stage 3 development. New agencies were appointed to devise the tests in science and in English. For the agencies in English, technology and Welsh, the piloting of tests with a 2 per cent sample was to be the main task in 1992. But it was mathematics and science once again to the fore as preparations were made for a national pilot of the new model tests on 8 and 9 June. Schools were not required to take part but were strongly encouraged to opt in and, if only to find out what was happening in advance of 1993 when there were to be statutory tests with the results published, the majority did so. Approximately 75 per cent of all schools with 14-year-old pupils opted in to the pilot tests.

When 14-year-olds sat the tests in June the new style of testing was the subject of more favourable press comment than its predecessor. Continuing criticisms from teachers and headteachers were noted but the majority of press reports of the mathematics and science tests were broadly accepting of testing through timed written examinations and did little more than set out the main features of the tests. For one of the main critics of the TGAT approach, the *Daily Mail*, there was much to celebrate. Less than two weeks after the pilot mathematics and science tests, the *Mail*'s education correspondent, under the headline 'School tests win top marks', reported that:

> (a) confidential interim report by inspectors on tests for 14-year-olds shows that concentration by pupils was 'excellent', the tests them- selves were 'rigorous', and teachers generally thought the questions set were good. (*Daily Mail*, 23 June 1992)

But, if confirmation were needed that the new-style tests were not quite as unproblematic as advocates of them suggested, it came in the same week as problems with the pilot tests in English surfaced. SEAC announced that it had terminated the contract of the agency it had appointed only a few months earlier to developed the Key Stage 3 examinations in that subject. Already, before the exercise had gone beyond a pilot in a 2 per cent sample of schools, the Council was looking for its fourth agency to devise tests in English.

By mid-1992 the first of the Key Stage 3 examinations had been tried out in schools. But the majority of pupils had encountered tests in only two subjects; the full range of examinations in seven subjects (eight in Wales) was still to come. Furthermore, schools had yet to experience the impact on them of publication of the test scores achieved by their pupils at this Key Stage.

Towards a Watershed in Policy

With a newly re-elected Conservative Government installed and a new Sec- retary of State, John Patten, signalling his intention to press ahead with in- troducing the tests, SEAC proceeded to implement plans already in place for 1993. Key Stage tests were scheduled in the core subjects together with tech- nology (and, in Wales, Welsh second language in those schools where Welsh was not a core subject). In addition, a small-scale pilot in approximately 2 per cent of schools was to take place in geography and history. SEAC was also beginning to look ahead to the spring of 1993 when it was anticipated that development work in the last of the subjects in which tests would be set, modern foreign languages, would begin. Thus there was every reason to expect that, by Easter 1993, work would be in hand in all seven of the subjects (eight in Wales) in which Key Stage 3 tests were planned.

Apart from technology and Welsh, the tests would take the form of time- limited written examinations timetabled over a period of ten days in mid- June. In those two subjects, exceptionally and in addition to some written examinations, extended tasks carried out over several weeks during ordinary lessons would form part of the statutory end-of-stage assessment. Thus, even after Kenneth Clarke had ensured that formal examinations would become the norm, a little of the TGAT ambition of assessment integrated into routine classroom work was still in evidence.

Those responsible for test development, in the contracted agencies and in SEAC as the body which advised on policy, were tackling some of the problems thrown up by the new model they were required to work to. For the most part, those problems remained a matter for debate among those engaged in the development process but they were numerous, complex and far from easy to resolve. How, for example, to sample adequately in perhaps two hours worth of examination questions the range of content specified in the Key Stage 3 programmes of study, covering as they did three years of schooling? How to set questions in those aspects of the Statutory Orders where considerable discretion had been given to the teacher to determine the precise topics the pupils in a particular school should study? How to organize the sets of question papers which, taken together (with each paper targeted at a limited range of attainment levels), would enable pupils whose attainment ranged from level 1 through to level 10 to show what they were capable of? How many opportunities should there be within a question paper for a candidate to show s/he had mastered any one of the statements of attainment? How to devise marking schemes for teachers to use which would make it possible for them to reach consistent decisions across all the schools involved? How to turn the series of decisions on whether the requirements of each individual statement of attainment had been satisfied into the award of levels in each of the relevant attainment targets (and then of a level in the subject as a whole)?

The way in which these problems presented themselves varied to some extent from subject to subject. In geography, for example, the sampling of 182 statements of attainment across five attainment targets in two one-hour examination papers was, to say the least, a daunting challenge for the development agency. In technology, the Order had left the contexts in which pupils would develop their technological skills and ideas to be determined by teachers in the schools, thus presenting the test designers with a very real difficulty in deciding which contexts should be used in the tests. But, while each subject presented a variant of the list of assessment problems referred to in the previous paragraph, all those problems were building up as the system moved from the TGAT design brief via development specification and piloting to full implementation.

The lead from politicians had been clear enough — timed unseen written examinations were to be the means of arriving at levels of attainment for every pupil in every subject tested. But it is doubtful if the politicians and officials who had determined that course were aware of the technical difficulties to be overcome. The nearest equivalent context in England and Wales where national testing was already in place — examinations for 16-year-olds (GCSE since 1986) — provided relatively few pointers for the Key Stage 3 developers because, in important respects, they operated on an essentially different basis. Those examinations were designed to supply only a single grade showing how well a candidate had done relative to the other candidates. They did not, therefore, have to design each question to test a specific attainment and a candidate's answer could be allocated a mark representing his/her degree of success in meeting the question requirements. The award of grades depended mainly on adding up those marks rather than on finding ways of turning a series of yes/no decisions, taken on each question in turn, into an attainment target level (and then a subject level) which would have some meaning in terms of the statements of attainment to which they should relate. Furthermore, in the case of the GCSE, the setting of questions, the marking of questions and the award of grades were all facilitated by the existence of a syllabus which was written with examinations in mind. Not only were the Key Stage 3 test developers having to come to terms with the strict (and often unfamiliar) disciplines of criterion-referenced testing, they were doing so in relation to documents — the National Curriculum Orders with their programmes of study and statements of attainment — which had been written as curriculum guidelines rather than as testing specifications.

The emerging public conflict about national testing during the winter of 1992/93, focussing initially on the English tests at Key Stage 3, was thus fuelled by very real technical problems being experienced by those contracted to develop the tests. The original TGAT-based concept of end-of-stage testing at Key Stage 3 had been abruptly terminated by Kenneth Clarke. But his preferred alternative, hastily introduced in the middle of 1991, was equally unproven as a viable approach to assessing the Subject Orders. It was also, as the events of the early months of 1993 were to show, less acceptable to the teachers who remained, as administrators and markers of the externally-set tests, a key factor in the success of the testing model now favoured by politicians (see chapter 7).

Key Stage 2

While SAT development at Key Stages 1 and 3 was the subject of significant debate and of shifts in policy, little was said about policy on the testing of 11-year-olds. Key Stage 2 would be the last of the stages to experience full implementation of the National Curriculum with even the core subjects not becoming statutory in year 6 until the school year 1992/93. Decisions on the form of testing to be required for that year group could therefore be deferred.

The potential for conflict in determining a testing strategy for Key Stage 2 was, if anything, greater than at the preceding and succeeding stages. Much of the original hostile reaction to the 1987 consultation document heralding a national assessment system was fuelled by strong feelings about one of the most hotly-debated features of post-war education in England and Wales — the 11+ examination. For many of the critics of national assessment, the 11+ had been (and remained so into the 1990s in a few areas) the inherently unfair determinant of access to the high status, grammar school, sector of secondary education. Further, even where secondary schools were all non-selective in character, any assessment of pupils at what was, in most areas, the main point of transition between schools, would give added significance to the assessment results of 11-year-olds. When it is also recognized that the published aggregate scores of that age group would be used as 'end-point' indicators of the quality of primary schools, it is obvious that very high stakes indeed were attached to Key Stage 2 assessments, for the schools as well as for the individual child.

For the first three years of national assessment development little was done to clarify policy for Key Stage 2 testing. Some relatively low-profile exploratory work was undertaken, looking at current assessment practice in year 6 and trialling with 11-year-olds some SAT materials from the other key stages. However, on the major questions relating to key stage 2, teachers could only speculate about government intentions for that age group. Would the Key Stage 1 style of classroom-based task be the main vehicle for testing 11-year-olds? Or would the stress on reliability of the results lead to something akin to the timed, written examinations for 14-year-olds which replaced the earlier TGAT-based approach after 1991? What place, if any, would 'teacher assessment' evidence have in summarizing pupils' attainments at the end of year 6?

When the issue first surfaced on SEAC's agenda, in February 1989, there were indications that DES officials favoured some kind of mix of the test materials already available from the other two stages. Yet, however much the levels of attainment were supposedly not age-related, stimulus material designed for 7 or 14-year-olds might not be appropriate for 11-year-olds and references to Key Stage 2 were dropped from the initial specifications for work at Key Stage 3. The first hint of what was to follow came in Kenneth Clarke's letter to SEAC of January 1991. While agreeing to an investigation of the way in which tests already developed for Key Stages 1 and 3 could be of value in testing 11-year-olds, he added: 'as in the case of 14-year-olds, we shall expect these tests (for Key Stage 2) to be predominantly written'.

The major decisions about Key Stage 2 were thus deferred until the rolling programme of National Curriculum implementation meant that development work must start if the materials were to be ready in time for use as planned in 1994. In its letter of advice to the DES (13 February 1992), SEAC made clear that it favoured an approach to testing that was much closer to the new (post-Clarke) Key Stage 3 model than it was to what was happening at Key Stage 1 where, while much modified, elements of the original TGAT intentions were still discernible.

> We have had a preliminary discussion about the nature of the compulsory tests for Key Stage 2. We see them as being predominantly written and concentrating on the basics of English, mathematics and science and, in Wales, Welsh.

As to whether these tests of the basics should take the form of timetabled examinations, SEAC was seemingly content to defer to the Secretary of State rather than offer clear advice of its own:

> We would like to know if it is your intention that the tests for 11-year-olds should each be taken on the same day in each school, as is the case for 14-year-olds.

The Government response was delayed until after the April General Election and it came from the new Secretary of State. In his decision, communicated to SEAC in a letter in June (12 June 1992), John Patten made it known that there would be 'separate, self-standing tests' in each of the core subjects' and that 'the tests will focus on pupils' knowledge and understanding, leaving practical skills to be assessed by teachers on the basis of ordinary classroom work'. The form which testing would take was to be 'time-limited written examinations' taken by all pupils simultaneously. Except in their more limited subject coverage, 'the tests already established at KS3 (which span the same levels) should prove a sound model'.

Not to be outdone, the Minister of State in the Education Department, Baroness Blatch, was soon writing on her own account to SEAC (23 June 1992). From her visits to schools it had become apparent to her that schools were eager to take part in a pilot of the Key Stage 2 tests in 1993:

> There was almost unanimous feeling that schools would welcome the opportunity to take part in a dry run in order to familiarize themselves with the tests themselves and to take stock of the curriculum demands which underpin them.

Following a further exchange of letters with SEAC, the Secretary of State was ready to announce, at the start of the school summer holidays (21 July), the tests for 1993 which, narrowing still further the scope of end-of-stage testing, would 'focus on the basics of reading, writing, spelling and arithmetic'. John Patten was in confident mood, declaring his belief in the course he was taking:

> I am determined to ensure that the tests for 11-year-olds are rigorous and rewarding for those who take them. Sensible testing of pupils is essential to inform teachers, parents and pupils about how well children are doing at school by highlighting both strengths and weaknesses, showing where help is needed.
>
> The success of this year's pilot tests for 14-year-olds has convinced me that we should adopt the same approach for 11-year-olds. I am sure they, like this year's 14-year-olds, will take these tests in their stride.

Given that the new-style Key Stage 3 tests, in mathematics and science, had been piloted nationally in secondary schools only a few weeks earlier, the Secretary of State had clearly come to a remarkably rapid conclusion about the soundness of that model.

John Patten's announcement brought Key Stage 2 testing back into the news for the first time since 1987 when the prospect of testing 11-year-olds had reopened the issue of 11+ selection. Typical headlines were: 'Return of 11+ brings new exam agony for pupils' (*Today*), 'Tests raise fear of backdoor 11+' (*The Guardian*). While for primary schools the realities of testing at Key Stage 2 were still some months ahead (a 2 per cent pilot being planned for 1993) and the consequences for them of results being published were two years away, the question of what the tests were for was once again crucial. As at the other Key Stages, politicians and officials were unwilling to declare unequivocally the purpose, or purposes, which were driving the development process:

> A spokesman for the Department for Education said they were designed primarily to assess pupils' progress and to place them in one of the ten levels of the National Curriculum. 'If some schools also choose to make use of them for selection, that is up to them.' (*The Independent*, 23 July 1992)

Government approval having been given for the development process to proceed, SEAC awarded contracts to four agencies which would be responsible, one in each core subject (English, mathematics, science and Welsh), for the pilot in 1993 and for the statutory tests in the succeeding three years. Before the whole of national assessment policy was put in jeopardy by the events of early 1993, Key Stage 2 testing was seemingly on course to fill the one remaining gap in the policy picture across the four Key Stages.

Other SAT Developments

Throughout the early period of development of national assessment the focus of discussion about national policy was firmly on what form the end-of-stage SATs should take. Other important features of the overall assessment model, notably the nature of within-key-stage 'teacher assessment', appeared to be regarded by national policy-makers as almost entirely for determination at the level of the individual teacher (see chapter 4). In spite of such preoccupations among the policy-makers, alternative approaches to 'standardness' in national assessment began to creep on to the policy agenda in two ways, both of them a consequence of the 'manageability' debate at Key Stage 1.

It was very clear from the first pilot SATS in the core subjects at Key Stage 1 that, not only would those SATs require drastic slimming down, but any idea of further SATs in the same mould in other subjects would be unrealistic. In the aftermath of the 1990 trials, ministers were faced with the prospect of the only elements of the national assessment arrangements which could seriously claim to be 'standard' being the SATs covering aspects of attainment in the three core subjects. Unprompted by SEAC, the Secretary of State (John MacGregor) proposed a new type of assessment instrument, the 'non-statutory standard assessment task' (letter to SEAC, April 1990). He wished to avoid placing 'an unduly heavy burden on primary school teachers' which could be expected if statutory end-of-stage tests were introduced in the non-core subjects. Instead, for technology, history, geography, together with Welsh as a second language in Wales, he proposed that optional SATs be developed nationally under contract to SEAC and then offered to schools. Thus 'teacher assessment would be the means of determining, and reporting on, what 7-year-olds had attained by the end of the Key Stage; but they would be guided by observation of pupils' performance in standard assessment tasks available at the choice of the school'.

However sensible and pragmatic it may have been, MacGregor's decision was, predictably, presented by Government supporters and critics alike as the first major modification of policy on national assessment and testing. 'A retreat on testing' (*Financial Times*), 'Exams climbdown' (*Daily Express*), 'Tories back down on school tests' (*Daily Mirror*) and 'U-turn in schools as tests are scrapped' (*Daily Express*) were among the headlines greeting MacGregor's announcement. What was in fact an interesting initiative — tests were standard in form but made available to teachers to use as and when they judged appropriate — was clouded by the inevitable rhetoric surrounding any apparent retreat from policy objectives.

The expedient of standard tasks for use in support of teacher assessment again came to the rescue of the national policy-makers later in 1990 when further problems were encountered with the manageability of the core subject Key Stage 1 SATs. Where the assessment of certain attainment targets proved problematic, the fall-back position of providing standard materials but allowing teachers to decide when (and whether) to use them was adopted. By 1992 this was the case to some extent in each of the core subjects, with optional SAT materials — 'SAT-type activities' in SEAC speak — being available for use at Key Stage 1 (in addition to the statutory SATs) as follows:

English:	AT1 — Speaking and listening
	AT2 — Written text of reading comprehension
Mathematics:	ATs 1/9, 2, 11
Science:	ATs 1, 13, 16
	All level 4 related materials

At Key Stage 3 also, the 1992 test materials included a significant element of optional SATs in mathematics and science. Manageability problems in the mathematics and science pilot had played some part in this but it was the decision to favour timed written examinations as the mode for end-of-stage testing which ensured that assessment of the 'process' attainment targets in those subjects and of speaking and listening in English would be assigned to 'teacher assessment'.

Thus, from 1990, the Government introduced a significant new variant into the already complex pattern of national assessment arrangements. It was a notable departure from the earlier twin-track model (teacher assessment and the SAT), forming a bridge between deriving results from the largely unregulated judgment of teachers and obtaining them from more tightly constrained end-of-stage tests. The idea of a non-statutory SAT did not emerge from a careful review, discussed with SEAC, of the viability of that model. In its origins and in the way it was presented, the decision to make use of optional standard materials was very much one of expediency, a product of piecemeal rethinking of policy as evidence from implementation made policy changes inevitable.

What had started as a twin track model for arriving at end-of-stage judgments had become a triple track route to those judgments. Teacher assessment was still expected to deliver, at Key Stages 1 and 3, decisions about attainment levels across all attainment targets in all foundation subjects. Statutory end-of-stage SATs (or 'tests' to use the now preferred ministerial style) would be used to assess a few attainment targets at Key Stage 1 thought to be of particular significance in the education of that age group. At Key Stage 3 they would also, in their very different form of timed written examinations, be used to assess most attainments in seven subjects (eight in Wales). The third track — the optional SAT — had crept into the picture largely unheralded. But by mid-1992 it had taken on a significant role in assessing certain attainments in the core subjects at Key Stages 1 and 3 and in supporting teacher assessment in other subjects at Key Stage 1. When, in June 1992, the Government announced its decision on Key Stage 2 assessment, the use of non-mandatory tests in technology, history and geography was extended across the full primary age range from 5–11. Thus, for the first six years of National Curriculum work in three of the foundation subjects (together with a fourth — Welsh second language — in Wales), the third track was firmly in place as the chosen route to standardness.

Conclusion

National assessment had been constructed initially on the foundations set out by TGAT — standard assessment tasks, scarcely distinguishable from normal classroom activities and used by teachers at all Key Stages to supply all the evidence needed, whether it be for formative, summative or diagnostic purposes. In the course of its early development, the system of standard tests evolved gradually into a complex series of arrangements differing from the TGAT model in three fundamental respects. Firstly, the tasks themselves had undergone such a transformation that few of the TGAT design features remained. Secondly, the 'SAT' had, without much publicity, taken on a meaning distinct from its usual association with the end of a Key Stage, as the optional SATs proliferated in non-core subjects and in areas of the core subjects which could not be covered in end-of-stage tests. Thirdly, the way standard tasks were to be used had become so variable, subject-by-subject and key-stage-by-key-stage, that it was no longer possible to identify a single set of characteristics possessed by all national tests across the Key Stages.

It was only at the secondary stage that a sharp divide between national tests on the one hand and locally determined assessment by teachers on the other had been clearly established. For 14-year-olds the tests were (except in technology and Welsh where 'long tasks' were retained) time-limited, unseen examination papers taken by students under exam conditions at a specified time. They were distinct from the the process of 'teacher assessment' carried out by the teacher throughout the Key Stage. At Key Stage 1 however, while 'teacher assessment' remained similarly ill-defined, some of the features of the SATs envisaged by TGAT had been retained. The core subject SATs were standard in form and accompanied by instructions as to how teachers should administer them. But, unlike their Key Stage 3 equivalents, they were administered within ordinary lessons at times chosen by the teacher over a period of several weeks. Their 'standardness' derived from their common form, the instructions to teachers using them and the marking scheme supplied to teachers to guide judgments about individual pupils' work.

These selective adjustments to the original model were among the indicators of what had become a notable, though largely unacknowledged, feature of national assessment. From being a unitary concept to encompass the assessment of attainment across the full eleven years of compulsory schooling, the system was gradually evolving into a series of Key Stage variants. As policy was implemented, the assessment procedures at each Key Stage had increasingly taken on their own distinctive features.

For the type of SAT most often in the public eye — the statutory end-of-stage standard assessment tasks — four years of development had seen a move from a form in which 'pupils would not necessarily be aware of any departure from normal classroom work' (TGAT, para 49) to something much closer to conventional tests. Even the Key Stage 1 SATs, though administered in the ordinary classroom, employed a more limited range of modes of presentation, operation and response than TGAT had advocated; ministerial insistence on more 'paper and pencil' tasks taken by whole classes of children simultaneously had had a growing influence on test design. Kenneth Clarke, who became Secretary of State in November 1990, had early on signalled his preference for the no-nonsense word 'test' and followed that up with policy decisions during 1991 which saw a new model emerging for Key Stage 3 SATs. Prime Minister John Major's clampdown on coursework in GCSE (see chapter 6) in the summer of 1991 further reinforced a shift away from classroom-based assessments towards traditional written tests and exams.

Development of standard tasks had passed through three phases, each characterized by concern with one aspect of task design. A major concern of the Task Group on Assessment and Testing had been to show that there could be a national assessment system which did justice to the wide range of attainments teachers judged important. The *validity* of their standard assessment tasks figures strongly in the TGAT argument for tests with 'a wide range of modes of presentation, operation and response . . . so that each may be valid in relation to the attainment targets assessed'. The second phase of development, beginning early on in the design of Key Stage 1 tasks, is dominated by concerns about *manageability*. If, as was soon obvious, the full range of attainments could not be assessed through end-of-stage tests, how to modify the tasks so that teachers and pupils could complete them within an acceptable period of time? Early in 1991, development entered a third phase fuelled mainly by the concern of policy-makers about the potential *reliability*, especially at Key Stage 3, of what were by now called 'tests'. Reinforced by a 'back to basics' theme echoed by the Prime Minister, John Major, as well as his Secretary of State for Education, Kenneth Clarke, the new exam-style tests would have to deliver the reliable indicators of school quality so prominent in the high profile 'Parents' Charter'.

Ultimately if the assessment system as a whole was to achieve its objectives, a balance would have to be arrived at such that assessment procedures were seen to be, to an extent which was acceptable publicly and professionally, valid, reliable *and* manageable. It is certainly arguable that both the particular balance to be aimed for and the relative importance of the several purposes of the system should vary from one Key Stage to the next. However, as SAT development proceeded at Key Stages 1, 2 and 3 during the second part of 1992, there were no signs of a willingness on the part of the Government or its advisers to look beyond the hectic schedule of implementation and revisit the fundamental principles on which the system had been constructed.

Note

1 For those schools in Wales where children are taught in Welsh, Welsh is also a core subject.

4 Teacher Assessment and Moderation

Introduction

The Task Group on Assessment and Testing had proposed that the national assessment system be based on 'a combination of moderated teachers' ratings and standardized assessment tasks'. The first part of this twin track approach was stated more fully in these terms:

> We recommend that teachers' ratings of pupil performance should be used as a fundamental element of the national assessment system. Just as with the national tests or tasks, teachers' own ratings should be derived from a variety of methods of evoking and assessing pupils' responses. (TGAT Report, para 60).

What was to become known as 'teacher assessment' — the judgment by teachers, without necessarily any reference to standard tasks, was thus given a prominent place in the scheme of things as envisaged by the Task Group. That recommendation was a natural consequence of the Group's overall view of the character and purposes of a national assessment system. Since one of their four 'principles' was that assessment should have a formative purpose, it would follow that teachers should be able to adjust their assessment methods and their response to the results to the needs of individual pupils. A system wholly dependent on external tests would be unlikely to succeed in those terms. The Group would also be aware that a broadly-based curriculum defined in criterion-referenced terms could not be assessed adequately by using only standard test methods.

That the system should be moderated was another of the Group's four principles. It is possible to imagine a system which had the formative purpose as its central concern paying relatively little attention to whether the judgment of one teacher was comparable to that of another. But such a system would be very variable in its operation and in consequence, even in the unlikely event of that purpose being the driving force behind developing national scale assessments, it would be so diverse as to scarcely merit the term 'system'. When a central aim at national level is to provide reliable indicators of individual pupils' attainments, some guarantee of the comparability of those judgments becomes necessary. When a national system seeks also, through publication of the aggregated scores of individual pupils, to measure the performance of teachers and schools, such a guarantee becomes a crucial element in establishing its credibility.

Thus both the provision for 'teachers' ratings of pupil performance' and the establishing of arrangements for moderation (defined in TGAT as 'the process of bringing individual judgments into line with general standards') were essential elements in the TGAT model of national assessment. Yet in the early years of developing the system neither was to receive the attention accorded to the SATs, the most obvious pillars on which the system was being constructed and the one of most interest to politicians. Both concepts — teacher assessment and moderation — remained poorly defined. Policy-makers relied instead on piecemeal responses to specific needs — perhaps some guidance needed by teachers or a decision called for on the form of statutory regulation of assessment arrangements. Five years into the national assessment system the concept of a SAT had undergone development and change, but the nature of 'teacher assessment' and of 'moderation' remained unclear.

Part of that uncertainty lay in the extent to which teacher assessment and moderation might be closely interlinked. To some extent they must be. If teachers' assessments are to be used for summative and evaluative purposes, something must done to 'bring individual judgments into line'. Yet the idea of moderation is not one which should be associated only with teacher assessment; it is also relevant to the SATs. The provision of standard test materials and of guidelines for teachers to follow when they mark pupil responses does not in itself guarantee 'standardness'. There are several ways in which variability could be substantial and widespread. Are the SATs being administered in comparable ways in different classrooms? Are different teachers interpreting the guidance on marking in different ways? Arrangements for bringing into line would therefore also be required for the SAT element in the twin track system. Moderation can thus be seen as potentially being applied both to teacher assessment and to the SATs. However, until the idea of 'teacher assessment' was clarified, any consideration of appropriate arrangements for moderation would founder on the question — moderation of what?

Teacher Assessment

Definitions and Purposes

TGAT clearly articulated (paras 56–63) the case for reliance on a mixture of standard tasks and teachers' own ratings. The curriculum was 'inherently complex', far more complex than could reasonably be assessed on a single occasion in each Key Stage. With sampling of attainments therefore inevitable, 'a broad range of assessment instruments sampling a broad range of attainments' would discourage 'teaching to the test'. Diversity in the contexts for assessment and the occasions on which judgments were made was essential — 'written test responses might be supplemented by teacher observation of skills made in a systematic way'. Further, the risks of misjudging a pupil's attainment would be 'minimized in teachers' ratings of longer term performance because those are based on many occasions and many different types of task'.

In that sense at least, teachers' ratings could be argued as being potentially more reliable as well as more valid than relying on the evidence from stand-ard tasks. The freedom of professional decision — 'an important aspect of the National Curriculum' — was also called in support of a case for teacher assessment.

Thus, on grounds of fairness to pupils, curriculum compatibility and the freedom of teachers to decide upon classroom activities, TGAT argued that teachers' ratings of their own pupils should have a major role in national testing. The standard tasks, however varied they might be in modes of presentation, operation and response, could not be expected to assess all the attainments defined in the statutory curriculum. What was soon to be gener-ally termed 'teacher assessment' was thus born and seemed to have a promising future. That it was still in its cradle some years later can be attributed to a combination of factors.

Teacher assessment was not seen by policy-makers in the Government and the DES as an important component of the system. Its lack of growth was in part simply because it was overlooked; it experienced a kind of benign neglect as the imperatives of putting other pieces of the system in place on a tight timetable controlled the agenda for development. But it was also true that TGAT's arguments for teacher assessment would not go unchallenged by those in, and close to, the Government who were setting the policy agenda. The purposes for which teacher assessment was best suited — the formative and diagnostic — were not a high priority for those policy-makers. And the elements in the curriculum which only the teacher could be expected to assess, such as oral work in languages and practical work in the sciences, were not on their list of curriculum 'basics'.

One factor which increasingly affected policy decisions on many aspects of national assessment, was the extent to which Government ministers dis-trusted teachers. Though Kenneth Baker had accepted the TGAT proposals there was a considerable gulf between the TGAT philosophy of teacher judg-ments being central to the system's achievement of its objectives and minister-ial preoccupation with developing tests which would supply the evidence for comparing differences in attainments.

Policy Development at Key Stage 1: Incremental and Incidental

It is difficult to discern in ministerial pronouncements, DES press releases and the growing file of policy letters exchanged between the Government and its Assessment Council advisers any serious attempt to take the concept of teacher assessment beyond those few paragraphs in the TGAT Report. While SEAC considered at length the arguments surrounding SAT development, 'teacher assessment' appeared as an agenda item at meetings of the full Council only once in the first three years of its existence. Passing references to it can be found when other matters were under discussion but its only brief appearance at centre stage came in the summer of 1990 when SEAC responded to a DES request for advice on the subject.

The first point at which the National Curriculum impacted on schools was with the introduction of the core subjects in year 1 from September 1989. The haste with which contracts for Key Stage SATs were let reflected anxiety that there was little enough time to prepare standard tasks in readiness for that cohort of pupils reaching the end of the stage in the summer of 1991. Teacher assessment was not part of the brief given late in 1988 to the three agencies which were to develop standard tasks at Key Stage 1, though it rates a mention in a paragraph with the heading 'teacher assessment and moderation'. Thus, from the very first steps in development, a close linkage of the two was already blurring the distinction between what should have been two distinct features of the system's design. One, teacher assessment, was to be a source of attainment evidence. The other, moderation, was a means of ensuring such evidence, and that obtained from the standard tasks, would be sufficiently consistent in quality for comparisons to be made between pupils and across the whole system.

Though all the attention (and the funding) was being concentrated on the standard tasks at Key Stage 1, the part of the national assessment system which infants teachers would encounter first would be teacher assessment. They were expected to accumulate throughout the two years of the Key Stage evidence of pupils' attainments across all the core subject attainment targets. When September 1989 came, and teachers found themselves expected to put into place their own interpretations of teacher assessment, they had received no advice, guidance or directions from the centre about what practices might be appropriate. Though work was in hand from January 1989 on developing the Key Stage 1 SATs which 7-year-olds would encounter in the summer of 1991, what was logically a higher priority — how day-to-day assessments would be tackled by teachers starting in the autumn term of 1989 — seems not to have been seen as something requiring development, or even guidance to teachers.

Among teachers, however, there was a widespread impression that the way in which they would be expected to carry out teacher assessments would, in due course, be laid down nationally. Teacher assessment was, after all, part of a national system being imposed through an Act of Parliament; it is therefore not surprising that many teachers were waiting for instructions on how to tackle it. But when something 'official' on the subject did appear in schools, it took the form of three booklets prepared by SEAC offering only very general guidance on how schools and classroom teachers might develop their own practices. *A Guide to Teacher Assessment: Packs A, B and C* was distributed by SEAC in December 1990, fifteen months after teachers had started teacher assessments with their year 1 pupils.

The packs had been commissioned from one of the SAT agencies as a spin-off from its main work and met with a mixed reception from teachers. One headteacher, referring to the views of his staff, was forthright in his criticism:

Their reactions were threefold: anger at the superior tone of the so-called guidelines; dismay at the direction in which they appear to be leading our teaching force; and incredulity at the assumption that so much could be incorporated into one school day.

We simply do not understand what the authors are trying to say and are left with a confusing picture of half-truths and unanswered questions. We also have an uneasy feeling that SEAC has taken the path towards formative assessment, as they term it, because they want it to fail. (Jack Cornall, *Junior Education*, April 1990)

Packs A, B and C were indeed long on generalizations and short on down-to-earth practical suggestions on the matters which by then teachers were grappling with. What techniques would be appropriate for judging performance in relation to statements of attainment? How to judge whether a particular pupil response could be regarded as sufficient evidence of the attainment having been demonstrated? How much evidence to retain as proof of attainment? What kind of record-keeping system was expected of teachers and schools? The booklets had little to say on such matters. After all, the authors, like their intended readership and indeed everybody else however competent in other ways, lacked any substantial experience of assessment against attainment criteria of the type to be found in the Statutory Orders. TGAT had only presented the *idea* of teacher assessment; it had not offered, even tentatively, any suggestions about the practices and procedures which would be needed to turn that idea into reality in many thousands of schools across the country.

Given that ministers and their advisers did not make any statement on the subject, it is possible only to speculate about the reasons for this implicit downgrading of the teacher assessment component of the system. There may have been a sense in which, since it was to teachers that responsibility had been given in 'teacher assessment', anything emanating from SEAC or from DES more directive than a set of guidance booklets might be an inappropriate curbing of teachers' freedom to reach decisions as they judged fit. Since in the original SAT development brief there was still a prospect of SATs covering most of the attainment targets the lack of central direction need not affect unduly the reliance which could be placed on results obtained from some sort of combination, as yet unclear, of the two elements. The possibility of a national development project, generating ideas about teacher assessment, which could then be the basis for a common framework of practices does not appear to have been considered.

Teacher Assessment: An Administrative Arrangement

Instead teacher assessment came to be lodged in the part of the policy agenda labelled 'National Curriculum Assessment Arrangements'. 'Assessment arrangements' were what would be imposed on the schools through regulations under section 4 of the Education Reform Act, covering such matters as the timing of assessments and how schools would finalize attainment levels in the foundation subjects. Thus teacher assessment, if it was discussed at all, came to be considered in the context of the bureaucratic control of the procedures and outcomes of assessment. As was to be the case also with moderation, it was perceived by those responsible for policy as an aspect of the administration of the system rather than a set of professional practices to be developed to serve both formative and summative purposes. Its location as a part of 'Assessment arrangements' also affected the timing of any discussion of teacher assessment. The first regulations governing assessment at Key Stage 1 were not due to appear until July 1990 so, although it was of little comfort to teachers of infants classes during 1989/90, any stance to be taken on it could wait until the regulations were published in draft form in May of that year.

This low key approach to teacher assessment continued through 1989 and much of 1990. Teacher assessment was excluded from the first Key Stage 3 SAT specifications, more narrowly focused than the specification for Key Stage 1. SEAC went no further than indicating informally to the DES that it would expect additional resources for work at a later stage (unspecified) on this and other types of work excluded from the contract. When it came to the second phase of Key Stage 1 SAT development later in 1990, teacher assessment was again mentioned only in passing. The successful agency might be expected to prepare further guidance on teacher assessment to update what had been included in the *School Assessment Folder* which SEAC had sent to all schools with year 2 classes.

When, in March 1990, teacher assessment did surface in the exchanges on policy matters between SEAC and ministers, it was in relation to fears about its manageability:

> . . . we have some reservations about the burden which the teacher assessment element of the statutory arrangements may impose on teachers. (DES letter to SEAC, March 1990)

Thus SEAC did not initiate a review of teacher assessment and its role but John MacGregor's request for advice gave the Council an opportunity to review policy in this area.

The SEAC reply (July 1990), its only public policy statement on teacher assessment, makes some comments on the extent of evidence to be retained by teachers and the nature of record-keeping arrangements. On both matters the Council tried to counter the belief apparently held in some quarters that teacher assessment implied cupboards full of work done by pupils plus exhaustive (and exhausting) record-keeping systems. But a reading of this letter would leave a teacher little the wiser about the practice of teacher assessment. For example:

> The judgement made by a teacher for the teacher assessment element of the statutory assessment at the end of a Key Stage is to be expressed as a level for each attainment target. That judgement must be based upon an assessment related to the statements of attainment supported by sufficient evidence to enable the teacher to show that the judgement is a reasonable one. In some cases such judgments can be based on extended classroom work reviewed as a whole; in other cases it

will be appropriate for teachers to assess particular pupils in relation to specific statements of attainment. It must be for the individual teacher to judge where different approaches are appropriate. (SEAC letter to DES, July 1990)

In his response to the advice, the Secretary of State also relied heavily on spelling out self-evident truths:

The important thing is that the assessment and recording methods should be manageable for the teacher, while also offering a sound basis on which to determine pupils' achievements in relation to the statutory attainment targets at the end of the Key Stage. (DES letter to SEAC, August 1990)

It would seem that, as long as how teachers assessed their pupils was manageable and, in ways which were not defined, offered a 'sound basis' for end-of-stage decisions, they were free to choose their own methods of determining attainment levels. Yet the same government, less than twelve months later was, in the name of unreliability and unfair practice, to curtail coursework at Key Stage 4, a system laden with rules and procedures designed to ensure that teachers' judgments were brought into line.

Policy Development at Key Stage 3

When it came to teacher assessment at Key Stage 3, the same order of priorities was apparent in the recommendations from SEAC and Government decisions. Development of the SATs came first, with teacher assessment a long way behind, in the amount of attention given to it, in the timing of action on it and in the funding allocated. The first generation of Key Stage 3 SATs had already gone through a complete cycle of origination, development and rejection by ministers before the first official documentation on teacher assessment appeared. It took the form of a leaflet, *Teacher Assessment at Key Stage 3* (March 1991) which offered general guidance to schools. More substantial booklets, with examples of practice explained and discussed were produced during 1991, dealing with mathematics, science and, more generally, *Key Stage 3 Teacher Assessment in Practice*.

These SEAC publications clearly located responsibility for decisions about teacher assessment in the school. It belonged with the planning and teaching of the curriculum by individual teachers rather than with the decisions on a National Curriculum and assessment framework:

Teacher assessment is part of everyday teaching and learning in the classroom. Teachers discuss with pupils, guide their work, ask and answer questions, observe, help, encourage and challenge. In addition they mark and review written and other kinds of work. Through these activities they are continually finding out about their pupils' capabilities and achievements. This knowledge then informs plans for future work. It is this continuous process that makes up teacher assessment. It should not be seen as a separate activity necessarily requiring the use of extra tasks or tests. (*Teacher Assessment at Key Stage 3*)

Why should SEAC be content for the practices and procedures of this important element in a national system to be determined by individual teachers and schools?

National Curriculum assessment has two main purposes: to indicate what levels of attainment pupils have reached at the end of the Key Stage and to build up a picture of pupils over a period of time in order to help carry them forward in their learning. Teacher assessment is mainly concerned with the latter. (*Key Stage 3 Teacher Assessment in Practice*)

A Clear Role for Teacher Assessment?

Thus, in the wording of the Council's guidance material rather than in policy statements, its thinking on teacher assessment was at last beginning to unfold towards the end of 1991. In the original TGAT conception, both standard assessment tasks and teachers' ratings would contribute to end-of-stage judgments. In the subsequent SAT developments, at Key Stages 1 and 3, it had been clear early on that there would be some attainment targets for which the only evidence would come from teacher assessment. But it was still unclear whether the judgments of teachers on aspects of attainment where there was also SAT evidence would have any effect on the levels reported at the end of a Key Stage (an issue discussed later in this chapter). What was obvious was that there would be some attainment targets for which the only evidence on which end-of-stage reporting could be based would have come from teacher assessment. In those attainment targets at least, teacher assessment would have to play its part in meeting the summative and evaluative purposes of the assessment system. Yet SEAC, when offering guidance to teachers, was associating teacher assessment very much with the formative purposes of assessment. It was not at all clear, even to the teachers required to make judgments on pupils' work in relation to those attainment targets, how the one source of evidence could be both useful formatively and supply results dependable enough to be reported and published.

What is revealed in such documents is not just that teacher assessment received little attention from policy-makers. It is also apparent that, in the attention which had been given to it, the *function* of teacher assessment within the system as a whole had not been clearly defined. Were the twin tracks in the system to be parallel, each contributing something towards each of the declared purposes? Or were they separate and distinct, with teacher assessment linked to one set of purposes, SATs to another? The same uncertainty had been evident in the evolution of thinking about SATs as, especially at Key

Stage 3, they changed character from classroom exercises which might have both formative and summative uses, to formal tests which, it was hoped, could be relied upon for summative and evaluative purposes.

It was not as easy to tie the process of teacher assessment to a limited range of purposes. As a week-in, week-out responsibility of classroom teachers it would inevitably be presented as formative, supporting teaching and learning. The number of references to formative assessment in official documentation about national assessment seems to have declined steadily from the TGAT Report onwards and the policy-makers showed little interest in investigating how best to use assessment as a source of constructive feedback to the learner. But by its very nature, with or without support from national agencies, teacher assessment would have some contribution to the formative purposes of the system. In addition, however, the standard tasks could not cover the full range of attainments, leaving teacher assessment to fill the gaps. Could the same set of procedures do both jobs? It seems unlikely, although the third track referred to in the previous chapter — optional SATs — might make the attainment judgments reached in that way somewhat more reliable than the judgments reached through the 'do it your way' teacher assessment of the SEAC guidance documents.

The step-by-step, piece-by-piece approach of moving away from the TGAT model had, by mid-1992, resulted in standard tasks at Key Stages 1 and 3 substantially different from those envisaged by TGAT. But the nature and purposes of what was supposed to be the other main source of attainment evidence remained far from clear.

The first published report on teacher assessment in practice, produced by the agency responsible for SATs at Key Stage 1, NFER/BGC (*A Report on Teacher Assessment*, SEAC) appeared in June 1991. Though teacher assessment had been a legal requirement since September 1989 there was evidently a long way to go in implementing this part of the national assessment system. The 'vast majority' of teachers were reported to be attempting to assess and record against individual statements of attainment, with the resulting heavy burden of record-keeping as each judgment was recorded against each of the numerous specific attainment criteria embodied in those statements. In addition:

> . . . many teachers were clearly anxious about the introduction of National Curriculum Assessment which they perceived as a highly threatening move to hold teachers to account for the attainment of their pupils;
>   . . . they mentioned a heavy time commitment, both in and out of school hours, often supported by supply cover or by the head or other members of staff;
>   . . . teachers were uncertain about retaining tangible evidence of pupils' attainment;
>   . . . the majority of schools had not used (packs A, B and C) as they found the content complex and inaccessible;
>   . . . there was considerable variation in the quality of the support and its extent.

An equivalent evaluation report at Key Stage 3, published eighteen months later, was no more encouraging in its observations and conclusions. Among the findings in the report (NFER/Brunel, *Teacher Assessment in Mathematics and Science at Key Stage 3*, SEAC, December 1992) were:

> . . . a general view that science and mathematics departments were learning as they went along and other subject departments would learn from them;
>
> . . . a 'wait and see' policy whereby practices were not being developed until absolutely necessary, i.e. until 'someone tells us we have to do it' as one head of science remarked;
>
> . . . in many schools there was no systematic approach to the monitoring of teacher assessment at anything other than the departmental level;
>
> . . . LEA support . . . varied considerably from non-existent to substantial. However, even in those authorities offering considerable support, confusion was apparent over some issues being advised on;
>
> . . . few teachers did any formal assessment in the classroom and many were finding differentiation, especially during science activities, a serious challenge.

These two reports confirm a picture in which, though central direction on practice had not been given, teachers believed they would, in due course, be held accountable for the judgments they had made. With or without local support, which varied greatly from LEA to LEA, they were thus engaged in an enormously time-consuming process of assessing the specifics of pupils' attainment, recording meticulously what they had found and storing the evidence of pupils' performance in readiness for the day when someone might ask them to justify what they had recorded.

Moreover, while practice was developing rapidly in some schools as experience was gained, teacher assessment was not capable of supplying consistent judgments about pupil attainment. This was becoming increasingly apparent and was true not only for attainment target results which would go no further than appearing in reports to a pupil's parents but also for the attainment targets in mathematics and science (Ma1 and Sc1) where teacher assessment would be the only source, in the absence of end-of-stage tests of those attainments, of end-of-stage attainment levels.

A Crisis of Manageability

As each year went by, more and more teachers across Key Stages 1 to 3 found themselves required to undertake 'teacher assessments' against the relevant attainment targets in each foundation subject. In the early days of implementation, during the school year 1989/90, trying to make sense of what was required was a problem only for teachers of years 1 and 7 and only in relation to the mathematics and science attainment targets. As the implementation timetable (figure 1) shows, by the autumn term of 1992 the nature and scope of teacher assessment was a matter for all age groups in the primary school and for almost all specialists in the secondary school.

Part of the difficulty faced by teachers was the sheer scale of the expectations imposed upon them. Secondary science specialists had from the beginning questioned the feasibility of assessing pupils in relation to more than 400 statements of attainment made statutory by the 1989 Science Order. Yet, by the autumn of 1992, year 1 teachers, the original guinea-pigs, were being expected to assess their pupils against each attainment target in every one of the nine National Curriculum subjects (ten in Wales).

There was also widespread uncertainty about the degree of discretion permitted to teachers in carrying out the required assessments. Across the country individual teachers and groups of teachers evolved their own ways of interpreting teacher assessment. Elaborate record-keeping procedures, some of them sophisticated computer-dependent systems, were invented by eager innovators, often those local education authority staff who had a responsibility to train and support teachers. A plethora of practices thus developed in the vacuum created by the unwillingness of policy-makers to offer anything more than occasional leaflets and booklets which would prove even less influential because they appeared long after teachers had had to find their own solutions to meeting a statutory requirement so minimally explained. To the inherent problem of manageability and workload was thus added the problem of uncontrolled diversity of practice as teachers understandably exploited the freedom available to them in the absence of national regulations or guidelines.

The requirement to assess all pupils across all attainment targets was, at the level of national policy, a means of ensuring that the whole curriculum, not just that covered by external tests, was covered by teachers and taken account of in judging pupils' attainment. But neither the problems of manageability of teacher assessment nor its extraordinary diversity need have fuelled to the extent that it did the discontent felt by teachers (leading eventually to ministers conceding a review of the system in 1993) if it had been clearer what teacher assessment was *for*. While some teachers were undoubtedly slow to rethink how they assessed their pupils to incorporate the idea of regular assessment against statutory targets, others laboured hard over the redesign of assessment, recording and reporting procedures.

For this latter group — the majority of teachers doing their best to try to make the system work — what made that task harder to justify was the absence of a clear sense of who would benefit from it all. Would pupils have a clearer picture of their attainments and thus be helped to progress? Would teachers learn more about their pupils, individually or collectively, and so be able to teach more effectively? Would parents know more about their own children's attainments and, as a result, be in a better position to assist and support them? Would parents looking for a school or others interested in judging a school's effectiveness be able to rely on the teacher assessment results as a basis on which to make comparative judgments about schools?

For even the most conscientious teacher trying to make a success of teacher assessment there was good reason to doubt whether any of these questions could be answered with a definite 'yes'. Did a good teacher need the elaborate structure of national assessment to tell him/her how well pupils were doing? Would the aggregated scores for attainment targets, profile components and whole subjects make more sense to parents than the kind of information they already received through school reports and parents' evenings? And could the teacher assessment results, derived by individual teachers in their own ways, really be regarded as comparable with the equivalent results from another school? In short, teacher assessment for formative purposes was of dubious value and teacher assessment for summative or evaluative purposes was deeply suspect. It was not only the volume of work which brought growing discontent as more and more teachers found themselves increasingly immersed in teacher assessment. It was the pointlessness of it all.

Policy on Teacher Assessment: 1992/93

As the groundswell of teacher dissatisfaction with teacher assessment grew, it might have been expected that the policy-makers would move to meet the very real concerns being expressed about this element in the national system, however subsidiary its perceived function was to that of the standard end-of-stage tasks. But, behind the convenient facade of 'it's your business really', SEAC allowed the design problems at the very foundation of teacher assessment to go unresolved.

The Council did step up its efforts to support teachers in making judgments about pupils' attainments. It produced and distributed, in addition to the general guidance booklets for Key Stages 1 and 3 referred to earlier, three further series of guidance materials. Leaflets on teacher assessment in each of the foundation subjects at Key Stage 3 followed up the initial general leaflet. Secondly, the optional standard tasks in certain subjects at Key Stages 1 and 2 (see chapter 3) were intended to support teacher assessment. In addition, at Key Stages 1 and 3, an extensive set of booklets to exemplify *Pupils' Work Assessed* (*Children's Work Assessed* at Key Stage 1) was published at regular intervals, beginning in 1991. Given the number of statements of attainment in each subject and the inevitable idiosyncracies of the work of individual pupils, such booklets could only go some way towards answering teacher demands for someone to explain what attainment level x on attainment target y really looked like. Nevertheless, as teachers, individually or with colleagues, worked to familiarize themselves with what were for most of them the novel requirements of criterion-referenced assessments, the booklets did at least offer some evidence of pupils' work with which they could compare the performance of their own pupils.

Yet at the level of policy, neither SEAC nor the Government seems to have been inclined to do anything to change the essentially laissez-faire approach to teacher assessment. They remained preoccupied with the redefining of the standard task element of the system. While GCSE coursework, its counterpart at Key Stage 4, was at the centre of the policy debate during the second half of 1991 (see chapter 6), teacher assessment at the other three Key

Stages appears to have remained a side issue for everyone except the teachers undertaking it. Having figured only once as an agenda item for SEAC Council in the first three years of the Council's existence, it was not on the agenda at all during the next two. Significantly, the words 'teacher assessment' did appear on the Council agenda on one occasion over that period (in November 1992) but only in the context of how it would be 'audited'. Having allowed teacher assessment to develop very diverse characteristics, the policy-makers were now, rather late in the day, looking for ways of controlling it.

The attempt to define teacher assessment was being made not because its significance necessitated it but because decisions on two other issues higher up the policy agenda could not be made without reference to teacher assessment. The first issue was the relationship of standard tasks to teacher assessment. What to do about reporting on the attainment targets where the only evidence available was from teacher assessment? What to do in those targets where there were standard task results as well as teachers' own assessments? The second issue concerned the moderation of the reported results. Though ground rules had not been put in place before teacher assessment had been introduced, it had become obvious that some post-hoc control would be needed of teacher assessment as well as of the way teachers administered and marked the standard tasks. Thus, during 1992, as a by-product of the need to resolve these two issues, long-overdue moves were being made to define what the TGAT Report, four years earlier, had seen as 'a fundamental element of the national assessment system'.

Moderation

There was ample experience available in the public examination system for 16 and 18-year-olds in England and Wales of methods for aligning judgments arrived at separately by those engaged in assessing attainment. Many factors could be shown to affect the consistency of judgment exercised by examiners, whether teachers marking their own pupils' work or people employed to set and mark examination papers. Some of those factors relate to what is done before the work is marked — training, clear guidelines on how to set tasks, feedback on previous judgments. Others refer to procedures put in place for checking whether or not judgments have proved to be consistent.

National Curriculum assessment would need to establish ways of influencing such factors if it was to be credible as a source of evidence for comparison between individual pupils and across the system as a whole. Sufficient doubts had been voiced about the efficacy of the moderation procedures in use in the GCSE examination at Key Stage 4 for the challenge of moderation in national assessment not to be underestimated. The TGAT model envisaged evidence of attainment being derived not just from the day-to-day experience of teacher assessment — an enormous challenge in itself for any set of moderation procedures — but it also relied on standard tasks set in different ways at different times by different teachers.

How to ensure these 'standard tasks' were standard enough for the results obtained from them to be used in the ways intended? How to train and prepare for teacher assessments which would be sufficiently consistent for the purposes to which they were to be put and, having done so, to check that they were indeed consistent from teacher to teacher, from school to school, from LEA to LEA? Further complicating the picture was the question of whether to link the answers to these two questions, i.e. having moderated the standard tasks, to use them in some way as a template against which to judge the consistency of the results obtained from teacher assessment. Faced with such questions the policy-makers would have to arrive at decisions, not only on appropriate procedures but also on what degree of consistency would prove acceptable for each of the several purposes of national assessment.

The TGAT Report and Moderation

Recognizing the significance of moderation for the overall credibility of its proposals, the Task Group on Assessment and Testing devoted a substantial section of its Report to rehearsing the options and justifying its recommendations:

> Methods of moderation have twin functions: to communicate general standards to individual assessors and to control aberrations from general standards by appropriate adjustments. Three methods are in common use:
>
> — scaling on a reference test;
> — inspection by visiting moderators;
> — group moderation bringing teachers together to discuss their assessments.
>
> Each differs in its relative emphasis on communication and control. (TGAT Report, para. 68)

Pointing both to the defects of the first two options for 'control' purposes and to their tendency to involve one-way communication from moderator to teacher, the Task Group argued strongly for the third, not least because, in the Group's opinion, it was the best way of providing for two-way communication about standards as well as acting as a mechanism for control:

> Group moderation allows examiners to clarify in discussion both the objectives of their syllabuses and the bases of their value judgments. It is the only one of the three moderation methods which would enable the professional judgments of teachers to inform the development of the National Curriculum. (TGAT Report, para. 72)

In a section of the Report headed 'How group moderation works' TGAT explained the way in which the deliberations of a group would affect the outcomes of assessment. A moderation group's 'general aim would be to adjust the overall teacher rating results to match the overall results of the national tests'. TGAT's chosen version of group moderation was thus a curious hybrid. In style of working it resembled the consensus moderation used in some GCSE subjects to moderate coursework. But its aim would be substantially different from groups which met in that context. Rather than looking at pupils' work with a view to reconciling differences of interpretation about work done as part of 'teacher assessment', it would be exploring discrepancies between the teacher assessment scores and the SAT scores of groups of pupils:

> The moderation group's aim . . . would be to arrive at a final distribution for each school or pupil group. In general this would be the distribution on the national tests, with the implication that teachers' ratings would need adjustment. (TGAT Report, para. 75)

Thus the TGAT proposal for moderation was in part about aligning to each other the teacher assessment decisions of different teachers but its main focus was the bringing of those decisions into line with the national tests. Even though the professional benefits of teachers meeting to discuss their judgments might, as TGAT argued, be considerable, it would be the national tests which would provide the standard against which teachers measured the quality of their own assessments. Moreover, oddly in a system where specific criteria were supposed to underpin decisions on individual pupils' attainment, it would be the rank order of a group of pupils which guided decisions on teachers' own assessments.

Returning to the subject of moderation in the first of its Supplementary Reports (March 1988), TGAT stressed the significance of group moderation for teacher assessment 'because teachers' own assessments have an important part to play'. These assessments 'can only be given the weight they deserve in the moderation process if teachers can produce and exchange substantial evidence of the basis for their assessments'. It was very clear also from the third Supplementary Report that, far from being seen only as a system of control over teachers' judgments of attainment, moderation in the Task Group's view was an aspect of the overall implementation at the local level of National Curriculum and assessment. 'Each local group could have a monitoring and communication role on INSET, and a coordinating role between curriculum, assessment and INSET developments' (para 18).

When the Secretary of State, Kenneth Baker, announced on 7 June 1988 to the House of Commons the Government's acceptance of the TGAT Report, it was the moderation proposals which were to be the exception to the generally positive tone:

> The suggestions made by the Task Group on Assessment and Testing in its third supplementary report on moderation appear complicated and costly.

The Government was evidently unenthusiastic about a system of moderation which gave groups of teachers at the local level the leading role in working towards a common standard. Not only did it not satisfy their view of what was needed in control terms, it could also prove disruptive (taking teachers out of the classroom) and expensive. But what would take its place? The Secretary of State went no further in his announcement than:

> in order to safeguard standards, assessments made by teachers should be compared with the results of national tests and with the judgments of other teachers.

Thus ministers adopted the convenient tactic of 'wait and see what emerges from developments'. A proposal from within SEAC Council, that alternative arrangements for moderation should be subjected to trials concurrently with the piloting of SAT materials, was not taken up. As with teacher assessment, it became clear that moderation would not take the form proposed by TGAT. But, again as with teacher assessment, no coherent alternative was put in its place.

SEAC's Alternative at Key Stage 1

In its advice to the DES on assessment arrangements for the National Curriculum (July 1989), SEAC put forward a view of moderation significantly different from that adopted by TGAT — 'some modification of this TGAT moderating model seems essential'. Four reasons were stated for preferring a different approach: minimizing the demands made on teachers, completing the process 'within a reasonably short period of time', overcoming the problem that for some attainment targets SAT results would not be available and the belief that moderation should focus on the performance of individual pupils (rather than groups as TGAT had envisaged).

Though these last two, more technical, reasons can take the discussion into the more abstruse corners of educational assessment, they are critical to the relative importance of teacher assessment and the SATs and therefore to any moderation system which attempted to relate one to the other. TGAT had suggested a 'pattern-matching technique', first within the local group, then at LEA level, the general aim of which would be 'to adjust the overall teacher rating results to match the overall results of (the same pupil group or school on) the national tests'. 'Departures from (the pattern of performance on the national tests) could be approved if the group as a whole could be convinced that they were justified in particular cases'. However, where departures from the test results pattern could not be justified, schools would be required to adjust the attainment levels given to individual pupils until the pattern of the overall distribution of levels matched what was required. Thus, even if a particular pupil's attainment level in a subject had been confirmed by national tests, the teacher might have to alter it to fit the distribution of levels required of the group. Implicit in the TGAT approach to moderation was that the national test results could be expected to be more reliable. The peer group of teachers could, however, decide that deviations from the national test pattern were permissible.

The Task Group may have been unrealistic in expecting the Government to approve the control of national standards being in the hands of teachers at the local level. It may also have been too much to expect the Government to accept that, as TGAT proposed, the moderation process should only affect a proportion of profile components in any one year. More fundamentally, the Group seems to have attempted to transfer from the public examination world of norm-referenced assessment to the new world of criterion-referencing the practices of adjusting the patterns of grades/levels awarded. If their moderation procedure had been adopted there would have been many teachers across the country trying to justify the unjustifiable. Though a pupil had shown in the test and during the school year that s/he had clearly reached a certain level, it might not be awarded if the moderation group decided the school's judgments about levels of attainment in the cohort to which that pupil belonged were unduly generous.

In place of the TGAT approach to moderation SEAC recommended (letter to the DES, July 1989) a different method. Teacher assessment scores would be passed to a local moderating group by the end of the spring term. After the SAT assessments, the TA and SAT scores could be compared:

> ... the SAT results, where available, should be used for recording and reporting purposes, instead of TA, except where this makes a change to a profile component result which the teacher wishes to query. We would anticipate a review procedure being established within individual schools, possibly involving an external moderator, to consider cases of this kind as the first stage of local moderation. Where, as a result of this procedure, the school judges it appropriate, the case should be referred to a local moderating group, which would include a representative of the school concerned. The matter would be resolved at that meeting on the basis of reliable evidence underlying both the TA results and the SAT results.

SEAC's alternative view of moderation was warmly received by Kenneth Baker: 'the procedures recommended have the considerable merit of simplicity and comprehensibility'. But it had a cool reception from former Task Group members and others. One sentence in particular in SEAC's July advice was picked up by critics: 'the SAT assessment is thus "preferred" to TA, where it is available'. Several articles and letters in the educational press challenged this as signifying a downgrading of the role of teacher assessment in the system as a whole. *The Times Educational Supplement* (4 August 1989) reported SEAC as having 'largely abandoned the central principle behind the TGAT recommendations' that local groups of teachers should determine the balance between SAT results and teacher assessment. 'It was this recommendation that helped sell the proposals to teachers who feared that they would otherwise end up teaching to the test and that external assessment would be used to judge their performance'. However, a *TES* editorial commented that 'all along it seemed something like this would happen when the chips were down' and 'some of the sophistication of the TGAT report (and some of its discreet fudge) was bound to go'. Former Task Group members regretted (*TES*, 20 October 1989) not only the assumption that SATs would necessarily prove more reliable than teacher assessment but also the loss of 'one of the principal ways in which National Curriculum could have improved the education of children'.

The discussion of moderation was already being bedevilled by uncertainty about the nature of SATs, and therefore how reliable they could be expected to be, and the nature of teacher assessment. One influential figure in SAT development work, Chris Whetton of the NFER, was quoted (*TES*, 8 December 1989) as saying that 'the difference between teacher assessment and a SAT is very fuzzy indeed'. In his view, the only significant difference was that 'there will be more instruction to teachers in SATs and he predicted that, in the longer term, 'the two may merge'. Those comments were made in relation to the early versions of SATs at Key Stage 1 but then SEAC also took care to point out that its moderation proposals too related only to Key Stage 1. How could SAT results be 'preferred' to teacher assessment if the two tracks in the assessment system were converging into one in the middle distance? How would the judgments made by teachers on attainment targets not covered by SATs be moderated? How would the SATs themselves be moderated? A start had been made on replacing the TGAT moderation model but much remained unclear.

When it returned to the subject, in its further advice of December 1989, SEAC claimed that its proposal that 'in certain circumstances a SAT outcome should be 'preferred' to a TA . . . had been widely misunderstood'. It offered a more detailed explanation as a corrective. The December letter of advice went much further in setting out how SEAC recommended moderation should operate at the local level. It did not however put forward any answers to the underlying questions about the relative nature and functions of teacher assessment and SATs. Moderation arrangements were being established without the assessment procedures and techniques being clarified.

What was also significant about the SEAC December 1989 advice was the context in which moderation was discussed. SEAC was making recommendations about who should be responsible at the local level for the administration of national assessment. In particular, it was anticipating the publication, during 1990, of regulations setting out the legal requirements for schools in relation to national assessments at Key Stage 1. The section of the SEAC letter dealing with moderation is headed 'local administration of the assessment arrangements'. Moderation as conceived by SEAC was not, as envisaged by TGAT, a professional process with both communication and control functions, helping to serve several purposes related to curriculum and teacher development. As with teacher assessment, it had clearly been moved by the Government and its advisers into the part of the policy agenda labelled 'administration' and concerned mainly with the regulation of assessment practices.

Administering Moderation at Key Stage 1

In this vein, SEAC amplified its proposals for moderation of assessments at Key Stage 1, hinting also that similar arrangements might also be appropriate for Key Stages 2 and 3. The Council proposed that local education authorities should administer national assessment at the local level 'since they will also have local responsibility for the provision and organization of the in-service training needed for the effective operation of the assessment system'. The link between training for assessment and the need to bring judgments, once made, into line was thus maintained.

In the first of three phases of an 'assessment cycle', in the first two terms of Y2, there would be training for teachers including 'agreement trials' in which groups of teachers would compare their judgments of pupils' work and realign them if necessary. The second phase, in the early part of the summer term, during which pupils tackled the standard assessment tasks, would be followed by a third, before the end of the summer term, when the final outcomes for pupils would be confirmed.

The idea of local groups of teachers working together thus continued to figure in SEAC's plans for moderation. However, the role of those groups in the sequence of activities comprising the moderating process was to contribute to the training of teachers in national assessment rather than (as TGAT had proposed) to come to agreement on outcomes. The training and 'agreement trials' were expected to promote consistency in decisions on teacher assessment but neither would have a control function in relation to those decisions. Control was to be given instead to 'moderators' appointed by the LEAs to oversee the whole cycle. The moderator would supervise the administration of SATs in a group of fifteen to twenty-five schools and act as referee of any cases in which teachers were not willing to accept the validity of an outcome determined by the 'SAT preferred' formula. Ultimately, a school could, if still dissatisfied, appeal to a panel of moderators established to consider cases where teacher and moderator could not agree.

The SEAC proposals did not receive immediate approval from the Secretary of State. Almost three months had elapsed — an age in the tight schedule ministers had set for implementing national assessment — when John MacGregor responded in March 1990. Before referring to the particulars of SEAC's advice, he was careful to point out that 'the Council should not assume that the arrangements which we have endorsed for assessing the core subjects at Key Stage 1 will set a general precedent'. Also, while accepting that LEAs were best placed to assume local responsibility, he was reluctant to be too specific in his requirements — 'effectiveness will best be secured by arrangements which, whilst conforming to the overall criteria of national policy, take account of LEAs' local circumstances'. The comparability of results in different schools and LEAs was, predictably, to become a major issue with the publication of the first batch of results, LEA by LEA, towards the end of 1991. Yet eighteen months earlier it was not SEAC but the DES which was advocating a light touch on the local administration of national assessment.

That the issues were being perceived in essentially administrative rather than professional terms is evident from the fact that the words 'moderation' or 'moderator' do not appear at all in John MacGregor's four-and-a-half pages of response to SEAC's December advice. The downgrading of moderation in policy terms is also apparent from the fact that it was not listed among the four functions of national administration of assessment arrangements stipulated by the Secretary of State in his letter. TGAT's elaborate proposals for moderation — one of the 'principles' on which the whole model was based — had thus, in the space of a few months, been buried without trace. Group moderation by teachers had been abandoned. It had been replaced, though without the term being used, by the second of the options rehearsed by the Task Group, 'moderation by inspection'.

For the most part, press comment on the evolving system understandably focused on the SATs themselves rather than the arrangements for ensuring that the SATs results could be relied upon to be a sound basis for comparisons across schools and LEAs. Only occasionally did such concerns surface while the assessment and moderation procedures were being developed and put in place. Under a headline 'School charter for cheats', the *Daily Mail* claimed in July 1990 that 'wangling results is set to become the new national sport as schools begin to tackle testing pupils at 7, 11, 14 and 16'.

Inherent weaknesses in the new model remained largely unacknowledged by SEAC and the DES. In particular the emphasis on local arrangements left unclear how the decisions in one moderation group or one LEA were to be aligned with those being reached elsewhere. The seconding of moderators across LEAs and national training, including cross-moderation, had rated a brief, one sentence, mention in the SEAC December 1989 letter and John MacGregor's reply had, without any indication of what he meant by it, referred to SEAC being 'the lynchpin of the system of quality control'. The original TGAT proposals had been criticized for failing to demonstrate how comparability at national level was to be achieved. But what the DES now put in its place was no better equipped to achieve that aim.

Implementing Moderation at Key Stage 1

From March 1990, work continued on putting into place the new approach to moderation devised by SEAC. A joint working party from SEAC and the LEAs produced a guidance booklet for those responsible for assessment within each LEA. Thousands of moderators were appointed by LEAs and the three-phase cycle swung into action for the first time in the school year 1990/91. The booklet spelled out the responsibilities of LEAs in respect of moderation:

> (Moderation) is concerned with the promotion of consistent standards of assessment among teachers within and across schools maintained by the authority. This will be achieved in three ways. First, by training on standards which could be based on SEAC's forthcoming anthology of assessed pupils' work; and by training on the operation of SATs. Second by support for teachers in their classrooms during the conduct of SATs. Third by monitoring and evaluating the outcomes of assessment in schools, both for internal consistency within the authority and for consistency with national standards. (*National Curriculum Assessment: Responsibilities of LEAs in 1990/91*, SEAC, July 1990)

The pattern for this Key Stage thus seemed to be set but when, as promised, the Government published, in December 1991, comparisons of performance across LEAs, moderation once more surfaced as an issue in national policy. Predictably, cries of 'unfair' came from those LEAs at or near the bottom of the comparative national tables, the first such national comparisons to appear. How much reliance could be placed on this picture of performance on standard tasks in the core subjects? For Bradford's Education Committee Chairman:

> This whole exercise has been rendered useless by the lack of any national monitoring or checking of the way papers were marked. It's been like asking pupils to award their own marks. (*The Guardian*, 20 December 1991)

The city's Director of Education, Sari Conway, pointed to action which would eliminate the perceived unfairness:

> In future results should be properly moderated, with differences in marking between authorities levelled out.

As with so many aspects of national assessment, it was the publication of results which exposed what was being implemented — the tests and the procedures surrounding them — to a wider, more critical, scrutiny.

By this time Key Stage 1 was already in to a second assessment cycle guided by a further, only slightly revised, SEAC booklet on LEA responsibilities. Its focus was still on reconciling differences at the local level rather than giving any serious attention to mechanisms which might result in greater consistency between Cornwall and Cumbria or even between Barnet and Brent. In the SEAC *Moderator's Handbook* (October 1991), eight pages were devoted to guidance on training and on 'support for schools and teachers' with the reconciling of SAT and TA results being dealt with in a page-and-a-half. The national perspective rates two paragraphs at the end with suggestions as to how cross-LEA contact might be made.

Further modifications of essentially the same model were made during 1992 in preparation for what would be the third national assessment of 7-year-olds the following year. In parallel with moves at other Key Stages, there was increased emphasis on the 'auditing' of results with the ambiguities in the role of the personnel responsible for this process being highlighted by SEAC's coining of a new term — 'audit-moderator'. Yet moderation remained, for this Key Stage at least, a light-touch affair which emphasized training and agreement trials more than formal controls on consistency. At the same time moderation practice and terminology at Key Stage 3 and, potentially, at Key Stage 2 were developing along rather different lines.

Key Stage 3: A Different Approach

Regulations would have to be drafted and finalized by July 1991 if procedures for the local administration of assessment at Key Stage 3 were to be in place in time for the 1991/92 school year. So, late in 1990, SEAC turned its mind to the same issues that had been addressed twelve months earlier in relation to Key Stage 1.

For Key Stage 3 SEAC proposed that the responsibilities given to LEAs at the earlier Key Stage should be shared between LEAs and the examining groups which administered the GCSE examinations for 16-year-olds. The LEAs would deal with administration, training and 'quality assurance' while 'the examining groups would have key responsibilities for moderation arrangements'. It seems that SEAC envisaged for year 9 a similar three phase cycle to that in place in year 2 though, in ways which were not specified, the GCSE groups would also be involved in determining national standards. As Kenneth Clarke's reply pointed out:

> this advice does not clearly identify who would be responsible for ensuring consistent and rigorous standards of assessment, nor how those standards would be applied uniformly to all schools, LEA-maintained and otherwise. (DES letter to SEAC, January 1991)

As in its signalling of the replacement at Key Stage 3 of standard assessment tasks by timed written examinations, so the January 1991 letter also marks the parting of the ways between the Key Stages in moderation arrangements. At Key Stage 1, with local responsibility wholly devolved to LEAs, the approach which linked training to the controlling of teachers' judgments remained. At Key Stage 3 LEAs were to retain their 'quality assurance' role in this, as in other aspects of the local administration of education. But the harder edge of 'quality audit' was introduced to describe externally managed control exercised on a regional basis by the examining groups.

The pace of change was also hotting up. SEAC was not only fighting a rearguard battle to defend its view of the nature of SATs at Key Stage 3. The Secretary of State, in a letter to SEAC (25 January 1991) requested further advice on Key Stage 3 administration including 'the precise means by which the examining bodies are to be involved'. From a proposed assessment and moderation model more akin to that being developed for Key Stage 1, Key Stage 3 was being realigned by the DES. As Kenneth Clarke asserted in a written answer to a question in Parliament (25 January 1991):

> Assigning responsibility for auditing quality to the examining bodies (which certify assessments at age 16) will help to ensure consistency of standards between the testing of 14-year-olds and the GCSE examination and across LEA-maintained, grant maintained and non-maintained schools alike.

An important change in the relationship between tests and teacher assessment proposed by SEAC in December 1990 was not given the same degree of attention as other changes in the Key Stage 3 assessment model in the early months on 1991. The process of moderation developed initially by SEAC for Key Stages 1 and 3 required teachers to complete their 'teacher assessment' judgments before the start of the SAT period. Now SEAC proposed that completion of the 'teacher assessment' record in 1992 need not be required until the mid-point of the summer term at Key Stage 1 and the end of June at Key Stage 3. In both cases these dates were *after* the pupils would have taken, and the teachers marked, the tests covering a majority of attainment targets in the core subjects.

Thus, from being prior judgments with which the later test result could be compared, teacher assessment decisions were timed so that the teacher could, if s/he wished, take account of the SAT evidence. While the characteristics of tests and teacher assessment at Key Stage 3 were diverging, their relative functions were becoming more indistinct than ever. If, as in the early developments at both Key Stages, SAT and TA results had been determined independently of each other and at separate times there was at least the potential for using SAT evidence when moderating TA results. By allowing, even encouraging, teachers to take account of SAT evidence, where available, when finalizing teacher assessments SEAC reduced the likelihood of spurious or chance differences between a pupil's TA and SAT scores. They also made it possible to report separately on a pupil's performance during the stage and in the end-of-stage tests thus giving due weight to each type of assessment evidence.

That potential merging of judgments by the teacher of what were previously presented as two separate decisions, arrived at independently of each other, meant that it would no longer be possible to use the SAT score as a moderating instrument with which the TA result could be compared and, perhaps, adjusted. Any differences between the two would be those consciously recorded by the teacher as indicating a real difference on the two assessment tracks. But confusion about the relationship returned when, for 1993, it was decided to revert to a deadline for completing teacher assessments which was, once again, before the end-of-stage tests (31 May for completion of teacher assessment record before the test dates of 7–16 June).

More to the fore in policy discussion of Key Stage 3 moderation were who should be responsible for it and how extensive it should be. For what was to be a voluntary pilot in mathematics and science in 1992, SEAC's booklet of *Information and Guidance for LEAs* (autumn, 1991) explained that a random sample was to be drawn of half the schools taking part in the pilot and a 20 per cent sample of what were now termed 'scripts' from each school was to be scrutinized by external moderators. In addition 'a small number of schools' would be asked to send samples of the evidence on which teachers had reached their judgments about the two attainment targets not dealt with in the tests. With that division of the effort and resource allocated to moderation it is clear that it had become a process which, in the minds of ministers at least, was to be mainly directed to reinforcing the reliability of the tests. There was no mechanism apparent for moderating teacher assessment across the full range of attainment targets. Even where teacher assessment would be the only source for end-of-stage reporting, the checking would be a light sampling of evidence supplied by teachers. One of TGAT's warnings about 'moderation by inspection' was becoming relevant: 'the control function . . . is not efficient because it must suffer from incompleteness of data; only the final outcomes of tasks can be retained for inspection'.

But the involvement of the examining groups in moderation was seen by the Government as an important step in establishing the credibility of the results which it was planned would, from 1993, be published. 'Audit' came to be a regular and prominent item in the continuing exchanges between SEAC and DES about Key Stage 3. In writing to SEAC in September 1991 Kenneth Clarke had made it clear he expected audit to cover all schools (not just a sample) and to influence results before they were reported (not just have an impact on decisions about the next cohort of students). In struggling to meet this formidable challenge, SEAC came up with a five-pronged strategy (letter to the DES, 27 February 1992) involving auditing all schools in each subject every year. For 1993, a sample of every school's marking would be checked by external assessors appointed by the audit agencies (the regional GCSE examining groups) with closer scrutiny of schools where marking was deemed unsatisfactory. Assessors would also receive teacher assessment results and a folio of evidence in respect of the attainment targets not covered by the end-of-stage tests. Such arrangements would, SEAC claimed:

> promote consistency of assessment within and between schools. It is intended to be simple, manageable, rigorous, and sufficiently flexible to cope with the demands of different subjects.

For the first time in the four years of evolution of national assessment, a system of moderation which had the controlling of consistency of results as its main aim was being proposed.

The new Secretary of State, John Patten, was evidently well satisfied with this new approach, describing what the Council had proposed as an 'excellent framework' (letter to SEAC, 12 May 1992). The one cloud on his horizon in this respect was not the proposed procedures themselves but how much they would cost. The scope of audit was already increased because of the number of subjects involved as well as the additional work resulting from the Secretary of State requiring that all schools be audited. In 1993, auditing in England would need to cover tests in mathematics, science, English and technology and would seek evidence in the five attainment targets where teacher assessment would be the source of evidence for attainment. In Wales, moderation of Welsh as a first and second language would also be required. In 1993/94 it was estimated that the costs of auditing Key Stage 3 tests and teacher assessment would exceed £6m, on top of the costs of preparing for, and administering, the tests themselves.

SEAC's projections of the operating costs of the audit across all secondary schools in England and Wales and across all the subjects for which tests were planned were alarmingly high and rising. Yet the Council was expected to manage the expanding testing system within an already agreed indicative budget. The time had come when the emerging national assessment system would have to face the realities not just of what was feasible in relation to its ambitious objectives but also of what was affordable. The Secretary of State stated his view of expenditure priorities:

(a) the writing, production and distribution of tests for 7, 11 and 14-year-olds;
(b) the establishment of rigorous audit arrangements at Key Stage 3 . . .

You should treat all other expenditure on ancillary objectives, including on support materials for teachers, on evaluation and monitoring and on conferences and publicity as of lesser priority. (Letter from John Patten to SEAC, 1 September 1992)

Never before as the system evolved had the Government's own policy priorities been more clearly stated. For the first time since TGAT, moderation of the assessments, if only for Key Stage 3, was back near the top of the policy agenda.

Key Stage 2: Which Model to Adopt?

Decisions on the nature of Key Stage 2 tests were needed during 1992 so that a pilot could proceed the following year. What was put in place would have to consider afresh for this Key Stage the issues raised when introducing moderation/audit at Key Stages 1 and 3. How wide a spectrum of subjects to include? How much emphasis on moderation of teacher assessment as distinct from the tests? How much to invest in training and support as against post-hoc auditing? Should there be visits to schools by moderators (as at Key Stage 1) or should reliance be placed on pupils' work being sent through the post to external assessors (as at Key Stage 3)? Which external agencies should be given responsibility for the audit? And how to keep the costs of it all within the planned budget?

In the event, when it came to pass, on Christmas Eve 1992, that SEAC submitted its advice on moderation at this Key Stage, the pressure from teachers to reconsider the whole assessment system was already building up. By the time John Patten responded (1 March 1993) he had given himself some breathing space by announcing that the publication of test results for 11-year-olds would not be a requirement until 1995. Final decisions about Key Stage 2 audit were therefore delayed until the autumn of 1993. Up to a point the Secretary of State was happy to endorse the model proposed by SEAC, which was similar in broad terms to what had been agreed at Key Stage 3 — 'an independent audit of schools' own test marking and assessments of school work' to be undertaken by 'competent independent bodies' which would manage the audit regionally. The word 'moderation' had disappeared entirely from the Department for Education's vocabulary; we were now in a world of 'audit' and of 'verifying standards'.

Moreover the Secretary of State indicated his interest in exploring further the separation of the quality assurance and quality control aspects of moderation:

I continue to see external marking of test papers in English, mathematics and science as a possible alternative to an external audit of schools' own marking standards. The merits of greater objectivity cannot be ignored. (Letter from John Patten to SEAC, 1 March 1993)

The shift in emphasis from the early intentions of ministers and SEAC is all too obvious from such a statement. John MacGregor had argued, only three years before, that:

To realize the improvements in teaching and learning potentially offered by the National Curriculum . . . we *must* ensure that assessment or testing is an essential part of normal classroom practice. (speech to Norfolk teachers, 10 March 1990)

Yet here was his successor suggesting that, in order to achieve the elusive degree of reliability (or 'objectivity') necessary for published results to be comparable, not only would the testing of 11-year-olds (and then other age groups?) not be part of routine classroom practice, the marking of those tests might be taken out of teachers' hands as well.

Moderation: Summary and Conclusion

Moderation of national assessment had thus gone through several developmental stages without the central issues and dilemmas being satisfactorily defined, still less resolved.

It was the first aspect of the TGAT model to be discarded; indeed, the only aspect to be dispensed with before policy moved off the drawing board. SEAC's preferred alternative for Key Stage 1, endorsed by ministers, has since then been the basis for practice. Independent studies (for example Gipps *et al.*, 1992) have suggested that those moderation procedures, together with the guidance published by SEAC nationally, were contributing something to the aligning of judgments by teachers from different schools. But such studies have also revealed tensions between the moderator's role as a trainer and supporter of teachers and her/his functions in ensuring consistency both of practice and of the interpretation of pupil performance (James and Conner, 1993). The personnel and practices involved in moderation at Key Stage 1 have been so diverse that, whatever else they are doing, it seems improbable that they are achieving a degree of consistency which would make it possible to use the results to make valid comparisons between schools and between LEAs.

By the time their pupils were taking the standard tasks, towards the end of year 2, teachers would have been made aware of the role of the moderator in relation to the SATs; in part concerned with consistency of presentation of tasks, in part with consistent interpretation of pupils' responses. But, certainly when Key Stage 1 teachers had embarked on teacher assessment, and perhaps even when they had finished, it was unclear how moderation arrangements would affect their judgments of attainment on the basis of routine classroom evidence. Unlike their loose equivalent at Key Stage 4, arrangements for moderating GCSE coursework, decisions on how moderation would operate in Key Stage 1 were not taken and publicized before the pupils started out on the Key Stage.

Teachers' perceptions of all this have been affected by the continuing uncertainty over how the SAT results would impact, if at all, on the teacher assessment results. First came the 'SAT preferred' publicity of mid-1989, then SEAC's correction of that 'misunderstanding' which still left teachers unclear about whether they were free to make their own teacher assessment judgments or could expect some checks on their judgments and on the evidence gathered in support. One year the TA scores had to be finalized before the SATs but then that was changed so that teachers could use the SAT evidence when finalizing teacher assessment. And then, for the next year, it was proposed that practice should revert, at Key Stage 3 at least, to finalizing teacher assessments before the SATs. To the open-minded and disinterested observer this could be regarded as proof that SEAC and ministers were willing to adjust the model in the light of experience. But the teacher at the centre of it all was left none the wiser as to how and by whom her/his judgments would be checked so that, even in common sense terms if not to a degree that would underpin league tables, s/he could feel that there was some consistency with the practice of other teachers.

As the second set of LEA comparisons was published, in December 1992, Key Stage 1 moderation remained an uncomfortable and only partially effective compromise between the activities designed to support teachers and those which might actually change a teacher's decision (on the SAT or on TA) on the grounds that it was out of line with equivalent decisions by other teachers.

But for Key Stage 3, and prospectively also for Key Stage 2, Kenneth Clarke and his successor, John Patten, had made a clear break from the TGAT notion, endorsed by SEAC with its Key Stage 1 moderation model, that what happened before teachers assessed was as important in aligning standards as what happened afterwards. The weaknesses in the model adopted at Key Stage 1 were recognized in the emerging research evidence and by commentators on the system. For example:

> . . . auditing is clearly a necessary part of any national assessment process. The Key Stage 1 SAT scores for 1991 were inherently unreliable because the standards were set locally — if they were set at all — and the outcomes were never reviewed or moderated. (Jim Sweetman, *The Guardian*, 28 January 1992)

All the policy decisions on moderation taken from early 1991 onwards were directed towards placing more emphasis on instituting external, independent checks on teachers' judgments, whether in the marking of SATs or in their teacher assessments. 'Audit' was now the term used and ministerial priorities were now spelled out in short, sharp phrases. As John Patten wrote to SEAC (12 June 1992):

(audit arrangements should)
— apply consistent standards nationwide;
— apply equally to schools maintained by LEAs, grant-maintained schools and such independent schools as choose to participate in the KS2 assessments;
— be credible to the secondary schools which receive the pupils assessed in year 6; and
— be cost-effective.

From being an essential feature of what TGAT proposed, moderation had for a time slipped down the policy agenda and been regarded, both by SEAC and by ministers, as an administrative matter which could be resolved as and when the time came to issue the necessary regulations to schools about end-of-stage assessment and reporting. Then, increasingly during 1991 and 1992, it reemerged as a major concern of ministers anxious to ensure that the performance tables, an integral part of their policy on school accountability, could be relied upon.

But when it did reappear, moderation was in a new guise. At last the very real difficulties of trying to ensure consistency of practice and interpretation of loosely-worded attainment statements were being faced up to squarely. It might not matter too much for formative purposes if one teacher's practice and interpretation differed from another's. But it certainly mattered if aggregations of what each had decided were to be used as an indicator of the performance of teachers, schools and LEAs. The most intractable moderation (or auditing) problem remained that of aligning the multiplicity of judgments made by thousands of teachers throughout each Key Stage. Since the standard tasks were not capable of covering all the statutory attainment targets, that problem could not be disregarded, though finding a solution to it does not seem to have been given as much attention as solving the parallel problem of moderating the SATs.

Even with the reduced variability resulting from deciding that there would be, for Key Stages 2 and 3, timed unseen examination papers, it was proving far from easy to find a way to ensure judgments about the awards of levels were indeed comparable. SEAC's own evidence from the 1992 pilot at Key Stage 3 in mathematics and science was far from encouraging in this respect. In reviewing the evidence about the way in which teachers and moderators struggled to match pupils' idiosyncratic answers to what they thought the assessment criteria really meant one is left doubting the feasibility of achieving the consistency needed for the results to be comparable. How far is it possible, however well designed the tests are and however conscientiously they are marked and moderated, to bring into line the millions of pupil responses marked by tens of thousands of teachers and checked by thousands of moderators? Within the long-established conventions of norm-referencing, the currency of moderation had always been marks awarded. Where a marker (or a moderator) was judged unduly harsh or lenient, the results of the pupils involved would be scaled upwards or downwards as appropriate.

But the manipulation of sets of marks is not an option available in a system where each judgment on each part-task is an either/or as to whether the pre-specified criteria have been met. With criterion-referencing of the kind embodied in the National Curriculum Orders, it may well be possible over a period of years, through procedures such as agreement trials and compilations of portfolios of pupils' work, to work towards a professional consensus as to the meaning of the terms used to describe attainments. Indeed, there is evidence of this happening as teachers have accumulated experiences over the first three years of assessment at Key Stage 1 (see James and Conner, 1993). But, even if there can be a developing consensus about what each statement of attainment really means, the demands on any moderation arrangements would be formidable. How to construct a moderation process which would check enough of those teacher judgments to satisfy the sceptical parent or politician that, when evaluative comparisons are the aim, the results can be relied upon? And can those politicians be expected to wait for several years until such a professional consensus emerges?

The cost implications of moderation on the scale needed to satisfy the policy imperative of performance tables were already being acknowledged in the exchanges about audit costs between the Secretary of State and SEAC during 1992. What was less in evidence, but beginning to appear at the margins of debate (see chapter 7), was a more fundamental questioning of the capacity of the testing and moderation model then in place to deliver what was required of it. TGAT had recognized the importance of moderation:

> the scales or grades should be capable of comparison across classes and schools, if teachers, pupils, and parents are to share a common language and common standards; so the assessments should be calibrated or moderated. (TGAT Report, para. 5)

However, after four years of development and with a satisfactory solution still not in sight, the time had come to redefine the problem.

5 Record-Keeping, Reporting and Publishing Results

Introduction

Decisions about what to assess and how were, perhaps inevitably, the central focus of the early development of a national assessment system. As each subject working group published its proposals, there was heated debate about the attainment targets and statements of attainment. As assessment in relation to those targets and statements evolved through the SAT development work and the 'teacher assessment' experience in schools, there was much discussion of the appropriate techniques of assessment, their timing and extent.

If the system had been designed within the norm-referencing conventions so well-established in the practices of schools and examination boards, questions about what happened to the evidence of pupil attainment would have ranged across the familiar territory of marking, standardizing and the award of grades. Record-keeping would have been a matter of taking note of marks; reporting and publishing a matter of making known the results to pupils, parents and public. The conversion from a detailed record of marks awarded to a single general indicator of overall attainment — total, percentage, grade — was a familiar part of assessment practice for teachers, pupils and parents, a fixed point in the educational landscape familiar in some form to all those who might be interested in that information.

But the system was not so designed. A central tenet of the TGAT Report was the use of a criterion-referenced approach to assessment. At the heart of such an approach is the requirement that, not only must criteria for assessment be defined in advance and evidence of attainment be judged against those criteria, but the recording and reporting of attainment must refer back to the criteria. The post-assessment processes which, with norm-referencing, involve aggregating marks and calibrating grading scales thus, with criterion-referencing, raise quite different issues. How, for example, is the diverse and idiosyncratic evidence of an individual's attainment to be recorded in a way that both refers back to the criteria and is also manageable for the teacher? At what point is the evidence of what the pupil has done regarded as proof that performance criteria have been met? How to maintain a pupil record which is capable of satisfying the various demands which may be made on it? How to report at realistic length, for example to parents, without the summarizing involved becoming so crude that the vital connection with the pre-specified criteria is lost?

To advisers and officials trying to keep to a demanding timetable for implementing an ambitious curriculum and assessment model it may have been tempting to see recording, reporting and publishing assessment out-comes as matters which did not require immediate attention. Deadlines for finalizing the curriculum design or for determining testing arrangements would inevitably loom larger than decisions about reporting to parents or publishing results. Yet the lessons from the experience of one local education authority, Croydon, which had already instituted a system of testing in its schools, had been spelled out clearly enough by its Director of Education:

> . . . the greatest attention should be paid during the earliest stages of designing and introducing testing to the ways in which its results and significance will eventually be conveyed to other teachers and inter-ested people, in particular parents and employers. (Donald Naismith, *TES*, 18 September 1987, p. 28)

From the original discussion of the TGAT model, immediately following publication of the TGAT Report, it was clear that how information about attainment was to be processed and communicated would be a critical issue in revealing which of its several declared purposes the new system would be best equipped to serve. And, as has been apparent from previous chapters, ques-tions about what to do with the evidence derived from assessment procedures constantly surfaced in the course of developing standard tasks and teacher assessment.

Record-keeping and Reporting in the 1980s

Pre-National Curriculum practice in the recording, reporting and publishing of information on pupil attainment was notably diverse and variable. Keeping a record of pupils' work was an established part of the business of teaching but it is difficult to generalize about the practices adopted. There were many examples of groups of teachers rethinking the way they kept pupil records, from infants schools looking for a more systematic charting of the young child's progress through to secondary school departments agreeing to a com-mon format for recording attainment in a subject. But for the majority of teachers in England and Wales prior to the National Curriculum, keeping a record of work done was a matter for decision by the individual teacher, sometimes within a loose framework set by the school.

Drawing on those records to report about individual pupils, whether within the school for monitoring of pupil progress or outside the school to communicate with parents, was similarly characterized by diversity of prac-tice from school to school. One school could have a complex procedure for checking regularly on pupil attendance, effort and attainment while its neighbour relied on casual staffroom conversation to identify problem pupils or, more rarely, to credit excellence. One school could have a well developed system of written reports to parents linked to appointments for parents to meet teachers while its neighbour was still using up the stock of report forms ordered from the local printer in the 1960s.

The third stage in the process of summarizing and transmitting information derived from assessment — the publication of results — was not even on the agenda of many schools and local education authorities. Only a minority of LEAs, notable among them the Inner London Education Authority (ILEA), had put in place systematic assessment arrangements across all their schools and developed ways of analysing and making available to parents summarized data on attainment. For secondary schools, the stress on publishing aggregate results which was to become such a significant feature of post 1988 developments was presaged by earlier legislation requiring them to make schools' examination results available. However, 'publishing' in the form of a document offered to prospective parents who enquired was very different in its character and its effects from the publication of league tables of schools and LEAs which was to follow the introduction of National Curriculum assessment arrangements. In most LEAs, apart from the results of candidates entered for public examinations at 16+ (typically the subject of controversy about how they should be interpreted), there was no LEA-wide information which could be published.

Records of achievement for individual pupils were, however, increasingly introduced into many secondary schools from the late 1970s to the mid 1980s. They had their roots in initiatives at local level to challenge the currency of test and examination results as the only indicators of attainment. By 1984 they had been given national recognition in the form of a Government policy statement which established the objective of all young people in secondary education having a record of achievement by the end of the decade. Together with the national system of examinations for 16-year-olds (GCSE after 1988) they were, therefore, the main areas of pre-existing Government policy at national level in the field of assessment which would have to be accommodated, modified or abandoned as the new national system was implemented.

Four purposes had been mentioned in *Records of Achievement: A Statement of Policy* (DES/Welsh Office, July 1984) — recognition of achievement, motivation and personal development, curriculum and organization, a document of record. To meet the first three of these purposes, schools would 'need to set up internal arrangements for the compilation of records throughout a pupil's period of secondary education' (para. 12). Such arrangements were expected to be more than bureaucratic book-keeping, being integrated into teaching and learning in such a way that pupils would be 'closely involved in the recording processes' (para. 36). The procedures of record-keeping and reporting were thus closely linked under the banner of 'records of achievement'.

During the 1980s, development of records of achievement continued at local level with Government backing, initially for nine pilot schemes funded through Education Support Grants and subsequently for further locally administered schemes. Reports from HM Inspectorate (1988) and from the National Steering Committee (1989) gave the impression that, while there were still problems to be overcome, the prospect of a national system of records of achievement was looming ever closer on the educational horizon. The first Government statement on National Curriculum, the 1987 consultation document, did not even hint at any incompatibility between developments to date and the new system:

> The Government aims to set in place by 1990 national arrangements for the introduction of records of achievement for school leavers. Such records . . . will have an important role in recording performance and profiling a pupil's achievements across and beyond the National Curriculum. (para. 32)

Yet, as Haviland's account of the responses to that consultation shows, the proposal which prompted the most hostile reaction was elsewhere in the same document — that schools and LEAs would be required to publish aggregations of results on national assessments. The stage was thus set in 1987 for the subsequent working through of tensions between recording and reporting procedures which focused on the individual and were intended mainly as a feedback loop to support learning, and their function as stages in the processing of aggregate data about attainment in preparation for its use mainly as an indicator of the performance of teachers, schools and local education authorities.

The TGAT Report on Record-Keeping, Reporting and Publishing

The TGAT Report committed itself to serving the several purposes of national assessment by using a common stem of evidence from assessments to feed the several distinct channels through which the summarized information could pass to potential users of it, including other teachers, parents, employers and those interested in aggregate indicators of performance. 'Each of the purposes of the national assessment system can be met by a separate report based on a different aggregate to which a different degree of confidence can be attached' (para. 81). From that proposition, challenged from the beginning by critics of the Report, it followed that the single stem would have to branch at some point during the procedures of record-keeping and reporting. Either a single composite record of attainment would have to be capable of feeding the various channels or the way records were kept would have to anticipate the different requirements of diverse 'users'.

The implications for record-keeping were not explored by the Task Group. However, as the National Curriculum was implemented, the nature of the record which should be kept was to become a major source of anxiety among teachers. Alongside the teacher assessment part of the system, in how much detail should a record be kept of each pupil's attainment? What evidence should be retained in support of a teacher's judgment that the criteria embodied in a particular statement of attainment had been met? With SATs, how elaborate (and therefore time-consuming) should be the form-filling expected of teachers?

Underlying all such professional questions was the central issue of purpose — what were teachers keeping a record *for*? (see chapter 4 for a fuller discussion of these issues).

Associated with it was another recurring source of uncertainty — whose business was it to decide these things? Was record-keeping an adjunct of teaching and therefore to be a matter for each teacher to determine as s/he judged? Or was it an aspect of the externally determined assessment require-ments and therefore something teachers could expect to be imposed from outside the school? The lack of clarification of such questions ensured that discussion and development of record-keeping would be confused and un-certain, the 'missing link' in the chain of procedures on which the success of a criterion-referenced assessment system depended.

The TGAT Report did, however, anticipate some of the issues which would arise in the reporting and publication of results. Four aspects of the reporting of attainment were given particular attention.

A clear and important distinction was made between reporting on indi-vidual pupils, for example to their parents, and using aggregate data at class, school, LEA or national level. For the former purpose the Task Group was firm in its view that 'final reports on individual pupils to their parents should be the responsibility of the teacher, supported by standardized assessment tasks and group moderation' (para. 80). Such reports should refer to attain-ment in each profile component and be positive and constructive in tone (paras. 126–7). Other audiences for information about the individual pupil — staff monitoring progress within and between schools, employers, further education — were also identified.

On the use of aggregate data, the Group believed that 'sufficient confi-dence would attach to these aggregations, target by target, to provide formative feedback both to inform schools and others about their work and to guide those responsible for developing the National Curriculum' (para. 83). They stressed, however, their preference for going beyond crude averages of the performance of groups of pupils and making use of information about the *range* of attainments within any group:

> We recommend that wherever schools use national assessment results
> in reports for evaluative purposes, they should report the distribution
> of pupil achievements. (TGAT Report, para. 84)

It was the prospect of aggregate results being published, as distinct from being communicated within the education system for monitoring the per-formance of schools and local authorities, which caused most concern among professional educators. A sub-section of the TGAT Report on 'reporting a school's performance' (paras. 132–138) anticipated this and explored how best to describe for public consumption the performance of a school. That four of the Task Group's forty-four specific recommendations emerge from this sec-tion of their argument is some measure of the importance they attached to the issue. The Group accepted the case for publishing information on a school's performance, drawing on the national assessment results of pupils at ages 11,

14 and 16, but argued against publishing the results of 7-year-olds. However, sensitive to the dangers of simple averages of the performance of a cohort of pupils being misinterpreted, the Group, having rehearsed the arguments for alternative approaches (including adjusting scores to take account of a school's pupil intake), advocated the placing of data aggregated at school level in context:

> We recommend that any report by a school which includes national assessment results should include a general report for the area, prepared by the local authority, to indicate the nature of socio-economic and other influences which are known to affect schools. (TGAT Report, para. 134)

Finally, in relation to reporting, the Task Group attempted to link what they were proposing to existing practice in the use of records of achievement. It is interesting to note that the submission received by the Group from the Records of Achievement National Steering Committee (RANSC) is reproduced in full as appendix I of the TGAT Report. The Steering Committee concluded that there were two 'key contributions' which records of achievement could make to National Curriculum development:

(a)   the formative process, with pupil-teacher dialogue essential to secure the Government's objective of diagnostic NC assessments; and

(b)   the setting of those NC assessments into the context of the totality of a pupil's achievements and experiences. (TGAT Report, appendix I, para. 22)

The use of records of achievement as a vehicle for recording progress and achievement within the national assessment system was endorsed by TGAT (para. 162) but that paragraph also glossed over some of the tensions within the broad field of work encompassed by the term 'records of achievement'. Whether they would, linked to the new national assessment system, serve primarily as vehicles for *record-keeping* and the associated formative feedback to pupils, or mainly as a means of *reporting* a wide range of pupils' attainments, is far from clear from the TGAT Report's relatively brief discussion of the subject.

   While the Task Group did devote substantial sections of its Report to reporting and publishing results, if not to record-keeping, some of the most critical issues which were to dominate the public debate in this area were scarcely touched upon. The prospect of one reporting purpose being incompatible with another or of the publication of results having a 'backwash' effect on the assessment process and the curriculum in which it is embedded may have been discussed by the Task Group but are not addressed directly in the TGAT Report. However, it must also be recognized that the Task Group envisaged a very different emphasis in the use of national assessment results than that which was to emerge from decisions taken as the system was implemented. For example, two of its recommendations made clear that aggregation of the results from each school for the information of parents with pupils at that school was how TGAT saw national assessment results being reported and 'published':

> National assessment results for a class as a whole and for a school as a whole should be available to the parents of its pupils. (para. 131)
>
> We recommend that the *only* form in which results of national assessment for, and identifying, a given school should be published is as part of a broader report by that school of its work as a whole. (para. 132)

Additionally, there is a brief reference to school governors and local and national providers of education needing aggregated information but it seems that what the Group had in mind there was an essentially private channelling of selected information required to inform decision-making. Seen as part of the TGAT 'package' of a variety of classroom assessments geared to helping the learner learn and the teacher teach, its recommendations on reporting aggregate results would complement that style of assessment by giving the individual parent information which could help support his/her own child's learning. If that had been the type of reporting and publication put in place as implementation proceeded it may be that record-keeping and reporting could have been developed along lines which were broadly neutral in their 'backwash' effect on the curriculum and assessment practices which supplied the necessary evidence. In practice however, reporting and publication of results took a markedly different form and most of TGAT's recommendations on these aspects of policy were disregarded.

Policy Development 1988–89

Records of Achievement or 'Administrative Arrangements'?

The National Curriculum policy agenda in the months following the passing of the Education Reform Act was dominated by the regular appearance of reports from curriculum working groups and, on the assessment front, by the first steps towards developing standard tasks for 7-year-olds. Record-keeping and reporting broke through into that agenda only twice and from two quite different directions. From one direction came the publication in January 1989 of the *Report of the Records of Achievement National Steering Committee* (RANSC), the culmination of a process of development and evaluation of records of achievement which pre-dated the moves towards a National Curriculum and assessment system. Secondly, during 1989, as a direct consequence of the 1988 Act, the DES was preparing the first of many sets of regulations which would set in place the administrative arrangements for the provision of information on the assessment of pupils under Section 22 of the 1988 Act. These were subsequently published as DES and Welsh Office circulars in July 1990. The flow of proposals from those two very different directions, both of them concerned with retaining and making use of information about attainment, would come together with predictably turbulent effects in the late summer of 1989.

As explained earlier, the RANSC Report was a stage in a development which had been given Government support in the DES/WO policy statement of 1984. The Report concluded with a series of recommendations designed to give effect to the expectation that a national scheme would be in place by the end of the decade. However, the wording of Kenneth Baker's letter to SEAC, asking the Council to consult on the Report and prepare advice, (DES letter to SEAC, 20 January 1989) is a clear indication of a rather more limited and lukewarm commitment to records of achievement than that contained in his predecessor's (Keith Joseph) statement of 1984. Specifically, the *process* of pre-paring records of achievement, so central to the 1984 argument, is uncoupled from the summative record and dismissed in two sentences as something for 'each LEA and each school to determine'. RANSC's advocacy of accreditation machinery which would help establish the credibility of records of achieve-ments as a national system is also quickly dismissed 'bearing in mind the cost and complexity involved'. Instead, the Secretary of State focuses attention on reporting the results of national assessments:

> Subject to your advice, I envisage that there will need to be a consist-ent basis for the presentation of national assessment results for pupils at each of the key ages of 7, 11, 14 and 16; and that annual if not more frequent reports to parents should include information about pupils' progress in a form to be prescribed in Regulations under Section 22.

A creature which had been nurtured in the undergrowth of individual schools and LEA development groups was already on its way to being confined to the cage of bureaucratic regulation.

Following receipt and analysis of the responses to its consultation, SEAC submitted its advice to the Secretaries of State (SEAC letter to the DES, 13 July 1989). It told the minister that there was 'strong and widespread support for the nationwide use of records of achievement in schools, underpinned by regulations'. SEAC expressed the 'firm view' that:

> regulations requiring all schools to maintain a record of achievement for each pupil between the ages of 5 and 16 should be promulgated under Section 22 of the Education Reform Act. The regulations should make it clear the central purpose of the records of achievement to acknowledge and give credit for what pupils have achieved in other ways as well as in terms of public examinations and National Cur-riculum assessments.

Thus, while the SEAC position favoured a more broadly defined record of achievement than that signalled by Mr. Baker in January, its advice challenged neither the rejection of national accreditation nor, perhaps more crucially, the redefinition of records of achievement almost entirely in terms of the summative document without reference to the process of preparing the record, seen by most of those advocating records of achievement to be central to their educational value.

Curiously, on the same day that SEAC offered this advice, it was writing separately to the Secretary of State about National Curriculum assessment arrangements, including how the results of assessments should be reported under Section 22 of the 1988 Act. Further advice on the issues raised in this letter of 13 July 1989 (headed 'National Curriculum Assessment and Testing') from Philip Halsey, SEAC Chairman, was promised for December 1989. The two sources influencing the development of reporting procedures had not yet reached a confluence.

From Recording Achievement to Reporting Attainment

The SEAC letter on National Curriculum assessment arrangements received a prompt reply from the Secretary of State (DES letter to SEAC, 24 July 1989) expressing reservations about the SEAC recommendation that reports to parents should give details of performance on each attainment target (as well as at the level of profile components and whole subjects). However, what was to be seen by many as a death blow to records of achievement as envisaged in the 1984 policy statement came three weeks later with the response of the Minister of State, Angela Rumbold (DES letter to SEAC, 16 August 1989) to SEAC's 'records of achievement' advice. In a few blunt paragraphs, the Minister completed the subjugation of records of achievement to the process of bureaucratic regulation. The Council's advice, she wrote, 'will serve as the starting point for the preparation of regulations under Section 22'. Her letter makes no mention of the issues of accreditation, breadth of achievement beyond National Curriculum or the formative process of pupil and teacher working together on completing the record. Philip Halsey's July letter had been headed 'Records of Achievement'; the DES press release announcing Mrs. Rumbold's decision in August was headed 'Reporting pupil achievement under the National Curriculum'. Within that month what had been assumed by those engaged in it to be a continuing process of recording *and* reporting a range of *achievements* had become officially in ministerial terms a matter of the *reporting* of National Curriculum *levels of attainment*.

Public response to the DES announcement of its decisions got off to a bad start with widespread misinterpretation of its implications for schools. Though the term 'record of achievement' does not appear at all in Mrs. Rumbold's response to SEAC advice on that subject, much of the national press presented the decision as end-of-term reports to parents being *replaced* by records of achievement. Headlines included 'Reports face axe' (*Daily Mirror*) and 'Yahoo! No more school reports' (*Daily Star*) while *The Times* introduced its report with: 'Traditional end of term school reports will be phased out from the summer of 1991 and replaced with "records of achievement" that will emphasize success and play down failure' (17 August 1989).

Press coverage of the issue was so wide of the mark that the DES issued a further statement the following day to clarify the position. Far from announcing the demise of school reports, the Government would be requiring every maintained school to report to parents at least once in each school year (more often if the school so decided). Far from signalling a new era of records of achievement, 'the requirements will be confined to National Curriculum subjects. Schools will have discretion to amplify them if resources permit.'

Such clarification underlined the minimalist approach of the DES on reporting to parents. For those committed to the very different philosophy of reporting the full range of 'achievement' in essentially positive terms it confirmed their fears that the Government had effectively buried the 1984 policy statement on Records of Achievement. One commentator, under the headline 'The month records died' lamented:

> The proven worth of records of achievement has been ignored in favour of the National Curriculum and its accompanying assessment system which is untried . . . (Stephen Munby, *TES*, 28 September 1989)

Chief education officers and examination boards were also reported to be 'angry over the Government's treatment of plans for pupils' records of achievement' (*TES*, 13 October 1989). Only in the quieter backwaters of the debate, such as the letters column of the journal *Education*, was a more measured, reflective perspective coming closer to the heart of the matter:

> . . . all those concerned with recording pupils' achievements (should) make a vital distinction between reports (for third parties and usually judgmental) and records (as being seen to be of benefit to those in the learning process and descriptively based on the outcome of dialogue with pupils). Attempting to make the same process fulfil different purposes is likely to result in the worst of all worlds.
> . . . neither the National Curriculum nor the GCSE attempt to differentiate between 'attainment' and 'achievement', and as a consequence it is assumed they are the same. The records of achievement movement should have attempted to raise the critical issues in this debate. (Letter from Frank Stote, *Education*, 25 August 1989)

As a footnote to what was, however dressed up, a clear shift in policy on reporting attainment it is interesting to note that 'Records of Achievement' was still sufficiently within the field of vision of ministers (or at least their officials) to merit a sub-heading in the text of a speech given by the Secretary of State, John MacGregor, to the Society of Education Officers the following January (25 January 1990). However, a truer indication of the Government's position on the subject may be that the section in question did not actually deal with records of achievement!

As the storm of protest over the Government's perceived failure to endorse records of achievement died down, the debate about reporting to parents came to be redefined as a facet of regulations under Section 22 of the 1988 Act. No longer were the principles underpinning the RANSC Report to the fore. Instead the what, when and how of informing parents about National Curriculum attainment levels became the subject of arguments expressed in more pragmatic terms.

The Government published draft regulations under Section 22 on 5, January 1990, to be followed by a three-month period of consultation. Some of SEAC's unease about records of achievement being subsumed under regulations headed 'The Education (Individual Pupils' Achievements) Regulations 1990' comes through in a letter from SEAC to the Secretary of State in March (SEAC letter to the DES, 28 March 1990). It urges John MacGregor to 'strengthen the limited encouragement for records of achievement' by modifying the wording to indicate his 'hopes that all schools will adopt schemes for records of achievement'. Also:

> The Regulations should make clear the central purpose of the records of achievement to acknowledge and give credit for what pupils have achieved in other ways as well as in terms of public examinations and national assessments.

In the event, the final version of the Circular, published in July (DES 8/90, WO 39/90), made more positive noises. The Secretary of State 'applauded' records of achievement developments, seeing them as 'the means by which achievement across the National Curriculum and beyond can be most effectively reported to a range of audiences'. However, it is notable that he stops short of committing the Government even to the 'hopes' suggested by SEAC. The change of the Circular's title to 'Records of Achievement' represents little more than a gesture to those who had accused the DES of abandoning its commitment to records of achievement. The statutory instrument, the part of the documentation with legislative force, is more prosaically headed 'The Education (Individual Pupils' Achievements) (Information) Regulations 1990' and the term 'record of achievement' is not used at all in its wording. In spite of the packaging, we are therefore still in the world of Government regulating what attainment information is reported to parents, a concept of reporting far removed from the principles the RANSC Report had sought to further.

Only in the work of the Training Agency's Technical and Vocational Education Extension (TVEE) were records of achievement to remain a significant part of Government policy. The 'National Record of Achievement', dubbed the 'This Is Your Life' report from its maroon-bound, gold-lettered format, was launched in February 1991 with the DES very much late recruits to an initiative fostered by the Department of Employment (see James, 1993 for a fuller account). As a *TES* Editorial (1 March 1991) put it:

> The guidance on completing the NRA draws on the work of the National Council for Vocational Qualifications; to all intents and purposes, it is as though the rest (of the development of records of achievement) never happened.

The NRA is a document of record for school leavers rather than the more broadly conceived record of achievement for which the RANSC Report came to look more like an epitaph than a launching pad.

Informing Parents

Extending the Role of the Government

If, by the end of 1989, it had become obvious that the DES did not favour records of achievement as an existing vehicle to which reporting for parents on National Curriculum assessment could be attached, it was by no means clear what form reports to parents would take and who would determine the style of report to be adopted. TGAT had recommended that 'final reports on individual pupils to their parents should be the responsibility of the individual teacher'. It was to become apparent during 1990 and 1991 that central Government was reluctant to allow schools much discretion in deciding the style and form of their communication with parents.

Early policy discussions in this area focused on the level of detail parents should receive about attainment levels and on the frequency of reporting. In respect of the former, in spite of continuing advocacy by SEAC that end-of-stage reporting should include levels for each attainment targets (argued as necessary for feeding back useful information about the extent of progress in each aspect of learning), the July 1990 Regulations and accompanying Circular settled upon reporting at profile component and whole subject levels. The Regulations also put in place the Government's intention, stated the previous August, of requiring a written report to parents at least once a year.

In addition however, the July Circular signalled a significant extension of central control in this area of policy:

> The Secretary of State sees advantages for parents and others con-
> cerned in seeking to devise an agreed common format for reporting
> ...(DES Circular 8/90, para. 25)

Early the following year, the DES issued a draft 'standard format for reporting to parents' and by March 1991 a 'model format' had been circulated to all primary and secondary schools. Though its use was not mandatory, schools were being encouraged to adopt that model format.

At about the same time, the DES issued a parents' guide to testing, *How is your child doing at school?*, explaining how to interpret the information which would be given to them in school reports. Interestingly, the section entitled 'why test?' puts the case for national testing entirely in terms of its value to the individual child and his/her parent(s). Nowhere is the possibility mentioned of test information, aggregated at school level, being useful evidence on which to base a choice of school. Very soon however, with the Government's flagship policy of 'citizens charters' empowering the public in their choice of services coming to the fore during 1991, publication of national assessment results would move to centre stage in the debate about Government education policy.

Towards the 'Parent's Charter'

From time to time since the initial presentation of the case for an assessed National Curriculum in the 1987 consultation document, the Government had made the case for parents being informed about the performance of schools by having aggregate data made available to them in addition to information about their own child's attainments. As with so much of policy on what should happen to the results obtained from national assessment procedures, it remained little more than a general statement of intent for the first two or three years of implementing the system, while other aspects of policy were to the fore. It was not until the first cohort of pupils was coming towards the end of a full Key Stage of National Curriculum courses in at least some subjects that the policy had to be more fully articulated and debated. By that time, the Department of Education and Science was led by a different Secretary of State, Kenneth Clarke, and the new Prime Minister, John Major, had committed himself to introducing public service charters, including one for parents of pupils in maintained schools. The reporting of aggregate data on pupil performance was increasingly presented and argued in the context of parents' entitlement to information about schools rather than as a facet of policy on assessment. The perceived needs of the main target audience for such information, the parent choosing or monitoring a school as well as checking on his/her own child's progress, were to govern the action required.

The first 'Citizen's Charter' proposals, published in July 1991, outlined what schools would be required to make available to parents, including truancy rates and the destinations of school leavers as well as results of examinations and national assessments. Local education authorities would also be expected to compile, and publish in the local press, 'league tables' of the results achieved by the schools in its area.

Education: A Charter for Parents (September 1991) set out in more detail the nature of the reports a parent would be entitled to receive. A written report on the individual child, at least once a year, would tell the parent about:

- progress in the core subjects, including test results at 7, 11 and 14;
- 'results in other important exams or tests';
- achievements in other subjects and activities during the year;
- how the results in exams and in national tests compare with those of other children of the same age;
- the child's general progress and attendance record;
- who to talk to in the school.

Access on a regular basis to information of various kinds was thus to be a central feature of the parent's entitlement as a citizen and the results of National Curriculum assessments were to be a major source of evidence about the child's progress. Prior to the introduction of a National Curriculum a school report might well have provided much of the above information to parents; only the fourth point was entirely novel. Not only would the report contain information about the parent's own child; that information would be compared with the equivalent results at national level. The use of test results as performance indicators for parents was also prominent in another part of the parental entitlement, the annual report to all parents from the school governors, which would contain 'information about exam and National Curriculum test results for the school as a whole'.

One symptom of the increased emphasis on the parent as a purchaser of educational services who would require information on which to base choices was the DES insistence that SEAC should commission, during the summer of 1991, a market research survey on the information they received and would want to receive. SEAC's doubts about the value of such an exercise were not heeded.

Reporting to Parents on the Individual Pupil

The Parent's Charter had set out the Government's policy on providing information to parents in various ways but, as in other areas of policy, putting it in place was to be a matter for statutory regulations. The regulations issued in July 1990 had been the first indication of what control by central government of reporting to parents might mean in practice. Subsequent regulations revised and extended the scope of information which schools would be obliged to publish and/or make available to parents. In each successive year new sets of regulations, accompanied by a Government Circular, would appear. Some referred to matters such as what should be published in school prospectuses and the information to be supplied by central agencies. Others dealt with how parents should be informed about their own children's attainments.

The DFE Circular 5/92 on *Reporting Pupils' Achievements to Parents: 1992* was the first of these to appear in the wake of publication of the Parent's Charter. It included an extensive section on the 'minimum mandatory content' of all school reports. Key Stage 1 was again in the front line as the first of the Key Stages in which pupils had experienced national end-of-Key-Stage testing. Schools would, as previously announced, have to report the pupil's level of attainment on the 1–10 scale for each profile component and each subject. Information about the child's performance on the attainment targets in a subject would, in general, be made available to parents only on request. However, the results of the reading accuracy and spelling tests in English and of the arithmetic attainment target in mathematics would have to be conveyed routinely as part of the written report. The implicit hierarchy of importance of aspects of National Curriculum attainment was thus becoming clear in the way ministers and their officials defined the reporting regulations. While for the most part in the core subjects only profile component and subject data would be passed to parents, the reporting of test results in reading, spelling and arithmetic would be exceptions to that rule. At the bottom of the hierarchy, information about the non-core subjects (in which there were no end-of-stage tests) would be limited to 'brief particulars of a pupil's achievements'.

Subsequent regulations and Circulars (7/92, 14/92) amended these provisions in detail while reinforcing the messages about priorities implicit in what was to be reported and how the information should be presented to parents. They demonstrate how far the debate about recording and reporting had moved on from the SEAC — Rumbold exchanges of July/August 1990. Then the tensions had been very much in evidence between the Government view, that reporting was essentially a matter of informing parents about National Curriculum levels of attainment, and a widely-held professional view that recording and reporting achievements through a developing 'record of achievement' was an educative process in its own right. The Government's own preferred 'model format' for reporting to parents, issued to schools in March 1991, had reinforced the former interpretation. By the time of the 1992 and 1993 Circulars on Reporting, the Government no longer even seemed to feel it necessary to make gestures in the direction of records of achievement. The only reference to them comes in the context of the provision for all school leavers ('strongly encouraged' in 1992, made mandatory in 1993) of the National Record of Achievement (NRA). Given that the style of the NRA is very much geared to its use as a summative document for school leavers it would be surprising if many schools took up the invitation to 'consider its use to report annually to parents on younger pupils'. In these Government Regulations, if not necessarily in the practices of individual schools, reporting attainment had triumphed over recording and reporting achievement!

Perhaps more significant than this use of school reports as a vehicle for selective emphasis, according to Government priorities, on certain aspects of individual attainment, was the emphasis on comparing an individual pupil's performance with the aggregate scores of what were, in the Government's view, comparable groups. Regulations obliged schools to include in each pupil's report information comparing his/her performance with other pupils of the same age in that school and with the average performance nationally in each of the required aspects of attainment. Whatever form a school's report to parents had taken previously, any comparisons included in it had typically been limited to those which linked the individual's performance to that of the class, set or age groups of which s/he was a member. Under the new regulations for 16 and 18-year-olds, where national examinations were already in place, a pupil's results would be set alongside comparative information about other pupils in the same school and nationally. As national testing arrangements came to be fully implemented, similar requirements would apply to reporting the attainment of 7, 11 and 14-year-olds. Not only would such test data be published but it would be used on the reports of each pupil to demonstrate how his/her performance compared with the school and national averages.

Publishing Results: Information in the Public Domain

Early Skirmishes

In the context of a school reporting to the parents of its pupils, the use of aggregate data raises questions about validity, usefulness, and the effect of that information on parents' perceptions of the performance both of their child and of the school. But the making of that same information public in the form of data about performance levels in schools, across LEAs and across the whole country brings national assessment very much into the debate about 'standards' in the education system. When a parent is informed about the levels of attainment in his/her child's year group, s/he will inevitably raise questions about how well that child is progressing in comparison with children of the same age. When that same information appears in the press, together with equivalent data about other schools (or LEAs in comparison with other LEAs), the obvious questions to be debated by a wider public would inevitably focus on how well schools were performing relative to each other. From the TGAT Report onwards the publication of results was always among the most contentious of the issues relating to national assessment.

As discussed earlier, TGAT had advocated the placing of data aggregated at the level of the school in the context of 'a general report for the area, prepared by the local authority, to indicate the nature of socioeconomic and other influences which are known to affect schools' (para. 134). That had been one of the Task Group's recommendations which did not attract widespread support, criticized on the one hand by those who believed it should be a matter for parents to put their own interpretations on such 'raw' performance data and, on the other, by those who argued for the school's assessment results to be presented in terms of the 'value added' which that school could show when the results of pupils leaving it were compared with their performance when they entered the school. However, whatever the merits of the TGAT proposal on reporting school data, it remained one of the Group's recommendations on which, for a long time following the Government's general acceptance of the TGAT model, policy remained uncertain. As with other aspects of policy on record-keeping, reporting and publishing results, it was not resolved until the first cohort of pupils to complete a National Curriculum Key Stage (those embarking on Key Stage 1) was approaching the point where results would, in some form, be published.

During that time, there were periodic skirmishes as teacher organizations and opposition parties reiterated their objections to schools being judged by the public on the basis of raw, unadjusted national assessment scores. For example, Labour Party education spokesmen, Jack Straw, told a conference in September 1989 that publication of crude results 'could lead to wild and hopelessly inaccurate judgments about the performance of different schools' (*Daily Telegraph*, 9 September 1989). In a brief reference to the prospect of schools publishing results, SEAC was cautious and non-committal in its advice to ministers:

> This is a complex issue which will need careful investigation and judgment to discover the most useful form in which to present these results. (SEAC letter to DES, 12 December 1989)

The Secretary of State for Education and Science for much of this period, John MacGregor, sought to reassure teacher opinion rather than to draw attention to this aspect of policy. For example, in his speech to one of the teacher associations (AMMA) in April (9 April 1990) he confirmed that, for 7-year-olds, 'there will be no requirement to publish at all'.

For the Key Stages at the end of which aggregate data at school level was to be required, the argument continued about the way in which information about a school's 'performance' should be presented. From the early criticisms of the TGAT proposals on this point, some commentators (for example, Goldstein, 1988) had advocated the use of scores which were adjusted to take account of a school's intake. The debate continued on the sidelines as the policy-makers moved from statements of intent to specific regulations and draft legislation. Professor Desmond Nuttall was among those questioning the value of 'raw' results:

> The argument that raw results are not good measures of school quality, and that they must be placed in the context of the calibre of the intake to look at value added, is now widely accepted. (*TES*, 13 September 1991)

In a briefing paper for the National Commission on Education, Andrew McPherson argued in similar terms:

> Unadjusted test scores should be accompanied by information on how much a school has contributed to the progress of its pupils. (*TES*, 21 February 1992)

Key Stage 1 would be first in line for publication of results but the publishing of school-level data was not, at least initially, to be compulsory at that Key Stage. It was therefore comparative results LEA-by-LEA and across the system as a whole which were at issue when the first round of public discussion of national assessment attainments took place. The opportunity for the press and public to scrutinize and comment upon the performance of individual schools would have to await the collation and publication, in late 1992, of data from Key Stage 4 examination results.

Distortion of Performance Data: The 1991 Test Results

The worst fears of those who opposed the publishing of results were confirmed by the furore which accompanied publication of the 1991 data on attainment at the end of Key Stage 1. The publicity for, and misinterpretation of, national assessment results began with a *Sunday Times* story (27 October 1991) based on a leak of an analysis, undertaken by the National Foundation for Educational Research, of the performance of a sample of 7-year-olds in the 1991 assessments. Mathematics appeared to be a problem: 'one in three can't count'. This was the paper's way of summarizing the evidence that a third of the pupil sample had not reached the anticipated average attainment level (level 2) in mathematics attainment target 2. No doubt if fewer than a third of the age group had been 'below average' there would have been an outcry in the press that the tasks had been 'too easy'. But, quite apart from the fact that the TGAT ten level scale was actually designed on the assumption that a substantial proportion of 7-year-olds would demonstrate attainments below that represented by level 2, the press reporting was based on a fundamental misconception as to what was required for a pupil to be recorded as having attained that level.

To have achieved level 2 a pupil would have had to demonstrate that s/he could successfully carry out several different arithmetical operations; 'one in three can't count' was an inaccurate, and unduly pessimistic, interpretation of the results. It was, however, much closer to the mark than some of the even wilder reporting which followed in the wake of the *Sunday Times* story. The *Daily Express* somehow contrived to conclude, on grounds which are difficult to discern, that 'only one in every thirty 7-year-olds can read and write after two years in primary school'. The stage was set for sections of the press to seek the necessary 'evidence' to support their well established assumption of low standards of attainment.

During a lull of several weeks pending DES publication of Key Stage 1 results LEA-by-LEA, there were some signs of more balanced presentation of the results. *The Times Educational Supplement*, commenting (8 November 1991) on figures about the reading attainments of 7-year-olds given by the Government to a Select Committee of the House of Commons, referred to evidence that 'more than a quarter of them cannot read without help'. The core subject results for pupils in Wales, published a month ahead of those for England, were analyzed by the broadsheet press under headlines like 'Welsh pupils find maths a test at 7' (*The Guardian*) and 'A quarter of Welsh pupils unable to master three Rs' (*Daily Telegraph*). The 'good news' from the same source, for example 88 per cent of pupils achieving the expected level (level 2) for the average seven year old in science and only 12 per cent falling below that level, was given less prominence.

However, the press was to have even more of a field day in misinterpreting the findings and highlighting the 'bad news' when the results for England were published in mid December. For *The Independent* 'the first national tests for 7-year-olds (showed) that 28 per cent cannot read or do simple sums' (20 December 1991). For *The Daily Telegraph* (20 December 1991):

> The release of nationwide exam results for 7-year-olds confirms that primary education in Britain is not far short of a national disgrace. The exams, strenuously opposed by the educational establishment, revealed that over a quarter of the age group cannot identify three letters of the alphabet, let alone read a story.

In what the *Times Educational Supplement* described (20 December 1991) as 'the near hysteria being worked up over standards of basic education', even those reporters who troubled to look at the data for the most part failed to understand two crucial design features of the ten level attainment scale.

Those who had framed the statements at each of the levels (the subject working groups) had been asked to design the system so that level 2 would represent the attainment of the average 7-year-old. The first results showed a pattern of attainment remarkably close to that which might have been anticipated. The *Financial Times* (20 December 1991) was one of the few papers to explain and report the figures in these terms:

> They divide 7-year-olds into three main groups: those performing at the level to be expected of a 5- or 6-year-old (level 1); those performing as expected (level 2); and those at the level of a typical 9-year-old (level 3). Overall, performance in science and English was better than in maths. In science, 90 per cent were at level 2 or above, with 23 per cent at level 3; in English, 78 per cent were at level 2 or above and 17 per cent at level 3; in maths 72 per cent were at level 2 or above, with 6 per cent at level 3.

The second point most reporters failed to understand was that, to achieve a particular level, several attainments, set out in the Statutory Orders for the subject in question, would have to be demonstrated. Thus, as *The Times Educational Supplement* editorial carefully explained (perhaps to colleagues in the press as much as to its own readers):

> Nor does the fact that pupils have not achieved level two mean they 'cannot read'. The standard represented by level two amounts to rather more than that. As many as a third of those recorded as level one may well read with some fluency, but simply fall down on one or two of the more stringent level two requirements — they may, for instance, not be able to use a dictionary. (*TES*, 20 December 1991)

The contribution of the Secretary of State, Kenneth Clarke, in all this showed him to be more attuned to the political benefits to be gained from trumpeting low standards (and therefore the need for changes in teaching methods and in the administration of schools) than a concern for accurate interpretation of the evidence:

> Parents can rightly be concerned at the new education 'league table' which I intend to publish later this week. It is the result of the first national tests for 7-year-olds — which I ordered — and shows that nearly a third of such pupils cannot even recognize three letters of the alphabet and one in four cannot do such simple sums as five times five. (*Mail on Sunday*, 15 December 1991)

The fact that the test results showed no such thing was conveniently ignored as the minister went on to use them as a stick with which to beat those responsible for this sorry state of affairs — local education authorities, teacher trainers and the 'educational establishment', all of them in Clarke's view tainted by 'sixties ideologies'. Results which had shown patterns of performance close to what the designers of the national assessment system might have anticipated — most pupils at the level expected of the average 7-year-old — were thus being used, by the Secretary of State for the Department responsible, as 'evidence' to support the direction of Government policy on schools. As the *Mail on Sunday* headline to Clarke's article put it: 'For our children's sake, these bureaucrats *MUST* be broken'.

Some of those most directly under fire, the local education authorities, protested not just about ministerial misrepresentation of the results but also about the unfairness of comparisons between authorities. In some areas the standard tasks had been given to a higher proportion of 7-year-olds than in other LEAs while the rigorousness of the testing and the associated moderation had also clearly varied from one LEA to the next. One education committee chairman expressed his concerns thus:

> It is clear that many LEAs did not submit returns from all their schools, with as little as 50 per cent in some cases, and in some schools only a sample of children were tested. This, together with the lack of standardization across authorities, we think accounts for Bexley's relatively low position in the table. (Brian Sams, *Education*, 21 February 1992)

In those circumstances, how much trust could be placed in the results which gave rise to the league tables? While such arguments were overshadowed by the press outcry about 'standards' and could be easily, perhaps too easily, dismissed as special pleading, one of the recurring themes in the development of national assessment had surfaced again. How much reliance could be placed on results from tasks administered and marked by tens of thousands of teachers of year 2 classes? Whatever it was claimed the results showed, were they reliable enough to be a basis for evaluating the performance of schools and local authorities? And — the most important question of all — was there reason to believe that publishing such results would have the hoped-for impact on the standards of pupils' work? The engine on which the Government was depending to drive up standards in schools was self-evidently close to stalling and there was as yet no convincing evidence to back ministers' faith in it as a powerful mechanism for improving pupils' attainment.

1992: More League Tables

By the time results of the 1992 tests were available for publication, the Conservative Government had won a General Election and a new Secretary of State for Education, John Patten, was in post. His Department even had a new title, Department for Education. On the publication of results, his hand was strengthened by the passage of the 1992 Education (Schools) Act which added extra teeth to the Parent's Charter by giving the Secretary of State power to obtain and publish:

> such information about the school as may be prescribed . . . with a
> view to making available information which is likely to:

(a)   assist parents in choosing schools for their children;

(b)   increase public awareness of the quality of education pro-
       vided by the schools concerned and of the educational
       standards achieved in these schools. (Section 16)

When doubts about the validity of the 1991 results had surfaced in May (based
on HMI reports and SEAC's own evidence), the Minister of State, Baroness
Blatch, had taken the opportunity to restate the Government's commitment
to the publishing of performance tables:

> Tests are the key to the parent's charter goal of opening up schools
> to scrutiny and raising standards. Assessment will give parents a secure
> means of measuring the progress, not only of their own children but
> also [of] individual schools, local authorities and the education service
> nationally. (*The Guardian*, 22 May 1992)

With November and December becoming established in the educational world
as the season of league tables, the results from Wales for Key Stages 1 and 3
were first in the field in 1992. Some improvement in pupil performance at
Key Stage 1 was acknowledged. The Welsh Office Minister, Sir Wyn Roberts
was 'very encouraged by the results for 7-year-olds. They show an improvement to just over 81 per cent of pupils achieving level 2 or above in the core
subjects.' But the good news was overshadowed by results of the pilot tests
for 14-year-olds in maths and science taken by pupils in about two-thirds of
the schools of Wales. The fact that they were *pilot* tests and had not been taken
by all pupils in the age group did not inhibit those intent on accentuating the
negative:

> Half of the Welsh 14-year-olds who sat exams in science and 40 per
> cent of those who took maths did not reach the 'average' level for
> their age. (*Western Mail*, 21 October 1992)

Next in line were the first official national tables of GCSE and 'A' level results
in England and Wales, school by school. As the broadsheet papers printed
special supplements to give the results in full, the Secretary of State claimed
they represented:

> (an) information revolution, bringing an end to a system which has
> too often denied parents the right to know how schools are perform-
> ing. Until today, comparative results have been the private preserve
> of local authorities which, with certain and notable exceptions, seemed
> to believe that parents cannot be trusted to understand or use the fig-
> ures wisely. This attitude is now permanently consigned to the dust-
> bin of history. (John Patten, quoted in *The Independent*, 19 November
> 1992)

But the announcement of this 'information revolution' was clouded by
continuing criticism of it as a valid means of comparing the performance of

schools. 'Independent schools shun publishing exam results' was *The Times* headline while *The Guardian*'s report was headed 'Parents and teachers condemn "misleading" results'.

Finally in the sequence came the results for English local authorities of Key Stage 1 tests and the pilot tests in maths and science for 14-year-olds. The press comment was noticeably less prominent and more restrained than twelve months earlier but the continuing deep divisions of opinion about the usefulness of the data were clearly apparent. Both the Department for Education and SEAC urged caution in interpreting the results at Key Stage 3. As to Key Stage 1, *The Independent* (22 December 1992) reported a teacher union leader (Nigel de Gruchy, NAS/UWT) as dismissing the results with:

> This is a glorious day for the Philistines who insist on reducing education to a balance sheet with thousands of numbers to crunch.

But the Secretary of State, far from conceding to doubts about the validity of results, was using them as the starting point for an investigation into 'underachieving' local authorities:

> Why is it that some high-spending authorities are achieving results well below the national average, and similar authorities spend far less but achieve much more?

Moreover, as the *Daily Mail* reported on the same day, John Patten would be going one step further in 1993:

> The 21,000 schools tested remain anonymous, but next year they will be identified. Bad schools will be rooted out by inspectors who already have a hit list of 200.

Performance tables comparing test results school by school, local authority by local authority, were becoming, it seemed, a permanent feature of the system. Even the original TGAT recommendation that the school-by-school results of 7-year-olds should not be published was now being overturned. In time such results would be published across a range of subjects for pupils at ages 7, 11, 14 and 16. Prospective parents would use them as a source of evidence when choosing a school, inspectors would be guided by them when judging a school's effectiveness and ministers would draw on them for LEA comparisons as well as for indications of trends in standards at the national level. As those on the political right, notably Dr. John Marks, continued to campaign for freely available performance tables, teacher unions remained resolutely opposed to the publication of 'raw' data at school level. By mid-1993, just before the recommendations of the National Curriculum Review were published, *The Times Educational Supplement* was ready to concede something to Dr. Marks:

> we cannot be certain from the raw data which schools are the really good ones, but we can be pretty sure that those at the bottom of the lists are doing a poor job. (*TES*, 23 July 1993)

But by then the stage was already set for a Government rethink on that aspect of assessment policy together with much else.

Record-keeping: The Link not Established

While successive policy decisions clarified reporting to parents and publication of results, record-keeping remained a problem area, the uncertain link between procedures for assessment and the communication to others of the information those procedures revealed.

On the one hand, record-keeping was presented by policy-makers as a matter for teachers to resolve. As an aspect of teacher assessment, the Government and SEAC largely disclaimed responsibility since, it was argued, it would not be appropriate for them to dictate to the teacher on a matter which was properly the province of the professional. For example, in the summer 1989 issue of SEAC's newsletter, the Council stated:

> At this stage it is not expected that there will be any need to prescribe the form in which each teacher should keep records of individual pupils. (SEAC *Recorder*, No. 2, p. 1)

From time to time ministers and SEAC acknowledged the additional burden that national assessment record-keeping was proving to be for many teachers. As HMI reported in one of their surveys of schools implementing national assessment, referring in this case to Key Stage 3 and the school year 1990/91:

> The majority of departments were developing new systems of record-keeping for the National Curriculum. The quality of the new records was uneven. Some departments were merely recording pupils' experience of the National Curriculum rather than their achievements within it.
>
> Even where good practice was developing, many teachers were unsure about how detailed National Curriculum records should be and when and how often they should be updated. (*Assessment, Recording and Reporting, A Report by HM Inspectorate on the Second Year, 1990/91*, HMSO, 1992)

In some cases, teachers were developing record-keeping arrangements which were additional to, and separate from, established practices including 'records of achievement' systems. It is not surprising that many were finding themselves overburdened!

Reporting on the beginning of national assessment implementation at Key Stage 1, *The Independent* noted (7 September 1989) that 'how and what teachers must record is unclear'. If teachers were indeed expected to 'grapple with 6810 statements of attainment' (i.e. levels 1 to 3 of all the attainment targets in the three core subjects multiplied by thirty pupils in a class) it would not be surprising if:

> The fear among most teachers is that when the time for the first formal assessments arrives, they will be faced by a crippling workload. (*The Independent*, 7 September 1989)

It is interesting to note that, in the reporting of this anticipated problem, the purpose of record-keeping is perceived to be gathering evidence for an end-of-stage summative judgment rather than to use assessment evidence along the way to help children learn.

The comments of John MacGregor in a speech to an AMMA conference (9 April 1990) are typical of the stance of ministers and their advisers on this matter:

> ...there can be no question of requiring teachers to keep detailed records of their pupils' attainments against every one of over 200 statements of attainment. Nor should they feel under any pressure to hoard large amounts of evidence to support their assessments...
>
> Recording must support assessment, not become a substitute for it. That means, in my view, that teachers must be free to develop whatever approach to recording suits their own teaching style and best enables them — at the end of the Key Stage — to form a judgement of each pupil's level of attainment.

While superficially reasonable and also sensitive to teachers' concerns, such a statement avoids the main issues facing teachers as, with minimal advice from the centre, they struggled to devise manageable, useful record-keeping systems. For whose benefit was the record being kept — the teacher, the pupil, the parent, the headteacher, the next school or employer down the line? If it was be the source of information for each of those potential users, how to keep the record to manageable proportions? On top of all that, if, as clearly was the case, teachers might have to justify to external moderators/auditors the judgments they had arrived at during the Key Stage, what would those scrutineers expect to be shown? Perhaps 'hoarding large amounts of evidence' was unnecessary but, in this area of practice, which was clearly beyond what teachers could decide for themselves since it was part of a standard national set of procedures, what exactly was expected of them?

The recording of results was perceived by many teachers as an area in which guidance, and perhaps regulation, could be expected from the centre. However, as discussed in chapter 4, the practices of teacher assessment were signalled by ministers and SEAC as being for teachers to develop with a minimum of guidance and no regulation by central government or its advisers. Record-keeping, the essential interface between assessment and reporting, was, throughout the period under review, given the teacher assessment treatment by policy-makers — 'it's for you, the teacher, to decide how to tackle it'. Only in the way in which records of pupils' SAT performance should be kept, as a preliminary to their being passed on to parents and others, was clear guidance on record-keeping offered by teachers. And that type of recording — of performance in one set of activities with the data being used essentially for summative and evaluative purposes — was not the main source of difficulty for teachers.

Yet when the opposition of teachers to the demands of national assessment and the associated record-keeping reached a new peak early in 1993, it was to be the time the ordinary teacher was taking to keep comprehensive records of attainment which would prove a crucial element in the teacher union case that their workload was excessive.

Conclusion

Policy and practice in record-keeping, reporting and publication of results — the 'front end' of the whole national assessment system — had thus evolved in a piecemeal fashion. Largely unconsidered while policy-makers were defining the curriculum and devising standard assessment tasks, they came to dominate much of the debate as the system reached the point where the first cohorts of pupils had followed the National Curriculum throughout a Key Stage, first at Key Stage 1 and then at Key Stage 3.

By that time, both reporting to parents about their own children and the publication of results had come to be seen as central features of a policy in which parents, by the choices they made, would be the main influences on the quality of work in schools and therefore the agents of improvement in educational standards nationally. At a professional level, how teachers could be expected to meet the various demands on them for information about pupils, individually and collectively, was still not being fully addressed by those responsible for national policy.

What did not seem to be grasped by policy-makers, either initially or even after implementation was well under way, were the problems inherent in any system seeking to base its procedures on a frame of reference constructed on explicit attainment criteria. The characteristic and familiar conventions of norm-referencing led to outcomes being summarized in the opaque but manageable shorthand of marks, grades and percentages. In contrast, for the outcomes of criterion-referenced assessment to be communicated to whoever may be interested in them, judgments must be made about how to inform the 'user' about the individual's attainment at an acceptable, intelligible level of detail. The information on attainment which would help the struggling pupil to progress (one reason a teacher might keep a record) is going to be different, in its form and level of detail, from that which would be of interest to the prospective employer of a school leaver (another of the legitimate demands on the attainment record). In between, other calls on the same record, for example by a moderator seeking evidence to verify the teacher's end-of-stage judgment, would have different implications for the teacher's record-keeping. The multiplicity, and to some extent mutual incompatibility, of the demands on the teacher's record of attainment remained, even at the end of 1992, central to the confusion about appropriate record-keeping systems.

More fundamentally, as the first 'league tables' of schools' results appeared during 1992 and 1993, record-keeping and reporting were inevitably increasingly perceived as rather more than links in the chain from the pupil's teacher to someone — parent, another teacher or potential employer — interested in the individual pupil. The same assessment procedures — teacher assessments and standard tasks — which supplied information about the individual would provide the data which, in aggregate form, would inform public judgments about the comparative performance of teachers and schools. Recording and reporting the individual's attainment had proved a problematic aspect of implementing national assessment, with questions of manageability and purpose largely unresolved. But to require the links in that same chain to lead to an evaluation of the teacher and the school, a quite distinct and, to many teachers, threatening purpose, would place increasing strains on the teacher's ability to process attainment evidence in a systematic, disinterested way.

6 Key Stage 4: National Assessment and the GCSE

Introduction

For Key Stages 1, 2 and 3, the structures of national assessment were developed largely without reference to pre-existing systems and procedures. Each school, of course, had its own arrangements for assessing and reporting attainment. In many primary schools, externally devised tests were in use, most commonly to assess reading. In a minority of local education authorities, selective systems of secondary schooling meant that pupils were assessed at the age of 11. But none of these systems and procedures were established on a sufficiently general basis either for them to be incorporated in the foundations of national assessment or for them to become an obstacle to its introduction.

Key Stage 4 was different. A new national (England and Wales) system of examinations for the 14–16 age group, the General Certificate of Secondary Education, had been in operation for only a year when the Government published its consultation paper, *The National Curriculum 5–16*, in July 1987. The first cohort of pupils taking courses leading to the award of GCSEs were half way through their two-year programme. By the time they received their results, in August 1988, the outline of a new National Curriculum and assessment system had reached the statute book. The new world of the GCSE, highly coloured by the optimistic rhetoric of the mid-1980s, was soon to be clouded by the uncertain vision of National Curriculum Key Stage 4.

There are several elements in the context for Key Stage 4 which make for a more complex policy agenda than that which applied to the development of national assessment for the first three Key Stages. In part this is because the *curriculum* context was fundamentally different in the last two years of compulsory schooling and was to remain so. For Key Stages 1 to 3, the curriculum to be assessed was that set out in the Statutory Orders; each pupil would follow a scheme of work, developed within the school, based on the programme of study for each statutory subject. In formal legal terms this would also be the case for Key Stage 4 since the relevant section of the 1988 Act makes no distinction between the statutory requirements at that Key Stage and what is required up to the age of 14. But, in reality, several factors influencing Key Stage 4 provision combined to set it apart from the more truly National Curriculum and assessment arrangements which were to be developed at the earlier Key Stages.

At Key Stage 4 there was to be a continuing attachment, among most policy-makers as well as practitioners, to three significant elements in the variability of curriculum from one school to another:

- *devolved administration* of examinations to independent examination boards, a long established feature of public examinations for 16- and 18-year-olds in England and Wales;
- *flexibility* for each school to add to the statutory requirements and shape its curriculum provision at Key Stage 4 in a distinctive way;
- *choice* for pupils within that provision;

Thus at Key Stage 3 every pupil would follow a largely common curriculum up to the age 14 and his/her attainments would be assessed by a national system administered by SEAC in London. But at Key Stage 4 the pupil's experience would be influenced, to an extent which was uncertain in the early years of implementation, by the particular examinations adopted in his/her school, by the curriculum offered within that school and by the choices s/he had exercised.

How flexibility and choice were to be realized in practice and the extent to which they should be encouraged was to be a continuing source of debate. Several proposals would be discussed — short courses, combined courses, vocational courses — which would extend the range of possible provision well beyond the basic idea of GCSE certification in foundation subjects. Each had an assessment dimension to it but they were all put forward primarily as 'solutions' to a curriculum problem. That problem can be defined as how much of the statutory National Curriculum should remain a common experience for all pupils beyond the age of 14 and what should be available, and approved as a qualification by the Secretary of State (under Section 5 of the Act), beyond that statutory minimum.

A further factor complicating the curriculum picture at Key Stage 4 was the continued existence of the notion of *syllabus* between the statutory programme of study and the scheme of work which each teacher would devise. Whereas at the other three Key Stages the teacher would use the Statutory Order as the starting point for course planning, at Key Stage 4 s/he would, as in pre-National Curriculum times, await the development of syllabuses by the examining groups. The examining groups thus retained a curriculum planning role, albeit one restricted by the terms of Key Stage 4 programmes of study and ultimately subject to control through syllabus approval procedures by SEAC, as well as their role as assessment agencies. In the early years of policy development it seemed that Government, advised by SEAC, would use its powers to ensure that diversity of syllabus provision in the foundation subjects would be kept to a minimum. While there might be more than one syllabus in a subject, each proposal would have to demonstrate that it met a defined 'need'. However, once the free market ideology became firmly established in the thinking of the DES and SEAC, it became apparent that examining groups would be allowed to develop as many syllabuses as they judged there was a market for. The idea of a National Curriculum at Key Stage 4 was thus softened by the interposing of a layer of curriculum design between programmes of study and schemes of work and by the allocation of responsibility for developing that layer to the examining groups.

A third aspect of the distinctiveness of the Key Stage 4 curriculum was the extent to which there was to be a *common curriculum* for all pupils. Would every pupil, irrespective of ability or attainment level, 'have access to broadly the same good and relevant curriculum' (*The National Curriculum 5–16*, p. 4)? At the first three Key Stages the statutory programmes of study and the associated assessment arrangements were to form the basis for the learning programme for *all* pupils. Though the curriculum and assessment arrangements could be disapplied in certain circumstances, the assumption from the beginning was that such cases should be kept to a minimum. Even those pupils whose levels of attainment were outside the norms for their age group were to have an entitlement to the common curriculum experienced by their peers. The differing needs of high and low attainers would be met by differentiation of provision *within* a broadly common curriculum. At Key Stages 1, 2 and 3 that commonality of curriculum was at odds with previous practice in some schools, especially at lower secondary level, though in line with existing practice in others.

At Key Stage 4 schools were only just coming to terms with the new GCSE examination which had been represented as, potentially at least, 'a common examination at 16+'. The tripartite division of the cohort at 14 into GCE 'O' level candidates, CSE candidates and 'non-examination' pupils had only been partially broken down by the abolition of the 'O' level/ CSE divide. In at least some subjects in many schools it had been replaced by a new two-fold division into GCSE candidates and 'non-GCSE candidates' who were following separate courses provided for low attainers. Some schools did enter all year 9 pupils for GCSE examinations in English language and mathematics but commonality of curriculum across the full ability range was far from being firmly established for this age group prior to the National Curriculum.

The absence of a shared understanding, even among those working in the education system, of what was meant by a 'common examination' made for difficulties in the syllabus development process and in the decisions schools had to take about which courses to make available. Sir Keith Joseph's vision of 90 per cent of GCSE candidates attaining standards equivalent to those reached by only half of the age group was an aspiration rather than something which could be achieved overnight. The proportion of 16-year-olds embarking on GCSE courses did steadily increase and the wider range of assessment methods used in GCSE assessments did make some syllabuses more accessible to low-attaining students. But GCSE syllabuses were usually not designed for even 90 per cent of the 'ability range' and certainly not for every student in the age group. Moreover, subsequent policy decisions about the certification of attainment were to cast doubt on the commitment of policy-makers, at least at this Key Stage, to the goal of a broadly common curriculum experience irrespective of a pupil's attainment level.

And it is that feature, *certification*, which most of all distinguishes the debate about national assessment at Key Stage 4 from its counterparts at the earlier Key Stages. At Key Stages 1, 2 and 3 the body responsible for national assessment, SEAC, would commission the development of standard tasks from agencies appointed on a short-term basis specifically for that purpose. The attainment levels of each pupil at the end of each Key Stage were to be reported to parents but not certificated. When National Curriculum and assessment was at the embryonic stage, it was possible to envisage such arrangements displacing the GCSE and some influential critics (Moon and Mortimore, 1989) advocated just such a policy. However, it very soon became clear that at Key Stage 4 there was to be some kind of accommodation between the established provision of examination and certification through GCSE and the statutory requirement in the 1988 Act that pupils should be assessed 'in relation to the attainment targets' 'at or near the end of each Key Stage'. The common thread running through all the development of National Curriculum assessment at Key Stage 4 has been the attempt to settle upon such an accommodation. As one commentator put it in the title of an article: 'GCSE meets Key Stage 4: Something had to give' (Stobart, 1991).

If attainment at Key Stage 4 was to be certificated, with GCSE as 'the chief means of assessment' (to use the phrase often quoted by ministers), a whole series of consequences would further distinguish that Key Stage from its predecessors. Examining procedures would have to be adapted to produce a result, across ten levels in each attainment target in each subject, which examining groups could be sufficiently confident of to vouch for with a certificate. The established notions of combining marks from examinations (assessing certain objectives) and coursework (targeting objectives more appropriately assessed during the course) would have to be reconsidered to take account of the rather different distinction (see chapters 3 and 4) between teacher assessment (assessing everything during the course) and standard tasks (assessing certain attainments at the end of the course). And the whole examining process, from the design of syllabuses through to the award of grades, would require redefinition to enable it to deliver a criterion-referenced result. Such a process would differ markedly from the awarding of pre-National Curriculum GCSE grades, which depended on examiner judgment being exercised only at the grade boundaries in a system geared to rank ordering candidates on the basis of total marks gained. Each of these matters, together with others, would have to be addressed by the policy-makers. However, unlike the earlier Key Stages, they were not matters the formal resolution of which need involve only ministers and their appointed advisory body, SEAC. As the organizations which would be expected to implement policy decisions and the custodians of public confidence in the GCSE which ministers were keen to retain, the GCSE examining groups were a significant third force in policy-making at Key Stage 4.

Thus, to summarize the policy agenda at Key Stage 4, it very soon became dominated by the terminology and practices of that most summative of assessment structures, the public examination. The questions being posed were distinct from those under discussion in relation to the national assessment system which was developing *de novo* at Key Stages 1–3. For example:

- Syllabuses — how many? how related to programmes of study? how approved?
- Coursework — what proportion? what role in the overall assessment?
- Grade awards — how to arrive at them? how to link the new scale to the old?
- Certification — only or mainly through GCSE? certificate the lowest levels also?

All this would be complex and difficult enough even without two further elements which were to give the Key Stage 4 debate its peculiarly tortuous and seemingly intractable character.

One has already been referred to — the nature of the curriculum framework to be assessed. The adaptation of the existing full GCSE courses to the requirements of the new ten-level, criterion-referenced, TGAT-based assessment system would be a challenging task in itself. But if, as successive Secretaries of State were to suggest in 1990 and 1991, the curriculum framework was to be remodelled to accommodate 'short', 'combined' and 'vocational' courses, what would be the implications of that for assessment and certification?

The other element derived from an increasing tendency for the GCSE to be the arena for battles over more fundamental concerns as the swing to the Right in educational policy became more obvious during 1991 and 1992. The already complex curriculum and assessment/certification debate was to be overlain by responses to the battle cries of those on the political Right who had been convinced from the beginning (see for example, North, 1987) that the GCSE had been an insidious influence on the education system, a vehicle for all manner of dangerously progressive educational ideas.

The story of GCSE during the period under review deserves a book to itself because of the many-faceted character of that part of the policy debate. Throughout the period, in addition to grappling with the complexities of linking a largely norm-referenced certificated examination for some pupils to a criterion-referenced national assessment system for the whole age group, SEAC was dealing with a range of other Key Stage 4 policy decisions. Some of those decisions related to the Council's function of monitoring the work of the examining groups, responding for example to anxieties, periodically expressed, about the comparability of awards made across the several groups and in a wide range of subjects. Others were responses to curriculum initiatives which posed novel assessment and certification problems, for example how to link the proposed short courses to the GCSE examining process. Still others arose from the need to react rapidly to the concerns, increasingly expressed by Government ministers during 1991 and 1992, about the fundamental nature of the GCSE and the impact it was having on the education of older secondary school pupils. In that category were the marked reversal of the Keith Joseph inspired commitment to GCSE coursework, the Government's decision that examining bodies should be required to allocate a specified proportion of the marks in all GCSE examinations for what came to be known as SPaG (spelling, punctuation and grammar), and the more general tightening up of examining procedures instigated by John Patten when, in September 1992, he called into question many aspects of what had, until then, been celebrated by ministers as the successful implementation of GCSE.

With such a heady brew of issues to debate, it may not be surprising that so many fundamental questions about how national assessment should be implemented at Key Stage 4 remained unresolved even as, in September 1992, it became the last of the Key Stages to reach the point at which implementation would begin. The review of Key Stage 4 policy which follows will, while making reference to the wider issues identified above, focus on the attempt to bring together the significantly different curriculum and assessment models of the GCSE and of national assessment, matters left unresolved when Kenneth Baker accepted most of the TGAT Report's recommendations in June 1988.

Developments to 1988; Introducing the GCSE

The examination system to which national assessment had to be accommodated, the General Certificate of Secondary Education, had had a long period of gestation prior to its introduction in September 1986. The policies which led to the Government decision (June 1984) to introduce the GCSE have been fully documented and discussed elsewhere (Gipps, 1986; Horton, 1986; Kingdon and Stobart, 1988). In political terms, its significance was alluded to in the preamble, signed by the Secretaries of State for Education and for Wales, to the National Criteria which would govern all syllabuses and assessment schemes:

> We see publication of the national criteria as an historic step. For the first time, the partners in the education service have pooled their wisdom and experience in order to produce nationally agreed statements on course objectives, content, and assessment methods for all the subject areas most commonly examined in the final years of compulsory schooling. (DES/WO, 1985a, p. 1)

Behind this rhetoric was a first, relatively small, move towards the exercise by central Government of political control over the school curriculum and its assessment.

In assessment terms, Kingdom and Stobart (1988) identify the defining features of GCSE as:

> the concept of positive achievement;
> the use of differentiated assessment;
> the use of teacher assessed elements in all syllabuses (p. 38).

To these should be added a fourth, criteria-related grading, which, though it was never to get beyond the drawing board stage, was clearly central to the concept of a new system which was to be much more than a reorganization of the administration of public examinations for 16-year-olds.

Thus in one sense the GCSE was the precursor of a national assessment system. It set the political precedent for the exercise of Government control which was to be massively extended by the 1988 Education Act. It also established the ground of teacher assessment, differentiation and criteria-grading which would be more fully explored as that Act was implemented. Much of that GCSE experience, especially the attempt to move to criteria-grading, seems to have been regarded subsequently as of only marginal relevance to the new assessment system. But it did ensure that, at Key Stage 4 as at other Key Stages, practitioners and critics were able to draw on experience within the England and Wales system when responding to the way national assessment evolved.

In another sense the GCSE, as a recent innovation, constituted a potential obstacle to the development of a national assessment system in one of the Key Stages. Acknowledged except by a small minority who were opposed to it ideologically as a notable improvement on the preceding arrangements, the GCSE would prove more difficult to change to align it with national assessment than would an examination system which was ripe for change, as the 'O' level/CSE system had been.

But, by the time the major policy decisions on Key Stage 4 came to be made, it was neither GCSE as precursor nor GCSE as obstacle which was to dominate the debate. In the early period of implementation of the 1988 Act, Key Stage 4 was low on the policy agenda. With the introduction of new-style GCSE courses not due even in the core subjects until September 1992, assessments at Key Stages 1 and 3 were at the forefront of the debate about national assessment. When, in the summer of 1991, the GCSE came to the top of the policy agenda again it had become in the minds of ministers and their most influential advisers a symbol of much that was wrong in the education system prior to the 1988 Act. No longer was the GCSE, as Secretary of State Keith Joseph had envisaged, the very model of a new curriculum and assessment system with a curriculum for all, suitably differentiated, and associated assessments emphasizing positive achievement and taking full account of work done during the course. Instead the same examination was to be characterized, by a Government of the same political colour but in which New Right thinking on education had become dominant, as unwisely reliant on the judgments of teachers and the procedures of examining groups and giving insufficient emphasis to time-honoured techniques involving written answers to time-limited, unseen, end-of-course examination papers.

Origins in TGAT

Though the GCSE had been the major curriculum and assessment innovation for the schools of England and Wales in the 1980s, the Task Group on Assessment and Testing refer to it relatively infrequently in framing their recommendations (DES/WO, 1988a). This is not surprising in some ways since an established examination for school leavers had little to offer the design of a system which was to be, in terms of two of the Group's principles, *formative* in its emphasis on purposes and geared to charting *progression* in learning. Only in respect of the third of the TGAT principles, *moderation* of assessments so that they could be compared with each other, could the GCSE have offered national assessment much in the way of relevant experience.

However, to anticipate how the TGAT model could apply to Key Stage 4, it was necessary for the Group to make recommendations on how, if at all, the GCSE should be modified to take account of national assessment. They rejected both the possibility of two independent systems of assessment operating alongside each other and the idea that 'GCSE should be revised and extended to provide appropriate targets for the entire age group'. Instead:

> We recommend that the formal relationship between national assess-
> ment and GCSE be limited, in the first instance, to this one reference
> point: the boundary between levels 6 and 7 should correspond to the
> grade F/G boundary. (DES/WO, 1988a, para. 105)

The question of equivalence between GCSE grades and the levels of attainment determined at Key Stages 1–3 was to be one continuing source of difficulty as attempts were made to create a 'new GCSE' from a mixture of the features of National Curriculum assessment and pre-National Curriculum GCSE. (In the event SEAC was to recommend, in July 1989, that the GCSE F/G boundary should correspond to the 5/4 boundary on the ten level scale.)

TGAT's recommendation was, in effect, no more than an indication to those who would frame the attainment targets subject by subject of the level of demand they should bear in mind when defining which attainments should be specified at level 6 or level 7. The Group talked in terms of 'a dialogue between the GCSE system and the curricular approaches characteristic of the earlier years of education', recommending that 'GCSE be retained in its present form until the national assessment system is initiated at earlier ages' (DES/WO, 1988a, para. 107). A similar (and understandable) caution about the implications of both moving to definitions of the attainments associated with each grade and changing the well-established procedures of examining, awarding and certificating is also in evidence in a later section of the TGAT Report dealing with the phasing of change:

> It may . . . be necessary to revise GCSE in two stages, one to incor-
> porate the National Curriculum targets within present systems of
> assessment and grading, followed later by more radical changes to the
> latter when the rest of the national assessment system had been in full
> operation for at least a short time. (DES/WO, 1988a, para. 194).

The same air of 'let's wait and see before we decide anything other than that GCSE will continue to exist' is also present in the ministerial statement accepting most of the TGAT recommendations. In his written answer to a Parliamentary question (7 June 1988) on the TGAT proposals the Secretary of State, Kenneth Baker, went no further than:

assessment should be by a combination of national external tests and assessment by teachers. At age 16 the GCSE will be the main form of assessment, especially in the core subjects of English, mathematics and science.

All the difficult issues were being left for decisions at a later date. Did 'main form of assessment' mean in effect that the GCSE would be the only national accreditation approved for Key Stage 4, in all subjects, for all levels of attainment, for vocational as well as for 'academic' courses? Or could perhaps, against TGAT's recommendation, the national assessments through standard tasks and teacher assessment, co-exist alongside GCSE but without leading to a certificate? Would there be a common grading scale for the GCSE and the earlier Key Stages (certainly implied by Baker's acceptance elsewhere in his statement that 'pupils' performance in relation to attainment targets should be assessed and reported on at ages 7, 11, 14, and 16')? How would the examining procedures of the GCSE groups be modified to enable them to certificate each level of attainment in each attainment target as well as (or instead of?) the overall grade in each GCSE subject?

It is in this last area, relating to the fourth of TGAT's principles — 'assessment results should give direct information about pupils' achievement in relation to objectives: they should be *criterion-referenced*' — that the discontinuity between the 'new GCSE', post-1988, and its fledgling predecessor was to prove most problematic. The 'old GCSE', pre-National Curriculum, had been envisaged, not least by the minister responsible, Keith Joseph, as an examination in which each grade would have a specific meaning attached to it. Development work on grade-related criteria had been undertaken by the Secondary Examinations Council, encountering ever greater difficulties as the practicalities of defining and using such criteria became increasingly obvious from pilot studies and reports of parallel experience in Scotland (Murphy, 1986). Working parties in the main GCSE subjects boldly attempted to define attainment in a way which, it was hoped would offer workable definitions for those who would judge attainment as well as meaningful summaries which could be of value to the 'user' of the examination results. None of this work had been subject to any serious trialling but TGAT chose to put an optimistic face on some very discouraging evidence:

> . . . there has in the past been a variety of attempts to derive written criteria from GCE and CSE grades. That experience suggests that no more than four sets of levels can be identified in relation to the GCSE population. (DES/WO, 1988a, para. 104)

What a cool appraisal of the evidence would actually have showed was that there was little reason to be confident about the use of criteria-related grading in GCSE, whatever the potential gains of an examination system reporting on specific attainments. Though the National Criteria for GCSE had implied that it was only a matter of time before criteria-related grading would be in place, in reality the idea never came close to being implemented in the pre-National

Curriculum GCSE. Grades were still awarded on the basis of overall marks in a subject rather than being determined by pre-specified criteria. The GCSE subject criteria settled instead for composite 'grade descriptions' which sought to find forms of words to cover the inevitably diverse attainments of those candidates achieving selected grades (inevitably diverse because the only thing definitely common to the work of all candidates awarded the same grade, even on only one syllabus in a subject, would be their mark totals). In spite of the flaws in that device, exposed some years before (Orr and Nuttall, 1983), such grade descriptions found their way into the GCSE system. In spite of the evident problems with the more ambitious notion of grade-related criteria (not inherently unsound like grade descriptions but yet to be proved workable in practice), they found their way into the 'new GCSE'. Having advocated a criterion-referenced system for all pupils from 5 to 16, TGAT could hardly do other than propose a variant of criterion-referencing for Key Stage 4. But to suggest as the Group did that even four 'sets of levels' could be identified and implemented for GCSE was to allow hopes and aspirations to obscure the already available discouraging evidence as to the feasibility of criteria-related grading.

The TGAT legacy to the subsequent policy debates on Key Stage 4 assessment was thus relatively modest. When the time did come for policy decisions on that Key Stage it was existing practice in GCSE, rather than what TGAT had proposed, which was usually the starting point for debate.

Key Stage 4 Policy 1988 to 1990: Calm Before the Storm

In the early years following the introduction of the GCSE a series of reports from HMI presented a generally positive picture of the new examination and its impact on schools. For example:

> The GCSE has encouraged many beneficial changes in teaching and learning in the classroom. There is a high level of commitment and enthusiasm from teachers for the GCSE and most teaching now offers wider and more varied opportunities for learning. (HMI, 1988, p. 8)

However, some of the differences in interpretation of the evidence about GCSE which would colour the subsequent debate were early in evidence in the way the press greeted publication of that HMI report. While for some the HMI conclusions were overwhelmingly favourable — 'An impressive beginning by any standards' (*The Times Educational Supplement*, 21 October 1988), 'Lessons better with GCSE' (*Teachers' Weekly*, 24 October 1988), others picked up the cautionary side of the HMI message — 'Must try harder, school inspectors report on GCSE' (*Daily Telegraph*, 19 October 1988), 'New exam may fail the less able, say inspectors' (*The Guardian*, 19 October 1988).

In its reports to the Secretary of State during 1988 and 1989 SEAC also struck a generally positive note. In his response to one such report, Kenneth Baker was equally upbeat:

This further report confirms that the GCSE has been successfully introduced. I agree with that conclusion. It reflects considerable credit on the Council, the GCSE examining groups and the teaching profession. (Letter from Kenneth Baker to SEAC, July 1989)

But, in respect of the practices of examining, the same letter also stresses:

The GCSE will be the chief means of assessing pupils' performance within the National Curriculum at the end of Key Stage 4. It is therefore all the more important that it be subject to scrutiny and that identified weaknesses are tackled. (*ibid*)

The need for appropriate means of differentiating attainment, for effective moderation of coursework and for consistency in the award of grades across the five examining groups were all mentioned as requiring further attention.

Oddly enough in view of its emergence two years later at the centre of an attack by the Prime Minister on GCSE, the place of coursework in the assessment of attainment was endorsed by the Secretary of State in his July 1989 letter:

The balance — characteristic of most GCSE courses — between coursework and an externally set and marked terminal examination has worked well. I accept the Council's judgment that assessment by means of coursework is one of the examination's strengths . . . (*ibid*)

For the moment at least the GCSE design principles, formulated by Baker's predecessor, Keith Joseph, remained intact.

During 1989 SEAC was beginning to work on the agenda of issues left over from TGAT concerning the relationship between the GCSE and national assessment. In this, the centrality of the GCSE as 'the chief means of assessing pupils' attainment at 16' was never seriously in question. The debate, at a technical level as well as in relation to broad policy objectives, focused instead on how to develop a single unified system of reporting which in some way linked the existing GCSE A-G scale to the National Curriculum ten-level scale already approved for the other Key Stages.

In his response (letter to SEAC, August 1989) to further SEAC advice on these matters, the newly-appointed Secretary of State, John MacGregor, established the main lines of policy which were to be maintained through subsequent challenges until the Dearing Review of 1993. In spite of reservations about SEAC's recommended model for relating the two grading scales (principally because there would be no direct equivalent to the GCSE grade C, widely regarded as representing a 'pass' at GCSE), MacGregor approved that model as 'the only practical solution', welcoming in particular the inclusion of a level 10 grade which 'will stretch the brightest pupils further than at present'.

The Secretary of State was not, however, willing to accept SEAC's recommendation that every level on the ten-point scale should be certificated, however modest in relative terms achievement at the lower levels might seem. In MacGregor's view 'level 4 on the National Curriculum scale (equivalent to the lowest grade, G, on the existing GCSE scale) should mark the minimum level of attainment for the award of a GCSE'. Thus, while GCSE would be the main means of *assessing* attainment at 16, when it came to *reporting* the outcomes, those achieving levels 1–3 would have to settle for recognition on their Record of Achievement rather than a GCSE certificate. The growing sense that candidates expected to reach levels 1–3 were not part of the GCSE-based curriculum and assessment system at Key Stage 4 was confirmed when SEAC abandoned preliminary work on syllabuses designed for such candidates.

The other significant step announced by John MacGregor was a decision that the new, National Curriculum-related, GCSEs would require a combination (in proportions as yet unspecified) of coursework assessment and terminal examination. The course which he had thus set to guide the convergence of GCSE and national assessment had a generally favourable reception from the press:

> Less than three weeks into his new job as Secretary of State for Education, Mr. John MacGregor has revived two concepts which seemed threatened with extinction: end-of-course examinations and the possibility of failure. (*The Times*, Editorial, 10 August 1989)

Even *The Guardian* supported the Minister:

> . . . the idea that 16-year-old school leavers should be given a grade, even though their level of attainment is equivalent only to what a bright 5-year-old or average seven-year-old could achieve, is absurd. (*The Guardian*, Editorial, 10 August 1989)

Yet doubts among those most closely involved in navigating this course surfaced only two months later in the form of a nine-page letter from the GCSE examining boards to SEAC expressing concerns about several aspects of Government policy on national assessment and the GCSE:

> Until teachers have reassessed their own pupils against the (National Curriculum) criteria, and experience has been gained from operational use, the outcomes of assessing children against attainment targets will be simply a matter of conjecture . . .
>
> In this situation it will be extremely difficult, if not impossible, to carry forward GCSE standards and to impose general standards on subjects. Either GCSE standards will have to be abandoned subject-by-subject or the attainment targets will have to be adjusted in the light of experience. (Letter from the Joint Council for the GCSE, quoted in *The Times*, 23 October 1989)

In March 1990 one of the GCSE examining groups, the Northern Examining Association, was also reported to have told SEAC that it could not overcome the problems of aligning GCSE with national assessment in time to meet the Government's deadline.

At the same time there were the first of what would become a chorus of calls from organizations representing teachers and schools for an end to the uncertainty about how GCSE would be remodelled to take account of national assessment. The Chairman of the Headmasters' Conference was voicing the anxieties of many when he wrote to *The Times*:

> . . . there must be an early resolution to the problem of Key Stage 4 of the National Curriculum for 14 to 16-year-olds and GCSE. Simply to go on saying that this is a difficult problem which will require much thought will no longer do. (Martin Marriott, letter to the editor, 22 November 1989)

There were few signs in the months which followed that either the GCSE boards' concerns or such calls from schools were prompting a policy rethink in SEAC or in the DES. Instead the developing Key Stage 4 debate was to be dominated by curriculum issues. The most significant event during this period was the statement of general policy on Key Stage 4 made by Secretary of State MacGregor when he spoke to the Society of Education Officers on 25 January 1990. While the detail of his proposals is only indirectly relevant to a review focusing on assessment it is worth noting the implications for assessment of several of the ideas which first surfaced in that speech:

- 'short courses' (half the length of typical GCSE courses) in non-core subjects;
- combinations of such short courses in foundation subjects, either with each other or with non-National Curriculum subjects;
- able pupils to be allowed to drop certain foundation subjects (but not the core subjects, technology or modern languages) before the end of the Key Stage;
- vocational examining bodies to be able to offer qualifications at Key Stage 4, in foundation subjects and in non-National Curriculum subjects.

This last proposal, perhaps appropriately for the first month of the new decade, was the first Government move in what would later become a major policy issue for the 1990s, the 'vocationalizing' of the Key Stage 4 curriculum.

John MacGregor's SEO Conference speech marks an important step in what was to be a long drawn out process of trying to solve the Key Stage 4 curriculum problem (or 'The disaster of Key Stage 4' as the then Chairman of the NCC has described it — Graham, 1992). But, in taking that step, he added greatly to the complexity of the scenario for assessment and certification. Would short courses be certificated through GCSE or in some other way, as yet unspecified? If such courses in foundation subjects were not to be certificated, how would the statutory requirements of assessing attainment 'at or near the end of the Key Stage' (as the 1988 Act required) be met? For combined courses, what rules would govern the awarding of a grade in, for example, geography and history, each with its own set of attainment targets? Where did vocational bodies, with their distinctive assessment procedures and traditions, fit into the National Curriculum assessment picture? And how would assessment and certification be arranged for the able pupils who could complete their studies before the end of year 11?

The Secretary of State had released a large flock of pigeons from the loft without any obvious signs of attention having been given to the implications of his proposals for assessment and certification. As the flock came home to roost at intervals in the ensuing years a marked tendency developed for them to collide with each other; the ground around the loft would increasingly be strewn with the bodies of the pigeons which Mr. MacGregor had sent out into the world with such high hopes in August 1989 and January 1990.

Key Stage 4 Policy 1990–1991: Approaching Implementation

Most of the public debate about Key Stage 4 during 1990 concentrated on the curriculum issues raised by MacGregor's proposals. The National Curriculum Council, rather than SEAC, was to the fore in the exchanges between the Secretary of State and his advisory bodies. In retrospect the Government decisions of January 1990 and January 1991 can be seen as a major episode in the retreat from the idea that the Key Stage 4 curriculum should be as broad and as common as the curriculum in preceding stages.

By the time assessment and certification issues came once again to the top of the policy agenda a new Secretary of State for Education, Kenneth Clarke, was in post. As the deadlines approached for putting GCSE syllabuses and assessment schemes in place in time for schools to prepare for a September 1992 start in the core subjects, the first signs of problems encountered in the behind-the-scenes development work surfaced in advice offered by SEAC to Clarke:

Current policies under the Education Reform Act. . . . require examinations in 1994 in the core subjects to provide:

(i) reported outcomes for each attainment target, not for inclusion on certificates, on the ten-level scale;
(ii) reported outcomes for each profile component and subject, possibly for inclusion on certificates, on the ten-level scale;
(iii) certificated outcomes for whole subjects which carry forward current GCSE standards;
(iv) a mix of coursework and terminal examinations, so that assessments are fit for purpose.

Extensive consultations with examining bodies and others have led us to conclude that requirements (i) and (iii) above cannot both be secured in 1994 in mathematics and science . . . For English, with its smaller number of attainment targets, the difficulties may be less acute — though not negligible. (SEAC, Letter to DES, 18 December 1990)

SEAC's diagnosis led the Council to the conclusion, not that the certification of components of subjects and the continuation of awarding standards from the old to the new GCSE were inherently problematic, but rather that those goals were attainable if the Statutory Orders in mathematics and science were to be rewritten so that the number of attainment targets in those subjects (fourteen and seventeen respectively) was drastically reduced.

In a separate letter, also dated 18 December 1990, SEAC offered reassurance to the new Secretary of State on other Key Stage 4 assessment matters. The proposed short and combined courses could, it argued, be assessed and certificated on the same basis as the more familiar full GCSE courses. Also, the suggested introduction of more vocationally-oriented Key Stage 4 courses could be managed within a 'quality assurance' framework, broader than the existing GCSE General Criteria, which could be applied to all approved examination courses at Key Stage 4 including those offered by vocational examining bodies. There was just one discordant note in a letter which generally endorsed the policies set out by John MacGregor the previous January. Returning to the issue of how the National Curriculum ten-level scale should be applied at this Key Stage, SEAC reiterated its view that 'GCSE and equivalent qualifications involving National Curriculum subjects should be designed to lead to certification across the full ten-level scale'. On this front at least the Council was holding to its position that assessment arrangements for Key Stage 4 should be based on the national assessment (or TGAT) model rather than perpetuating the idea that the only attainments worthy of recognition were those in the middle and top ranges of the scale.

In the period between his receipt of this advice and his response to it, the Secretary of State, Kenneth Clarke, in a speech to the North of England Education Conference, followed up the ideas of the Key Stage 4 curriculum floated by his predecessor twelve months earlier. Encouragement for more vocational courses was reaffirmed, certain National Curriculum subjects would become optional at this Key Stage while in others the minimum requirement would be a short course. Only in the core subjects would a full course, probably certificated through the GCSE, be compulsory.

On the curriculum front, the concept of a broad common curriculum at Key Stage 4 was fading fast but, for the moment at least, the policy-makers were holding on to the idea that assessment arrangements for the more variable curriculum programme now envisaged would be recognizable as at least first cousins to their counterparts at earlier Key Stages. The early months of 1991 saw the consolidation of advice given, and decisions taken, in late December and early January. The Secretary of State announced a revision of the Orders in mathematics and science and SEAC confirmed that it would be possible, with difficulty, to keep to the original target date of introducing the new GCSE in these subjects from September 1992. Kenneth Clarke also dismissed in a few short sentences SEAC's attempt to reopen the question of certificating levels 1 to 3:

> I consider it important that the minimum standard required to gain a GCSE certificate should remain the same as now. I do not see that the public will find any conceptual difficulty with this. And I believe that they would see the issuing of a GCSE certificate to those attaining no more than levels 1–3 as a devaluation of the GCSE. (DES letter to SEAC, 8 February 1991)

In July SEAC returned to the question of how to link the way in which grades were awarded in the existing GCSE to the procedures which would be in place for the new, National Curriculum-based, courses which would be introduced in the years following 1992. Several options had been considered and there was no clear consensus among Council members. A majority favoured applying the rules of aggregation which were already being applied at Key Stages 1 and 3, viz. the accumulation of evidence of performance in relation to statements of attainment in each attainment target leading to attainment target scores which would then be arithmetically combined to supply a whole subject score. But the Council acknowledged that, if that option was proceeded with, 'there can be no assurance that the proportions of candidates obtaining the various grades or levels in 1994, subject by subject, will closely match the corresponding proportions for earlier years' (SEAC letter to the DES, 13 July 1991). However, clearly not of one mind on this matter, the Council left the way open for the Secretary of State to back one of the alternative options, each of which involved applying procedures which would make it more likely that the patterns of grades awarded after 1994 would not be dissimilar from those received under existing arrangements.

In many ways this was a highly technical issue for the examining boards to advise upon. But syllabus development teams and schools needed to know how candidates' work would be marked and how grades would be awarded if they were to complete the design work and preparation for the new syllabuses and assessment schemes. The need to put in place the foundations of the new GCSE was becoming ever more urgent as deadlines approached but, even in the middle of 1991, there was no clear line from the centre on whether the new, national assessment style, way of certificating attainment would prevail or whether the examining boards would revert to their established practice of making grade decisions on the basis of total marks allocated combined with examiners' judgments about the overall quality of a candidate's performance in each subject.

Key Stage 4 Policy 1991–1993: GCSE in Question

In the event, from July 1991 onwards, such questions of how to bring GCSE and national assessment together were overshadowed by a radical change of direction in Government policy on GCSE. Only the previous year John MacGregor had proposed, and ultimately received SEAC support for, a reduced emphasis on coursework so that any award in any subject would depend in part (a minimum of 30 per cent of the credit) on an externally-set terminal examination. GCSE schemes relying wholly on assessed coursework would therefore no longer be approved. In a speech to the Centre for Policy Studies on 3 July 1991, the Prime Minister, John Major, went much further:

> It is clear that there is now far too much coursework, project work and teacher assessment in GCSE. The remedy surely lies in getting GCSE back to being an externally assessed exam which is predominantly written. I am attracted to the idea that for most subjects a maximum of 20 per cent of the marks should be obtainable from coursework.

Later the same month, with Philip Halsey having been prevailed upon to resign as Chairman of SEAC and the Centre for Policy Studies Chairman, Lord Griffiths, having been appointed in his place, the Prime Minister and his Secretary of State ensured that the statutory advisory body on assessment and examinations was so constituted that it would be more likely to offer acceptable advice. The Government then attempted to turn the tide, at all Key Stages but especially at Key Stage 4, back from the 1980s thinking on assessment which had coloured both the original blueprint for GCSE and the thinking of the Task Group on Assessment and Testing.

It was the criticisms of the GCSE, and in particular the further limitations on coursework assessment, which would receive most of the public attention in the months following the Prime Minister's speech. The hostile reactions of most teachers and their representatives were in contrast to the vocal support the Secretary of State received for those who had been calling for a return to a system in which most of the credit depended on end-of-course examinations. But the decision on new coursework limits did nothing to help resolve the continuing uncertainty about how the new GCSE would be linked to national assessment. Indeed, by changing the ground rules which syllabus developers in the GCSE examining groups would have to observe, it complicated the already difficult task faced by the groups as they struggled to draw up new syllabuses and schemes of assessment based on the National Curriculum programmes of study and attainment targets.

During the second half of 1991, issues relating to the GCSE dominated the exchanges between ministers and their statutory advisory body. The reductions in coursework, proposed by John Major in July, were worked through in detail and announced by the Secretary of State in November. Other correspondence between SEAC and the DES ranged across topics such as differentiated assessment at Key Stage 4, ensuring that the new level 10 would challenge the most able GCSE candidates, the place of modular courses in the new GCSE, allocating marks for spelling, punctuation and grammar, SEAC procedures for scrutinizing GCSE practice in the examining groups, and the list of qualifications (through GCSE and through other forms of certification) which SEAC recommended should be approved for use in schools over the period 1992 to 1994. Key Stage 4 had certainly shot up to the top of the assessment policy agenda. And yet, while public attention was being focused on the merits of the GCSE examination then in place, the less high profile questions of how to adapt GCSE procedures to fit the national assessment requirements of statements of attainment and the ten-level scale were still to be decided. Following up the earlier correspondence about how decisions on GCSE awards should be made in subjects covered by National Curriculum Orders, SEAC advised (in a letter dated 29 October 1991) that there should be further discussions with the examining groups leading to agreement on detailed procedures within proposed 'general rules'. The basic principles — of using the ten-level scale, of reporting by attainment targets and of subject levels derived by aggregating attainment target scores — were restated. On the basis of those policy decisions development continued through 1992. The core subjects of mathematics, science and English were first in line, with implementation of the new arrangements due for the cohort of students who would embark on courses in September 1992 and be certificated in the summer of 1994.

The problems faced by schools and the examining groups in trying to implement not only new National Curriculum-related syllabuses, but also novel procedures for marking candidates' work and for awarding grades, were substantial. As in 1989 for Key Stage 1, a radically different model for assessing and accrediting attainment was being introduced on a tight timetable with many of the implications not yet fully explored. But it was not those matters, the technical and professional dimensions of the new GCSE, which were to the fore when Key Stage 4 once more hit the headlines in September 1992.

Closely following publication of the aggregated results of the 1992 examinations the Secretary of State used selective quotations from a not yet published HMI report to announce an urgent inquiry into the GCSE. Whereas previous years' results had been welcomed by ministers as evidence that the GCSE was raising standards of performance by the nation's 16-year-olds, the continuing picture of more students receiving higher grades was, in 1992, interpreted by ministers (as it had been all along by the examination's opponents) as showing that the GCSE was too easy. Focusing on a quote from the HMI report that there was evidence which 'could point to a gradual erosion of standards' since 1988, the GCSE's critics in the press opted for headlines such as 'Easy-Peasy' (*Sunday Times*, 6 September 1992) and 'A confidence trick' (*Daily Telegraph*, 2 September 1992). John Patten's very public criticism of GCSE had struck a chord with many who had long been suspicious of the curriculum and assessment innovations associated with GCSE. The damage caused — to the examination's public reputation, to the students receiving GCSE awards and to the morale of teachers who were committed to the educational principles underpinning GCSE — was considerable. As *The Times Educational Supplement* wryly observed in an editorial on the matter:

> . . . instead of speaking up for education and for the millions of pupils and thousands of teachers who have no alternative but to put their faith in the GCSE decreed by the Government, he has found it politically expedient to be seen to join the pack baying for its blood.
>
> For Mr. Patten then to say that pupils and teachers should not feel that any of this devalues their efforts in any way is rather like

hoping that Mrs. Lincoln's enjoyment of the play was not unduly marred. (*TES*, Editorial, 4 September 1992)

The direct result of the inquiry instituted by John Patten was a series of exchanges involving the DES, the examining groups and SEAC (who were reportedly angered by the Secretary of State's criticisms) leading to publication in January 1993 of a Mandatory Code of Practice for the GCSE:

> This new Code will put beyond doubt the credentials of the GCSE as a reliable way of measuring achievement at the end of compulsory schooling. (John Patten, DFE press release, 27 January 1993)

The indirect results of a very public discrediting of the GCSE by the Secretary of State responsible for the examination are harder to estimate. However, there can be no doubt that the resentment felt by many teachers about the Government's handling of the issue helped fuel the climate of confrontation between Government and the teaching profession which was to have major consequences for curriculum and assessment policy at all Key Stages (see chapter 7).

While the attention of the public and of most teachers was concentrated on the reputation of the GCSE in broad terms other decisions were being reached affecting the way in which the GCSE and the National Curriculum assessment model were to be linked. It was announced that the proposed short courses in non-core subjects would normally only be certificated through the GCSE if they were to form part of a full 'combined' course leading to a GCSE award. On the question of giving credit at the opposite ends of the ten level scale, 'performance descriptors' were under development to guide level 10 awards and it was confirmed that the National Record of Achievement (NRA) would be the vehicle for reporting attainment at level 1, 2 or 3.

As late as March 1993 the main lines of policy on marrying national assessment to the GCSE were thus, officially at least, still intact. The four 'requirements' of SEAC's December 1990 letter, including using the ten-level scale to report on each attainment target as well as whole subjects, continued to be the basis for the new generation of GCSE courses and the awards to be made from 1994. In measuring attainment leading to such awards, syllabuses and assessment schemes would refer to the relevant statements of attainment when designing and marking assessment tasks. And, in all National Curriculum subjects except art, music and physical education, the whole process would operate within the framework of the programmes of study and attainment targets of the Statutory Orders.

However, as with so much else in national assessment policy, all that was to change as the Dearing Review made its mark. The full scope of the major review, announced in April 1993, of the National Curriculum and its assessment is considered below (chapter 7). But, insofar as it dealt with Key Stage 4, it was to see a distinct parting of the ways, an end to the prolonged courtship of GCSE and national assessment.

One of Sir Ron Dearing's first actions following his appointment in March as Chairman-designate of the new School Curriculum and Assessment Authority was to recommend that the GCSE A–G grading scale be retained for 1994, together with a new 'starred A' grade to reward outstanding achievement. By the end of July, when his Interim Report on the review was published, he was ready to recommend retention of the A–G scale until at least 1995. By January 1994 Dearing was recommending, and the Secretary of State was agreeing, that the A–G scale, plus a starred A grade, should be confirmed for the years beyond 1995. What had been John MacGregor's 'only practical solution' in 1990 was discarded. Dearing went on to recommend that the ten-level scale should not be used at all at Key Stage 4, though how to recognize the achievement of the less able student whose efforts were insufficient for him/her to be awarded a GCSE certificate would be for the SCAA to investigate 'as a matter of urgency'.

The uncoupling of grading at Key Stage 4 from the ten level-scale was the clearest possible signal that assessment at that Key Stage would stand apart from the earlier Key Stages. Not only would the attainment of 16-year-olds lead to certification but the scale for reporting that attainment would be the familiar one introduced back in 1986. While details of how syllabuses and assessment schemes would be related to the National Curriculum Orders were yet to be decided, the assumptions which went with use of the ten-level scale would obviously also be revisited.

Conclusion

In 1988 assessment at Key Stage 4 had been well down the list of policy priorities for national assessment. During 1991 and 1992 it had been a key battleground on the wider front of a changing education policy. By 1994 the debate about curriculum and assessment at Key Stage 4 had become strikingly similar to what had been argued about in pre-national curriculum days. Many of the arguments in chapter 5 of Dearing's Final Report echoed a longstanding debate about whether diversity in the curriculum, and in the forms of certification associated with it, should be a planned feature of provision for students beyond the age of 14.

The 1988 Act had envisaged a common curriculum and assessment framework for the whole eleven years of compulsory schooling. Through a series of steps taken by Secretaries of State MacGregor and Clarke the extent of statutory commonality in the Key Stage 4 curriculum had been steadily reduced. That trend was to culminate in the minimal core curriculum requirements for Key Stage 4 proposed by Dearing and accepted by John Patten. Only the core subjects were to be compulsory for all students, together with, in England but not in Wales, short courses in technology and in a modern foreign language. For the other foundation subjects the National Curriculum would be a nine-year, 5–14 curriculum. Following Dearing's lead, the Key Stage 4 curriculum was also to be reconceptualized in terms of distinct 'pathways' — 'academic', 'vocational' and 'occupational'.

Over the same period, from 1988 to 1994, the idea of Key Stage 4 assessment and certification becoming a close relative of national assessment at the earlier stages had gradually foundered. The decision to use a fundamentally different grading scale marked the culmination of a retreat from the prospect of a fully criterion-referenced examination designed, marked and graded on the same principles as the TGAT-based system at Key Stages 1–3. Though the alternative, pre-National Curriculum, GCSE model of assessment and grading did not have complete supremacy (there were to be some non-GCSE certificates available as well), it was abundantly clear what had had to give when national assessment met GCSE.

7 The System Reviewed

After four years of development the national assessment system remained more or less on course for implementation on the timetable set in 1989. Each component of the system had encountered problems but none of these had been sufficient to stop the development process or even, except in a few specific instances, to delay it. The standard assessment tasks had been modified year-by-year and distinctive approaches to test design and moderation were emerging at each of the Key Stages. Teacher assessment, especially the recording of it, remained a considerable burden for teachers and its role in the system was far from clear but at least some published guidance materials were beginning to clarify what was expected. Although the reporting and publication of results brought more deep-rooted objections from the teaching profession the Government appeared to have ridden out the storm of protest at the early league tables. Not everyone was happy with the decision to align the GCSE with national assessment by introducing criteria-related grading on a 1–10 scale but the preparatory work for introducing the first of the new GCSE courses was on schedule.

Ministers were focusing public and professional attention on some of the fundamental questions raised in the course of implementation. For the most part these were matters of curriculum rather than of assessment, with their origins in doubts, especially on the Right of the Conservative Party, about whether the 1988 Act was proving radical enough in its impact on schools. The decisions to launch a high-profile review of the primary curriculum and to review the Statutory Order for English were the decisions of ministers pressing ahead with their own policy agenda rather than drawing back in the face of criticism.

The re-election, in April 1992, of a Conservative Government seemed to confirm the general expectation that curriculum and assessment policy would stay on the course set four years earlier. The new Secretary of State, John Patten, defended the reforms vigorously and spoke optimistically of the benefits emerging as they were implemented. *The Daily Mail*'s report on his keynote address to an international conference in Basle in May was headlined: 'Patten's world class: Other countries queue up to study British school reforms'.

Writing in *New Statesman and Society* on 17 July 1992, John Patten made it very clear what purposes he saw national assessment serving:

> (Regular assessment) will enable teachers to pick out schools . . . whose
> results suggest their methods are worth following. It will allow parents

to exert influence through their choice of school. And it will give governors the evidence on which to compare performance within their school and from one year to the next. Published tests and assessment will break the producers' monopoly, demystify education and provide real data about real education. (p. 21)

The new Secretary of State apparently did not think it necessary to make even token references to national assessment's role in helping pupils learn and teachers teach, the formative purposes of assessment.

To build on the claimed success of the Government's educational reforms, another phase of change was heralded by the publication in July of the White Paper, *Choice and Diversity*:

The reform programme introduced following the Education Act 1988 has begun to raise standards. Its full implementation will, however, require further organizational changes to create choice, diversity and better standards. (DFE/WO, 1992, p. 15)

A by now familiar ideological thrust was also very clear in these proposals. As one sceptical editorial put it:

. . . schools are in for a huge, generation-long bureaucratic reshuffle. The connection between this upheaval and the theory of parental choice is evident. The connection with what goes on in the classroom is not. (*Financial Times*, Editorial, 29 July 1992)

The early months of the new Government, leading up to publication of the White Paper, was a time for confident noises about education policy for the long-term future ('Patten writes school rules for 25 years' — *The Guardian*). And yet, within twelve months, the National Curriculum and assessment system, and in particular the assessment requirements, were to be challenged to such an extent that the Government would be forced to concede the need for a fundamental review. The policy issues which ministers had, until then, been able to deal with one-by-one came together in a groundswell of increasingly hostile opinion. How did it come about that a Government with a fresh mandate and with little serious dissent on education policy among its own backbenchers announced, in April 1993, that the system would be reviewed?

Pressing Ahead with Reform

Changes on the curriculum front continued throughout 1992 at the pace set by the Government. Early in the year a wide-ranging critique of established practice in primary schools had heralded a Primary Review led by the Curriculum Councils in England and Wales. During the summer term the last of the Statutory Orders to be completed (in modern languages, physical education, art and music) reached the schools in time for implementation to begin in September. The existing, first generation, Orders for Technology and for English were subjected to a growing volume of criticism and the Government initiated the process of revising them. None of these events was free from controversy but nor was the weight of opposition sufficient to deflect the Government from its declared intention to maintain the momentum of change.

At the National Association of Headteachers' Conference in May, its General Secretary, David Hart, argued for recognition of teachers' anxieties about managing change:

> I am sure the government understands that as far as possible we must slow the pace to allow those responsible for managing the service to cope with the reforms we've seen in the last few years. (quoted in *The Times*, 28 May 1992)

But, whether he understood or not, there were no signs that the new Secretary of State, whose reluctance to meet teachers' associations was already being noted, was inclined to heed such advice.

During the summer an impressive array of critics emerged from the ranks of those who had been in key positions during the period when policy on National Curriculum and assessment had been taking shape. Speaking at a conference in July, Eric Bolton, Chief Inspector of Schools in England until his retirement in 1991, argued that education policy was 'beset by uncertainty, confusion and incoherence'.

A month later Professor Paul Black, as Chairman of TGAT, the main architect of the original national assessment proposals, also voiced concern about the speed with which changes were being introduced into schools:

> If this were a new drug, its application, even for those in dire need, would not be allowed with this degree of untried novelty. (*Education*, 28 August 1992, p. 8)

He argued that his Task Group's proposals had been 'abandoned' by successive Secretaries of State ('death by a thousand cuts') and was especially critical of 'current ideas (which are) based on prejudice rather than evidence and are set fair to do serious harm to children's education'.

The Government's main adviser on curriculum from 1988 until 1991, Duncan Graham (Chairman of the National Curriculum Council) was reported as fearing that the impact of the new curriculum could be lost in a 'welter of counter-initiatives . . . and distractions' (*The Guardian*, 7 September 1992). Later the same month his successor as NCC Chairman, David Pascall, acknowledged that the National Curriculum was placing 'considerable pressures on hard-working primary classroom teachers' (*The Independent*, 25 September 1992).

Several themes can be recognized as recurring in the general criticism directed at Government curriculum and assessment policy during 1992. The *pace of change* was still hectic. The Orders in the last four of the foundation subjects began to impact on work in schools from September and the phased introduction of national tests at each key stage was making new demands on teachers and schools as they struggled to come to terms with what would be expected of them next.

Not only was the pace hectic but the *workload* associated with National Curriculum and assessment seemed to be on an inexorably rising curve. For headteachers, the Government circulars came in a steady flow, with instructions on organizing tests, on providing data for use in league tables, or on how to report to parents. Among classroom teachers, those responsible for pupils in the last year of a key stage were faced with planning, managing and marking the statutory tests. All teachers were now having to cope with what many perceived as the onerous and bureaucratic business of making, recording and reporting teacher assessments.

A third theme in this growing body of criticism was the *complexity* of it all. As primary teachers at last found themselves with a complete set of Curriculum Orders the complex requirements they embodied were difficult enough even to interpret; turning them into a coherent programme of teaching and learning for a class of primary school children was a curriculum design problem of daunting proportions. On the assessment side, not only were the demands on teachers exceptionally detailed but as policy decisions had been taken on each specific aspect of the system it had become increasingly difficult to discern the grand design of the original TGAT Report. Complexity without a coherent overview was thus a feature of national assessment as well as of the National Curriculum it was supposed to complement.

In spite of the crescendo of criticism the Secretary of State made it abundantly clear that he would be pressing ahead on the already published timetable and with only minor modifications to curriculum and assessment policy. Indeed, some of his decisions, such as the early revision of the Order for English or the intention to publish Key Stage 1 results on a school-by-school basis, represented a hardening of the Government's position in the teeth of fierce opposition from teachers and schools.

It may be that this 'press on regardless' line was doomed to fail anyway as the weight of the system's demands coupled with the unresolved tensions in its design opened up cracks along lines of weakness and threatened a complete collapse of the whole edifice. What is undoubtedly the case is that certain specific aspects of policy were to become, during the winter of 1992/93, the catalysts for the wide-ranging review announced in April 1993.

English as a Battleground

The most obvious such catalyst was the long-running debate about the testing of English at Key Stage 3. In one sense the arguments about the Key Stage 3 English tests can be seen as a sub-plot of the by now already epic story of National Curriculum English. For much of 1992 it even seemed to be a relatively minor sub-plot as ministers and some sections of the press continued to highlight English, and the teachers responsible for the subject in schools, as a major cause for concern. John Patten, speaking in his constituency in June, heralded the decision to revise the English Order with an attack on teachers and advisers:

> Though there are many fine teachers with a commitment to real education, there are still some in the grip of dated theorists whose progressive orthodoxy has led so many children up an educational blind alley. (quoted in *The Guardian*, 15 June 1992)

The inclusion of a reference to television drama in one GCSE examining group's syllabus was a gift to the 'back to basics' campaigners. The Prime Minister weighed in with his response to a question in Parliament:

> The basics of education are fundamentally important and the teaching of the classics of education are, I suspect, rather more valuable to children than that of soap operas. (John Major, quoted in the *Daily Express*, 20 May 1992)

But once the furore surrounding this episode had died down and the Secretary of State had announced a review of the English Order, it was the testing of 14-year-olds which became the battleground between, on the one side, Government and its advisory body SEAC and, on the other, teachers of English and the teacher associations.

At the end of June, as part of the general move to place greater emphasis on time-limited unseen examinations at the end of Key Stage 3 (see chapter 3), John Patten announced his decision on the form which the English tests would take in the summer of 1994. The changes, he argued, were necessary 'to secure rigour and a proper test of the breadth and depth of pupils' reading'. The aspect of the proposals picked up by all the press headlines was, as the *Daily Express* put it: 'Shakespeare for all' — questions were to be set on a Shakespeare play. However, there were other significant moves away from the classroom-based tasks pioneered by the agencies which had been awarded the original contracts for developing what were then called SATs in English. There were to be separate tests of reading, comprehension and imaginative writing and there were also to be questions on an anthology, distributed free to schools, of extracts from selected texts.

Many of the crucial decisions about these English tests were still to come. For example, *which* Shakespeare play and what would be included in the anthology? Teachers, even those not vociferously opposed to this new style of testing, wanted to know the answers to such questions as they began to teach the year 9 classes of pupils who would take the tests in June 1993. Yet not only had such inevitably controversial decisions not been taken but the job of developing the tests was to be given to an agency new to the task of designing National Curriculum tests. When the award of the contract to the University of Cambridge Local Examination Syndicate (UCLES) was announced in August it was represented as a 'Victory for traditionalists in battle for English tests' (*Sunday Telegraph*, 9 August 1992). According to Fran Abrams, the *Sunday Telegraph*'s Education Correspondent, members of SEAC

Council had been impressed by 'the emphasis that the syndicate placed on the importance of grammar in English teaching'. UCLES was the fourth agency in three years to be involved in Key Stage 3 English tests, following in the footsteps of the two groups responsible for the early trialling and piloting and another examining board, the Northern Examining Association, which had designed and administered the 1992 pilot tests.

A leaked draft list, prepared by SEAC officers, of texts to be studied by 14-year-olds was the first aspect of the new English tests to provoke hostile comment. Under the headline 'Adrian ousts Dickens' the *Daily Express* reported (14 September 1992) that:

> A proposal for Adrian Mole to replace Charles Dickens's David Cop-
> perfield as a set book in English lessons has angered traditionalists.

But the list didn't only upset traditionalists; everyone invited to comment, from the National Association for the Teaching of English (NATE) to the Secretary of State himself, who had 'neither seen nor approved it', found fault with SEAC's preferred texts. SEAC's curriculum counterpart in England, the NCC, was equally unhappy that a list of texts to be used as a basis for testing might be seen as pre-empting the question of which books and authors should be specified in the new English Order which would emerge from the review on which, together with the Curriculum Council for Wales, it had only re- cently embarked. When, in November, a revised list surfaced minus Adrian Mole and with the Secretary of State's approval, at least the *Sunday Telegraph* was able to give it a cautious welcome, recycling its August headline as: 'Triumph for tradition in round one of books bout'.

The test anthology was another focus for criticism. Three months into the new school year *The Times* reported (27 November 1992) that agreement had still to be reached on what to include in the anthology and schools would not receive the final version until February. In the event publication was brought forward to the beginning of January. For the *Daily Telegraph* the extracts included were another sign of 'the return of the English classical tradition to the nation's classrooms'. For Terry Furlong, past Chairman of NATE and former English test developer, it was but one small, grudgingly accepted, piece in the assessment jigsaw:

> Teachers will be just as mystified about what is going on but they
> will be glad that the anthology has at least been published. (quoted in
> *The Times Educational Supplement*, 8 January 1993)

But it was neither the list of books nor the anthology which aroused most criticism and led to calls by teachers for the English tests to be boycotted. It was the lack of trialling of the new-style tests to be used in a 'national pilot' in 1994, the results of which, following a decision by Patten's predecessor Kenneth Clarke, would be published. The test agency, UCLES, had only had limited time in which to devise and trial tests according to the brief given them when they had been awarded the contract in August. Trial versions were taken in November in thirty-two schools by 15-year-olds, the age group a year ahead of the pupils who would actually sit the tests. SEAC admitted it had hoped to make use of at least some of the trial questions in the final test papers but that plan was thwarted by the leaking to the press in January of the questions trialled. SEAC also attempted to persuade an increasingly concerned and sceptical teaching profession that the work of UCLES drew on evidence from the earlier pilot SATs carried out by its predecessor agencies. Lord Griffiths, Chairman of SEAC, concluded a stout defence of his Council's actions with a confident claim:

> I know of few other public examinations which have had so extensive and thorough a preparation. I have every confidence that the (English) tests will provide us with a valid and reliable assessment, and with information of great value to parents, pupils and teachers. (*Times Educational Supplement*, 29 January 1993)

Something of the state of mind of the Secretary of State, John Patten, can be gleaned from an article in his name published in *The Sun* (28 January 1993). Seeking to represent the campaign against the English tests as the work of a minority of left wing 'wreckers' associated with the National Union of Teachers he declared:

> These people have tried every trick in the book to try to derail the tests. They must not win . . .
> New tests are already being prepared and will be used in June.

Unwilling to make even the slightest concession, such as not publishing the results, a course urged on him by the moderate teacher union, the Association of Teachers and Lecturers and many others, he pronounced himself as determined as ever not to be deflected from the course set before the series of events which had led to Key Stage 3 English testing being called into question: 'Nothing will stop the tests going ahead as planned'.

But as General Patten, together with his adjutant, Lord Griffiths, pressed forward, he either failed to notice or failed to take seriously the fact that almost all the troops he needed behind him, not just the rebellious left wing, had lost any faith they might have had in his battle plan and in his leadership.

1992/93: A Winter of Discontent

While the English testing saga was unfolding, other events were occurring which sapped the confidence, both of teachers and of the others concerned with developments, in the National Curriculum and, more especially, in national assessment.

Several of the matters on which the Government and its critics had disagreed in the preceding three years were still rumbling only just beneath the surface of the policy debate, occasionally surfacing when a further point in the policy-making process was reached. While it was the English tests for 14-year-olds which received most public attention the testing of mathematics and science was still far from being fully accepted by teachers and the tests in other foundation subjects, notably technology, were widely criticized. A survey of headteachers, published in December, highlighted a range of criticisms, focusing in particular on experience in the maths and science pilots:

> Tests for 14-year-olds were yesterday attacked for being unfair to the children taking them next year. Exam chiefs have been warned that the 'free response' maths and science questions could result in wildly inconsistent marking. (*Daily Express*, 10 December 1992)

Decisions on the approach to be adopted in testing 11-year-olds were announced in July 1992 as the first step towards what would be a 2 per cent pilot in the summer of 1993. Almost all the teacher organizations commenting on the announcement wondered aloud whether in the proposals they were hearing echoes of the system of 11+ selection which had been abandoned in almost all parts of England and Wales. Their fears and those of their members were hardly assuaged by either the press coverage — 'Return of 11+ brings new exam agony for pupils' (*Today*) — or the way in which the uses to which test results might be put was explained by the Department for Education:

> A spokesman for the Department for Education said they were designed primarily to assess pupils' progress and to place them in one of the ten levels of the national curriculum. 'If some schools also choose to make use of them for selection, that is up to them'. (quoted in *The Independent*, 23 July 1992)

Once again the unwillingness of national assessment policy-makers to associate particular parts of the process with particular purposes was giving rise to confusion and suspicion in the minds of teachers and their organizations.

At the key stage where it had all started back in 1989, Key Stage 1, the testing and teacher assessment arrangements were being further modified in preparation for testing pupils who would reach the end of year 2 in 1994. The tests, announced in October 1992, would include compulsory testing of spelling and reading comprehension and were, according to the minister responsible, 'essential to good teaching':

> I have no doubt that next summer's tests will be of great value in raising standards still further and in providing objective and reliable information for teachers and parents about the achievements of their children. (Baroness Blatch, quoted in the *Daily Telegraph*, 16 October 1992)

But many teachers remained unconvinced of the value of end-of-key-stage testing. At a conference of the National Association of Headteachers (NAHT) in May the Association's General Secretary, David Hart, had been as firm as ever in his opposition to testing at Key Stage 1:

> The tests are too narrowly based and do not adequately assess children's progress across the whole curriculum. Many of our members have always been opposed to any form of testing for 7-year-olds. I have no doubt the Government will set its face against us, but that does not mean we should abandon our position. (quoted in the *Daily Telegraph*, 28 May 1992)

The conference unanimously approved a motion to end the tests because they were 'too simplistic' to produce useful results or to improve children's learning.

Also at Key Stage 1, the extra work of teacher assessment in the last three foundation subjects implemented (from September 1992) added to the already heavy burden on teachers. They were now expected to record, report and keep evidence of attainment across all nine National Curriculum subjects. It is little wonder that when, during the winter of 1992/93, teacher organizations began to ballot their members on a boycott of national assessment, the frustration felt by many Key Stage 1 teachers lent support to opposition which was sparked off initially by events at Key Stage 3.

Fuelling such opposition was continuing teacher unease and resentment at the publication of performance data in national league tables. In a consultation paper published in October 1992 the Government had restated its view that publishing such information was an essential part of its whole policy for schools though it did for the first time accept the principle that, in due course, 'value added' measures might be used alongside raw scores:

> National Curriculum assessment provides an opportunity for the first time to calculate reliable measures of the extent to which schools have enhanced the attainment of pupils over time.

Publication of tables of GCSE and GCE 'A' level results in November was accompanied by the now familiar chorus of protest from teachers' organizations that league tables of any kind were a poor indicator of the quality of a school. Speaking on behalf of those who were intended to benefit from the availability of such information, the parents, a spokeswoman for the National Confederation of Parent Teacher Associations was equally dismissive:

> There are lies, damned lies and school exam statistics. They can be distorted and misreported in as many ways as you can count. (Margaret Morrissey, quoted in *The Guardian*, 19 November 1992)

Apparently undaunted, and discomfited hardly at all by errors in the statistics and the fact that many independent schools had withheld their results, John Patten reiterated the case for publishing, school-by-school, the results of national assessments and public examinations:

> Until today comparative results have been the private preserve of local authorities which, with certain notable and praiseworthy exceptions seemed to believe that parents cannot be trusted to understand

or use the figures wisely. This attitude is now permanently consigned to the dustbin of educational history. (quoted in *The Guardian*, 19 November 1992)

When the latest set of Key Stage 1 test results were published just before Christmas, set out for that Key Stage LEA-by-LEA, the Secretary of Stage added a new twist to the familiar exchanges between him and the critics of league tables. He reinforced the message that such tables were valid indicators of the quality of provision by announcing an urgent investigation by his Department into why there continued to be 'unacceptable variations' in attainments across different local education authorities.

Throughout their early months in office the new team of ministers in the Department for Education had not been slow to take a confrontational line with organizations representing teachers and schools. In July Baroness Blatch, Minister of State responsible for schools, had mounted one of several vigorous attacks on critics of Government policy, directed especially at the National Union of Teachers (NUT):

They are against tests. They are against Shakespeare. They are against grammar and spelling and against greater rigour in the GCSE. They seem to be quite indifferent to the importance of raising standards. (*Evening Standard*, 23 July 1992)

Given more press coverage, no doubt because it was more surprising, was her reaction to criticisms voiced at the annual conference in November 1992 of the Girls' Schools Association, representing schools in the independent sector. According to *The Independent*, headteachers of girls' schools 'queued up to disown the tests (of 14-year-olds)' and several announced that they would not take part in them. In a wide-ranging critique of Government policy on testing the Association's outgoing President, Elizabeth Diggory, warned of the danger 'that oversimplified testing will have the very opposite of the results intended' (*Daily Telegraph*, 11 November 1992). Her successor, Joan Jefferson, went further when she described the tests as a blunt instrument and a complete waste of teachers' time. Clearly stung by her reception at the GSA, Lady Blatch came back with a rejoinder:

Miss Diggory's outburst was ridiculous and full of old 1960s arguments . . . Miss Diggory and other independent school headteachers — thankfully a minority — are looking backwards at a time when most schools and most teachers are looking forwards. (*The Guardian*, 12 November 1992)

Once again the ministerial tactic was to represent critics as being a vocal, backward-looking minority but Lady Blatch in turn found herself being rebuked by the Chairman of the Headmasters' Conference, Dominic Milroy, among whose members are almost all the leading independent boys' schools:

> It is a bad sign when Government ministers react so badly to criticism, and appear to give such little weight to the considered views of professional teaching associations. (quoted in *The Independent*, 13 November 1992)

What was striking about the climate of opinion at the end of 1992 was the range of organizations which had expressed open opposition to the Government's assessment policy, opposition which was often linked to criticism of education policy more broadly and frequently focused on the way in which policy decisions were being taken. In a speech at Leicester in December, Sir Malcolm Thornton, a Conservative MP and Chairman of the House of Commons Select Committee on Education, reaffirmed his support for the 1988 curriculum and assessment legislation but launched a strong attack on Right wing pressure groups which had gained an increasing hold on policy-making:

> Sadly whole sections of our nation once respected for common sense have been brainwashed into an acceptance of their dogma. I could not let this occasion pass without standing up for the voices of sanity and experience in education. (quoted in *The Times Educational Supplement*, 4 December 1992)

1992 had seen a marked polarization of opinion as opposition to many aspects of Government policy had hardened while John Patten had made it very clear that he was unwilling to concede even an inch to his critics.

The Call for a Boycott

Threats by teachers to refuse to carry out what was required of them by National Curriculum and/or assessment legislation and subsequent regulations run like disconnected threads through the fabric of the policy debate from even before the passing of the 1988 Act. However, unlike the equivalent situation in Scotland where non-cooperation by a majority of teachers and parents had forced the Government to back down on testing, such threats had had little apparent effect on Government policy in England and Wales.

Some of the threats had related to piloting of the tests. For example, in April 1992 the then Secretary of State, Kenneth Clarke and the NAHT had clashed over Clarke's declared intention to publish, at national level, the results of Key Stage 3 pilot tests. The NAHT said it would encourage schools not to make the results available if the Secretary of State persisted with his plans to publish them. Later in the year the same Association, having seen what form the proposed testing of 11-year-olds would take, urged its members not to volunteer to take part in the pilot tests scheduled for 1994:

> Heads and deputies in England and Wales are not willing to assist in the introduction of untrialled and unproven assessments which will damage the education of the children for whom they are responsible.

(David Hart, General Secretary of NAHT, quoted in *The Guardian*, 21 December 1992)

But by then moves were already afoot in other teacher associations to mount a more direct challenge to Government policy by threatening some form of boycott.

In early December, the *Times Educational Supplement* reported that, as a response to the plans for testing English at Key Stage 3, several branches of the National Association for the Teaching of English (NATE) were discussing 'a mass campaign of non-co-operation'. The following week *The Guardian*'s Education Correspondent reported 'the first steps towards a national boycott'. Not only had the National Executive of the National Union of Teachers (NUT) decided to canvass its members on a possible boycott of the Key Stage 3 English tests but the NAS/UWT had 'pledged full support for members deemed to be pursuing a legitimate trade dispute over "workload and unreasonableness"' (*The Guardian*, 11 December 1992).

The first signs had thus appeared of a twin-pronged attack on national assessment policy by the two largest teacher unions; one was challenging a specific test, the other was mounting a broader assault by questioning whether the overall workload on teachers arising from the statutory requirements was, in legal terms, 'reasonable'. In early January 1993 the same workload issue was taken up, but without the accompanying boycott threat, by the other major union, the Association of Teachers and Lecturers (ATL), formerly the Assistant Masters' and Mistresses' Association (AMMA). In a statement the Association spelled out the pressures teachers and schools were experiencing:

> The question remains whether the complexity of National Curriculum assessment, recording and reporting as currently conceived is in fact manageable by all schools.

The sense of a growing crisis was increased by the reported success of the NAHT's call (referred to above) to its primary headteacher members not to volunteer to take part in the piloting of Key Stage 2 tests. According to *The Independent* (27 January 1993):

> The Association says its patience with ministers is exhausted after their refusal to listen to teachers' views and a series of broken promises.

The results of the NUT's ballot of its members showed overwhelming support for a boycott among those who would be involved in the Key Stage 3 English tests. By the beginning of February *The Guardian*'s Education Correspondent was reporting that 'education ministers are facing their most serious confrontation with the teaching profession since the mid-1980s pay strikes' (*The Guardian*, 1 February 1993).

The response of Baroness Blatch to the talk of boycotts was typically uncompromising:

> The tests are vital if we are to raise standards . . . Parents will be given the information they have always sought . . . This information enables teachers and, indeed, parents to build on the strengths, and to address the weaknesses, of pupils. How can anyone object to this? How can anyone seek to deprive children, parents and teachers of this valuable information? (quoted in *The Independent*, 15 January 1993)

When a boycott by teachers was being threatened, it was to the formative uses of assessment, so long overshadowed by the rights of parents to use aggregate results to help them choose schools, that the Minister chose to refer.

Behind the confident rhetoric however, education ministers were clearly under mounting pressure to find a way of resolving their differences with the teaching profession. Following meetings in mid-February 1993 with representatives of most of the main teacher organizations John Patten announced that the results of the 1993 pilot tests at Key Stage 3 in English and technology would not now be published. That concession was enough to mollify some of the critics; for example, the ATL's General Secretary Peter Smith pronounced it 'a statesmanlike decision'. But, writing later the same month, Peter Smith warned the Secretary of State that the crisis was of his own making and that 'one conversation does not make a dialogue':

> John Patten and his advisers almost certainly misread the situation. As far as one can tell, Mr. Patten judged that mounting opposition to KS3 English testing was an orchestrated and essentially political campaign against the Government's entire reform programme . . .
>
> It seems certain that Mr. Patten was determined to prove that he could out-Clarke his predecessor; he would stand his ground, deride his critics and point to genuine public concern . . . (*The Times Educational Supplement*, 26 February 1993)

However, the NUT and the NAS/UWT (whom Patten had refused to meet because they were threatening a boycott) were not satisfied with a response from the Secretary of State which dealt with only one of their many grievances. In early March the NAS/UWT announced the result of its ballot of members. Eighty-eight per cent of those voting supported a boycott which would include not only the end-of-stage tests at Key Stages 1 and 3 but also teacher assessments judged to be imposing an undue burden on teachers. The Union Executive followed this vote by instructing its members to boycott all 'unreasonable and unnecessary elements' of national assessment. In a by-now desperate attempt to hold the Government line, Baroness Blatch again referred to the supposed formative value of assessment as she sought to represent the union's threatened action as being harmful to children's education and their stance as not reflecting the majority view among teachers:

> No wonder they are finding themselves increasingly isolated within the teaching profession. Only through testing can the strengths and

weaknesses of children be identified. (quoted in *The Guardian*, 10 March 1993).

At this point in the confrontation the action moved to the courts as the Conservative Council in Wandsworth initiated an action in the High Court to declare unlawful the NAS/UWT's proposed boycott. But at the beginning of April the High Court refused the Council's application for an injunction against the industrial action planned by the NAS/UWT in its schools:

> (The judge) ruled that the teachers had a legitimate trade dispute in breaking their contracts of employment and had no statutory duty to assess and test children under the Education Reform Act 1988 . . . (*Daily Telegraph*, 3 April 1993)

For some time thereafter the possibility of that decision being overturned by the Court of Appeal was a consideration for both the teachers and the Government in deciding their next moves. In the event, the Appeal Court hearing in late April cleared the way for a boycott when it ruled that, by focusing on an increasing workload, the NAS/UWT action was within the terms of the relevant trade union legislation. Wandsworth Council decided not to take its legal challenge any further. The only consolation John Patten could find in all this was to draw attention to the fact that the courts 'had not ruled on the merits of this summer's tests nor on the desirability of industrial action' (quoted in *The Independent*, 24 April 1993).

Pressure on the Secretary of State increased further as all three major teacher unions now lined up to challenge his Government's policies on testing. The NUT's annual conference voted to ballot the membership on a total boycott and even the ATL, widely regarded as the most moderate of the three, voted unanimously at its annual meeting for a vaguely worded motion calling for a membership ballot on a boycott.

During the first three months of 1993 what had seemed to be a more focused challenge to only one set of tests, those in English at Key Stage 3, had turned into a widely-supported vote of no confidence in the national assessment system. Even on the Right of the Conservative Party those who had been among the most influential of advocates of national testing were coming out openly against Government policy.

At a seminar in mid-March, organized by the Centre for Policy Studies, some of those who had been closest to policy-making were forthright in their criticisms. For Donald Naismith, Wandsworth's Director of Education:

> What we have now is not what was intended. Chickens are coming home to roost. The Government will have to rethink it on original lines. It is over-bureaucratic and unworkable. The sooner it is buried the better. (quoted in the *Daily Mail*, 18 March 1993)

Dr. John Marks, prominent among those on the political Right advocating a more radical approach to education policy and a participant in the formal policy-making process as a Council member both of SEAC and of NCC, returned to his long-standing criticism of the complexity inherent in a ten-level scale with numerous statements of attainment:

> The way this ten-point national curriculum scale has been drawn up is highly questionable. The whole thing is unnecessarily complicated. (*Daily Mail*, 18 March 1993)

Some of the strongest language was used by Lord Skidelsky, another disillusioned Right-winger who had been brought in to join Dr. Marks as a SEAC Council member and provide Right-thinking support for Lord Griffiths, the SEAC Chairman (and also Chairman of the Centre for Policy Studies):

> He (Lord Skidelsky) criticised the 'bewildering and bamboozling' features of the tests, which he described as a product of 'loose-thinking', 'hair-raising' methods and an 'insane' proliferation of unnecessary details. (*Daily Mail*, 18 March 1993)

In the course of an article in the *Sunday Telegraph* (20 March 1993) explaining his position, Lord Skidelsky, while apportioning some of the blame to teachers, said:

> I agree with the teachers; the new testing system *is* over-complicated, bureaucratic and time-consuming. Moreover, as often as not it doesn't even produce good tests.

The more moderate language used by the Office for Standards in Education in its report on the third year of implementation of national assessment offered little comfort for the Government:

> . . . the improvements in educational standards (as a result of the 1988 reforms) are tangible: in higher expectations of what pupils can and should achieve; in better planning and preparation; in ensuring broader curriculum coverage.
> . . . This year, however, and for the first time, the benefits and costs are finely balanced. There are some clearly discernible signs that the impact of 'teaching to the test' and the complexities of the assessment requirements could lead to a distortion of the positive relationship between teaching, learning and assessment. (*Assessment, Recording and Reporting: Third Year 1991–92*)

By Easter 1993 few voices were to be heard in defence of the system as it then stood. Its architects, such as Professor Paul Black, had disowned the modified version of their original design, the product of a series of specific policy decisions by successive Secretaries of State. The teacher unions were untypically united in threatening action to force on the Government a fundamental rethink. And the Conservative Right, increasingly in control of education policy-making since the arrival of John Major as Prime Minister and his appointment of Kenneth Clarke as Secretary of State, were thoroughly disillusioned with what they saw as the Government's failure to be radical enough in implementing a straightforward system for testing 'the basics' and providing parents with the information needed to empower them.

There was even a noticeable convergence in the language used in the chorus of criticism. 'Teachers' boycott aims to stop 'tests juggernaut' was *The Guardian*'s headline over its report of the NAS/UWT vote for a boycott. 'Stop this juggernaut' was the way the *Daily Mail* chose to headline its report of Lord Skidelsky's contribution to the CPS seminar a week later. Faced with such unanimous opposition from such diverse directions, even the previously intransigent Mr. Patten was finally forced to accept the case for a fundamental policy review.

The Decision to Review

One important ministerial decision made in March 1993 was to have a significant effect on the course which assessment policy would take in the period after John Patten's decision the following month to instigate a thoroughgoing review of all aspects of National Curriculum and assessment. Under the terms of what was to become the 1993 Education Act, the separation of assessment from curriculum in policy-making, reinforced by the 1988 Act's provision for separate advisory bodies, was to end. The National Curriculum Council and the School Examinations and Assessment Council would be replaced from October 1993 by a single new quango, the School Curriculum and Assessment Authority (with a parallel Authority for Wales).

In advance of the establishment of the SCAA, John Patten had announced in mid-March that the Authority's Chairman would be Sir Ron Dearing. 'Sir Ron', as he was soon to be familiarly referred to in education circles, would also take over as Chairman of both the NCC and the SEAC for the months remaining until the SCAA was set up in October. Thus, when John Patten took the decision to review the National Curriculum and assessment he had available to him as formal sources of advice two outgoing quangoes and one incoming Chairman whose quango existed at that time only in name. He chose to give the incoming Chairman, Sir Ron Dearing, within weeks of his appointment, a personal remit for the review, consulting whoever he wished and submitting the recommendations requested in his own name rather than on behalf of the various organizations which he was chairing or was about to chair. After five years of Secretaries of State taking advice on curriculum and assessment from two statutory quangoes in England, John Patten embarked on the process of simplifying the system by placing the responsibility for advising him formally in the hands of one man.

There is some irony in the fact that the one man in question was neither Lord Griffiths nor David Pascall, the two Chairmen brought in by Kenneth Clarke in the summer of 1991 to chair the SEAC and the NCC respectively. Both men, and particularly Lord Griffiths, were on the political Right in their thinking on education and had done much to change the policy agenda from the earlier, less political, stance of their predecessors, Philip Halsey and Duncan Graham. David Pascall had, in fact, been the first senior figure in the policy-making process to advocate a full review of National Curriculum and assessment policy. In a speech to primary headteachers in September 1992 he had accepted that primary school teachers were suffering from overload and that the curriculum should be simplified. He had said then he was 'not yet confident that the testing system, any more than the curriculum, is as simple and practicable as it should be' (quoted in *The Independent*, 25 September 1992). But it was to his successor, Sir Ron Dearing, that John Patten gave the job of what was soon to become known as 'The Dearing Review'.

At the time of the announcement of the Review it was the fact that a review was to take place at all which was surprising, though an impasse had been reached in relations between the Government and the teaching profession which necessitated more radical steps than had hitherto seemed likely. The announcement was also notable for the fundamental nature of the questions John Patten was asking Sir Ron Dearing to consider. From a Secretary of State whose only previous concession to his critics had been not to publish the results of two sets of pilot tests the scope of this Review was extraordinarily wide.

John Patten needed a convenient peg, other than the need to meet teacher action with some concessions, on which to hang the case for a Review. He found it in the impending establishment of a new School Curriculum and Assessment Authority. This, he wrote to Sir Ron Dearing on 7 April, 'provides a unique opportunity to review the manageability of the curriculum and assessment framework within which this year's tests will take place'. The lack of integration of assessment with the curriculum was, he said:

> a concern which is shared by some teachers who tell me that the curriculum has become over-extended and that, as a result, the assessment arrangements are unduly complex. Much of this concern has focused on the tests for 1993, although it goes wider than the tests themselves.

There were, suggested Patten, four 'key issues for review':

(a) What is the scope for slimming down the curriculum?
(b) What is the future of the ten-level scale for graduating children's attainment?
(c) How can the testing arrangements be simplified?
(d) How can central administration of the National Curriculum and testing arrangements be improved?

Two of the themes — complexity and overload — which had coloured the debate of the preceding months were thus reflected in what, to judge from the sub-text of the letter as well as the DFE presentation of the Review, was to be a relatively open-minded search for solutions to problems of complexity and of excessive workload for teachers and schools.

But there were to be no concessions on the third of the themes identified earlier as a major concern of teachers, the pace of change. Moreover, though seemingly willing to look at simplifying both the curriculum and the testing arrangements, the Secretary of State was still standing firm on the end-of-stage tests which had been such a central issue:

> ... I am clear that the 1993 tests must go ahead.
> It is vitally important that this Summer's tests take place unhindered so that we may collect hard evidence about what improvements need to be made to the tests for the future.

In other words, the tests are here to stay even if they may be 'simplified' in future and we will need 1993 evidence to enable us to maintain the momentum of test development.

The Dearing Review Phase 1

The day following the announcement of the Review *The Guardian*'s education correspondents were reporting that:

> John Patten, the Education Secretary, last night appeared to have lost his gamble that a review of the National Curriculum and testing would head off chaos in the schools this summer. (*The Guardian*, 8 April 1993)

The NAS/UWT confirmed its intention to proceed with the boycott already approved by its members through a ballot, the ATL would be going ahead with its ballot and, as expected, the NUT took a conference decision three days after the Review was announced to proceed with its ballot on a possible boycott.

Moreover, the decision to review had not even won the support of those the Secretary of State might have expected to find backing him. Amidst continuing doubts being voiced about the wisdom of going ahead as planned with the 1993 tests the Vice-Chairman of the Conservative Backbench Education Committee, Alan Haselhurst, aligned himself with the doubters:

> I am extremely worried about the gulf which is opening up between most of the teaching profession and the Secretary of State. I wonder how it is going to be possible to have meaningful tests this year if, in large parts of the country, no action is going to be taken. (quoted in *The Independent on Sunday*, 11 April 1993)

The early weeks of the Review were dominated by this continuing confrontation between the Government and the teachers' organizations over the 1993 tests. When in mid-May Sir Ron Dearing formally launched the consultation process associated with the Review, the Government chose, in advance of the Review, that same point to deal with some of the concerns which had been expressed about testing. John Patten announced a series of measures which would simplify testing and reduce workload:

(1) End-of-stage tests would only be mandatory for 7-year-olds and 14-year-olds in the core subjects.
(2) These tests would themselves be 'streamlined'.
(3) The merits of external marking of tests (thus reducing teacher work-load) at Key Stages 2 and 3 would be looked at.
(4) The 1994 tests at Key Stage 2 would be a national pilot with statutory testing a year later.
(5) There would no longer be an obligation on Key Stage 1 teachers to record and report their teacher assessments in subjects outside the core.

There was some criticism that these decisions were effectively pre-empting the outcomes of the Review though little disagreement with the measures as such. However, from the teachers' point of view, there was one basic problem with this wide-ranging package; none of it related to the immediate issue of the 1993 tests since none of the decisions was to be implemented until 1994. The Secretary of State remained adamant:

It would be a betrayal of a further generation of pupils to postpone what are acknowledged on all sides to be much-needed educational reforms. It would be to set aside the tremendous efforts made by the great majority of hard-working teachers to implement the National Curriculum since 1989. Tests for 7-year-olds are in their third year. We know that they work. Tests in 1991 and 1992 have improved standards of teaching and learning. Last year's pilot tests for 14-year-olds were well-received: attendance went up on test days. (Statement to the House of Commons, 11 May 1993)

In a few short sentences John Patten had given the House an upbeat progress report on the implementation of national assessment. But he had done nothing to draw the sting from the teacher organizations already embarked on a course of boycotting the assessment requirements in 1993. The ATL had announced at the end of April a five to one majority of the Association's members in support of a boycott. A few days after the Commons statement the NUT announced the result of its ballot; an overwhelming 96 per cent of those voting favoured a boycott.

Editorials in the broadsheet press were, without exception, unimpressed by the Secretary of State's attempt to resolve the dispute. 'A messy compromise' was *The Daily Telegraph*'s judgment, 'A statement written in the ink of panic' that of *The Times*. Like its competitors *The Independent* argued that the Secretary of State should have proceeded with the 1993 tests on a voluntary basis, reluctantly accepting the obvious fact that widespread non-cooperation would make them invalid for the purpose of national comparisons. *The Guardian* (12 May 1993) summed up the continuing impasse in a sentence:

Promising a ceasefire next year means that there will be no peace this year.

Once again the military metaphor seemed sadly appropriate for what remained an educational battlefield.

By this time John Patten was looking increasingly isolated in his attempts to insist that the 1993 tests went ahead according to plan. A letter warning headteachers and governors of their statutory duty to ensure that the tests were implemented had a frosty reception from organizations representing those groups:

> We regard this (letter) as very bad advice. If governors felt that they might be at any time used as a coercion instrument you would get mass resignations. (Walter Ulrich, National Asociation of Governors and Managers, quoted in the *Financial Times*, 22 April 1993)

> The general exhortation to do one's duty will not go down well because this great difficulty is not of our making and we advised him time and again on how to avoid it. (John Sutton, Secondary Heads' Association, quoted in the *Financial Times*, 22 April 1993)

An advertising campaign to explain testing to parents was represented by the Opposition as a desperate attempt, using taxpayers' money, to justify Government policy on national assessment. To judge from opinion polls, many parents remained at best unconvinced of the value of the reforms which has been so central to Government policy. A Gallup poll reported in *The Daily Telegraph* found only 58 per cent of the public supporting the National Curriculum, 50 per cent in favour of testing at the ages of 7, 11 and 14 and no less than 62 per cent sympathizing with the teachers' boycott of the 1993 tests. An NOP poll for *The Independent* of parents with children aged between 5 and 16 reported 70 per cent of respondents believing league tables of test results to be misleading against 27 per cent supporting publication of them. Later in the month, a survey by the National Confederation of Parent Teacher Associations (NCPTA) found 76 per cent of primary PTAs opposed to the tests for 7-year-olds being completed in 1993 and 78 per cent of secondary PTAs against the tests at 14. A spokeswoman, Margaret Morrissey, for the Confederation commented:

> Most parents see no good reason for subjecting their children to hours of tests which are basically flawed, administratively cumbersome and time-consuming. (quoted in *The Guardian*, 28 May 1993)

On top of this, the erosion of support for the Secretary of State from the political Right was underlined by the much-publicized resignations from the SEAC Council of Lord Skidelsky and Dr John Marenbon who, as Chairman of the Council's English Committee, had been at the centre of the row over testing English. Both had been regarded as appointees who would strengthen the influence of the Right on policy advice from the SEAC but both had clearly had enough. In explaining his resignation, Dr. Marenbon described the English tests as 'inadequate and unfair' and the overall timetable for implementing testing as 'impossible' (quoted in the *Financial Times*, 6 May 1993)

Lord Skidelsky was equally outspoken in his criticism both of the Government's testing policy and of the Dearing Review. His verdict on the tests was damning:

> . . . they take an enormous amount of time to administer. They are not very reliable because they are not externally marked. The cost of getting them all consistent with each other is absolutely enormous. (writing in the *Sunday Mirror*, 9 May 1993)

His favoured solution was 'two forms of tests' — teacher assessment as part of routine classroom work and end of stage tests for use in published league tables. As to the Review, he believed it to have been set up in the way it had 'so it would be controlled by the Department of (sic) Education' which was 'looking for a superficial fix rather than a fundamental review of the system which is in crisis'.

By early June the Secretary of State was being given an angry, contemptuous reception by headteachers at the NAHT annual conference and teachers' union leaders were claiming that the boycott of Key Stage 3 tests was '99.9 per cent effective' (*The Independent*, 8 June 1993). Independent evidence from school inspectors confirmed the effectiveness of the Key Stage 3 boycott and the inspectors also found that, while most primary schools had conducted the tests for 7-year-olds, none of the forty-nine schools included in their survey would be passing on the results to LEAs, thus thwarting the Government's intended publication of league tables. The planned piloting of tests for 11-year-olds was also being jeopardized by the small number of schools volunteering to participate.

Supposedly national tests had reached the farcical point of the London *Evening Standard* reporting (7 June 1993) that 'only one school in inner London admitted to carrying out the English paper set by Whitehall for 14-year-olds'. In an attempt to regain the initiative the DFE published the Key Stage 3 English test and one newspaper — *The Guardian* — printed the test in full. But by now even the *Daily Mail*, usually an enthusiastic supporter of Government education policy, was conceding (8 June 1993) that 'teachers, also, have a point', referring to the English tests being 'bounced on the profession with inadequate preparation' and to the test marking scheme as 'a bureaucratic monstrosity sixty-six pages long'.

Towards Interim Recommendations

If there was one thing which Sir Ron Dearing had going for him in attempting to rescue Government policy from crisis it was the fact that the system he was reviewing had reached the point where no-one except the ministers responsible seemed to have much of a good word to say for it. Whatever the actual progress made in implenting curriculum and assessment policy, the public perception was of a system which was breaking down, with the teachers' action being seen as a symptom of deep-seated problems rather than the cause. Indeed, after the first of many meetings at which Dearing met groups of teachers, the *Daily Telegraph* headlined its report: 'Teachers are asked to rescue policy on testing' (11 May 1993).

From early on in the Review Sir Ron Dearing made it very much a personal initiative with his readiness to meet interested parties and to travel up and down the country attending consultation conferences. The absence of any previous involvement with policy on schools at a national level and his frequently asserted open mind on the matters he was reviewing enabled him to win the confidence of teachers, organizations in education and most sections of the press:

> He is a teamwork man, a prodigious worker, straight-dealing and apolitical having worked with ministers as politically diverse as Sir Keith Joseph and Tony Benn while a civil servant. (Clare Dean, *The Times Educational Supplement*, 28 May 1993)

It had been some years since the word 'apolitical' had been used to describe someone in a central policy-making role in relation to the National Curriculum and its assessment.

Through May and June questionnaires were sent to schools and organizations, conferences were held, articles soliciting responses were published in *The Times Educational Supplement* and the general impression was given of a man genuinely in search of answers which would take account of teachers' experiences to date and provide a workable model for the future. Some press coverage was given to submissions from the main teacher organizations, setting out their views on the issues, but there was no advance indication of the line which Sir Ron Dearing would take in his advice.

As the educational world awaited Dearing's report, the context for policy was in fact no different from the situation either side of Easter when the problems surrounding National Curriculum and assessment had been a regular headline matter for the press. The teachers' boycott was proving to be highly effective in undermining Government policy on assessment. Even at Key Stage 1, where pupils in many schools had already taken the tests, it was reported (*The Guardian*, 22 July 1993) that only between 3 per cent and a third of schools (the proportions varied in different LEAs) were passing on the information about pupil attainment, thus thwarting the Government's intended publication of league tables. But, while a solution was being sought, a temporary unofficial ceasefire in the hostilities between Government and the teachers came into effect.

When *The National Curriculum and its Assessment: Interim Report* was published at the beginning of August 1993 several of its recommendations related to the curriculum elements in Dearing's brief. Each Subject Order, it recommended, should be divided into a statutory core and an optional element, the teaching of which would be at the discretion of the school and the teacher. Further, there would for the first time since the 1988 Act be 'a clear policy framework for each Key Stage' and a specified 'appropriate margin of time' at each key stage for the teacher to make use of as he/she saw fit. Teachers' calls had been heeded both for a reduced statutory requirement and for sufficient flexibility to allow the teacher and the school to shape the curriculum to meet the circumstances of the locality, the class and the individual pupil. Decisions on how and when to implement this reduction in statutory specification and what to recommend as the common curriculum requirements for Key Stage 4 were deferred until the second part of the review.

In many ways the main thrust of Dearing's recommendations on curriculum was predictable. Once the Government had signalled the need to 'slim down' the National Curriculum it was the details of how far, when and by whom that remained to be decided and, perhaps, argued about. But it was the assessment of that National Curriculum which had brought the Government's education policy to the point of crisis and it was on his recommendations in respect of assessment that the success of Dearing's proposals would depend.

On some aspects of assessment policy the recommendations were, like the associated proposals on curriculum, a natural extension of the thinking which had informed the brief Dearing had been given. National testing at Key Stages 1, 2 and 3 should, it was proposed, be limited 'for the next three years' to the core subjects. These tests, he argued, 'have a key role to play':

> They provide a reliable means of establishing levels of achievement by pupils in schools throughout the country. In addition they contribute to the moderation of teacher assessment and provide hard information upon which a school can make judgments about the targeting of resources and the definition of in-service training priorities. They also, as the Office for Standards in Education has reported, play an important part in raising professional expectations about what pupils can achieve. (para 1.14)

No concessions there to those in the teaching profession who had argued for abandoning national testing but rather a reassertion, in terms which must have been welcome to Government ministers, of the case for standard tests if only in the three core subjects.

More welcome to teachers was Dearing's acceptance, at least in principle, of the importance of teacher assessment. His recommendations on this were couched in equally broad terms and again stressed purposes:

> Teacher assessment lies at the heart of the learning progress (sic) in that the new learning must be matched to what a pupil already knows and can do. It is the teacher in his/her classroom who, day in day out, undertakes this vitally important task of formative assessment. (para. 1.13)

The deliberate blurring of the distinction between teacher assessment and testing, a feature of the national assessment debate going back to the TGAT Report, was now being challenged.

But what would teacher assessment being 'vitally important' actually mean in practice? For the assessing of science at Key Stage 1 it was proposed that statutory teacher assessment should be, for 1994 at least, the means by which attainment scores would be determined. And for 'reporting to parents and others by whatever means' teacher assessment and national test results would be given equal standing at Key Stages 1, 2 and 3. However, the wider question of whether teacher assessment should be a statutory requirement in any of the non-core subjects at any of the key stages after 1994 was left until Dearing's Final Report, due in December.

In fact most of the difficult assessment issues, though discussed at the interim report stage, were left until the second part of the Dearing Review. The Interim Report was a redefining of the assessment policy agenda, including ideas about assessment of the value added by schools and alternative approaches to quality assurance in schools, both of which would be further investigated. Though a new model for national assessment was not yet apparent, the TGAT view of how pupils should be assessed was, for the first time in the five-and-a-half years since its publication, being officially questioned. This was evident from the first of the issues which would be considered in the course of further consultation prior to a Final Report:

> Should the ten-level scale be modified or should a new approach to the assessment of pupil progress be developed, which, while retaining a significant element of criterion-referencing, abandons the attempt to measure achievement from 5–16 on any single scale? (para. 1.8)

To add to the continuing uncertainty about every aspect of national assessment except what would be tested in 1994 (the May announcement), there was Sir Ron Dearing's unwillingness to becoming involved in what remained the most basic issue dividing the teachers and the Government:

> There have . . . been strong representations from teachers and their associations about the use of national tests for performance tables. The use of such tables lies outside the scope of this Review. (para. 1.11)

Sir Ron was not averse to redefining his remit when it suited him. For example, continuity of curriculum post-16 was acknowledged as 'not within my remit' but that did not prevent him from proposing (para. 3.28) further consultation on the issue. On performance tables, however, Dearing clearly understood that was one aspect of Government policy which was not for him to question in public.

Such a deflecting of the issue of league tables in the Interim Report meant that, when it came to a Government response, ministers were able to present their rethinking of that issue as an initiative on their part rather than a mere acceptance of what Dearing had put to them. It was the 'retreat' on league tables which attracted most publicity when, on the day Dearing's Interim Report was published, the Government's response was announced. 'Tables axed in schools U-turn' was the *Daily Express* headline explaining that 'league tables listing nationwide school-by-school results are to be scrapped' (3 August 1993). Only for pupils at 11 were national league tables of school results to be retained and they would only be introduced at the earliest in 1996 as the tests for that age group had 'settled down'. According to *The Sun*, taking a rare interest in education policy matters, 'teachers were cock-a-hoop at a massive Government climbdown on school tests and the National Curriculum' (3 August 1993). As well as the performance tables issue much was made by the press of the decision to halve the testing and marking time for tests at Key Stages 1 and 3.

For *The Guardian*, publication of the Report was 'humiliating' for the Government. Certainly the acceptance of Dearing's recommendations by Lady Blatch, standing in for the Secretary of State during John Patten's absence through ill-health, represented a backing down from the 'no compromise' line taken during the period leading up to the announcement of the Review. It was clear also that the Report had succeeded in winning over most of those who had been criticizing Government policy. The Association of Teachers and Lecturers pronounced it 'brave, bold and refreshingly pragmatic' (*Daily Telegraph*, 3 August 1993) while the NAS/UWT, whose action had brought matters to a head, was reported to have 'warmly welcomed the report for its "banning of bureaucracy and restoration of professionalism"' (*The Independent*, 3 August 1993). Some remained to be convinced, with the NUT offering the most cautious of the union reactions and Lord Skidelsky 'expressing strong opposition to the decision not to publish league tables for 14-year-olds or introduce external marking of tests' (*Financial Times*, 3 August 1993). But while much of the press chose the angle that the onus was now on teachers to make the new arrangements work there were few dissenting voices heard on the substance of Dearing's proposals.

And yet, how many of the fundamental points of difference between the Government and teachers had actually been removed by Dearing's Interim Report and ministers' acceptance of it? True, there would be fewer and shorter 'pencil-and-paper tests' but tests there would still be in the core subjects. True also that performance tables of school results at Key Stages 1 and 3 would no longer be published nationally but they were still to be made available for publication locally. And the prospect of national tables of 11-year-olds' results remained. Testing and league tabling were not being abandoned but they were being significantly reduced in their scope.

What of the future for those who were arguing against the over-simplifications inherent in short, written tests and in publishing raw results? Yes, it was proposed that teacher assessment would have equal status to testing and that ways of calculating the value added by a school would be investigated. But would 'equal status' mean equal priority for teacher assessment in policy and in resources? And was the promised investigation into value added anything more than a gesture to the critics of performance tables? There was no doubt that, in the short term, Sir Ron Dearing had won the confidence of many by listening to criticisms and producing a carefully crafted report to which most interested parties were able to give a warm welcome. A significant reduction in teacher workload could be expected from the combined effects of reduction in testing and the easing of expectations to record attainments in detail.

There was a renewed if cautiously expressed sense of hope, an almost palpable sense of relief that something had been retrieved from what the *Daily Express* (3 August 1993) referred to as 'five years of classroom confusion'. But a more considered judgment on Sir Ron Dearing's achievement ('it appears he may be a magician as well as a fixer' — *The Guardian*) would only be possible after two further stages in the process he had begun. Still to come in 1993 was the attempt to find a revised and workable model for national assessment. Beyond lay the practicalities of implementing that new model. It was easy to forget in the heady days of August 1993 that the TGAT proposals had been widely welcomed in March 1988.

The Dearing Review Phase 2

Through the autumn of 1993 a series of consultation meetings, on a smaller scale than in the first phase but still extensive, helped shape the Dearing Final Report which was submitted to ministers in December and published in January 1994. Again there was little indication in advance of the report's publication as to how Dearing would attempt to tackle some of the more intractable matters on which further work had been signalled in August. In respect of assessment, the major issue identified for consultation in the review's second phase had been: 'should the ten-level scale be modified to make it more effective or should a new approach to the assessment of pupil progress be developed?' (Dearing, 1993, para. 1.8).

One of the most striking characteristics of the Final Report is the forthrightness with which some of the judgments on the pre-existing system are expressed. For example:

> The ten-level scale is unnecessarily complex and excessively prescriptive. It suffers from duplication and inconsistencies. These failings explain some of the very real problems teachers have experienced in implementing the National Curriculum. (para. 2.28)
> . . . we have created an over-elaborate system which distorts the nature of different subjects, which serves to fragment teaching and learning in that teachers are planning work from the statements of attainment, and which has at times reduced the assessment process to a meaningless ticking of myriad boxes. (para. 7.25)

If the system was that bad, how did Dearing suggest such weaknesses could be eliminated?

Simplifying National Assessment

In part the remedy was to lie in carrying through the logic of 'slimming down' and 'simplifying' so that, not only would the curriculum content as defined in statutory programmes of study be reduced, but the assessment framework and the assessment procedures would also be more limited in scale and scope. On the attainment targets, there were to be fewer of them, especially at Key Stages 1 and 2. Within those fewer targets there would also be a 'substantial reduction in the number of statements of attainment' (para. 2.33). On end-of-stage testing, the tests would remain confined to the core subjects, SCAA would continue to simplify them and the time needed to administer them would be further reduced.

On statutory teacher assessment and on record-keeping there was also some reassurance for those teachers who saw the main problem as the scale of the undertaking and the burden that imposed on the teacher. Teacher assessment would remain a statutory requirement only in the core subject at Key Stages 1, 2 and 3. On record-keeping, for the first time since national assessment had been introduced and the form a teacher's record should take had become a major concern for teachers, there was an authoritative statement (appendix 6) on what was expected. Clearly designed to allay teacher anxiety and answer the charge of excessive workload in record-keeping and reporting, much of it is concerned to clarify what is *not* a requirement. For example:

There are **no requirements to keep records in any particular manner** nor to keep records against individual statements of attainment. Also, there is *no* requirement to keep evidence of the attainments of every pupil in every attainment target. (appendix 6, para. 6)

The other clear recommendation from Dearing was the decision to retain a GCSE seven-point grading scale from A to G with the sole addition of a 'starred A' for the highest levels of achievement. It would no longer be necessary for the examination boards to try to work out how to apply the ten-level scale to GCSE examinations and users of GCSE certificates would be spared the problems of trying to understand equivalences between the A-G scale and its ten-level replacement. In this respect, as in several others, the Dearing Final Report was conclusive in its separating out of Key Stage 4 curriculum and assessment policy from the three preceding stages. Not only would the established pre-National Curriculum grading scale for the GCSE be retained but there would be reporting of performance only at the whole subject level (not for each attainment target) and the trend towards a distinct vocational element in the curriculum was confirmed with the introduction of the General National Vocational Qualification (GNVQ) as an option for this age group. These decisions 'simplified' the National Curriculum policy picture only in the sense that they finally removed the link between Key Stage 4 and national assessment at Key Stages 1-3. In fact of course, they relocated the issue of how to assess attainment at that Key Stage and placed it within the policy debate about the curriculum and assessment framework for the 14–19 age group.

Some Issues not yet Resolved

Yet, for all the stated firmness of intention to continue to 'simplify' the national assessment system, there were many matters on which the Dearing Final Report signalled still further work before a policy decision would be taken.

On testing outside the core at Key Stage 3: 'after 1996, it may be right to consider the introduction of tests in other subjects' (para. 9.12). Exactly when statutory teacher assessment would be reintroduced in the core subjects at Key Stage 3 was also unclear; only that it would occur when the Curriculum Orders had been revised and 'the schools have had time to adapt to them' (para. 2.46). A similar uncertainty remained about future teacher assessment requirements in the non-core foundation subjects; that was another decision deferred until after the new Curriculum Orders had been implemented.

The optimistic teacher, impressed by Dearing's evident determination to simplify the assessment requirements, could read into the Report a future system with no more statutory testing and teacher assessment than would be in place in 1994. But the less trusting critic might read into the same Report the prospect of end-of-stage tests being reintroduced outside the core at Key Stage 3 and of statutory teacher assessment once more becoming a requirement in non-core subjects at Key Stages 1, 2 and 3.

On other matters, not so much of the scale and scope of national assessment but rather of how the system might be modified to respond to identified concerns, the Final Report was a model of reasonableness without giving a clear indication of how, if at all, policy would change.

A chapter considering 'Children with special educational needs' was evidence of a long overdue attempt to think through more clearly the implications of the system for pupils for whom 'the steps of progress may be small compared to those of other pupils, (although) they often represent huge progress for individual children' (para. 6.6). But Sir Ron recommended only that 'the assessment and recording of achievement by pupils with special educational needs should be reviewed' (para. 6.8).

The moderation of teacher assessment was another issue acknowledged to be important if teacher assessment was to have the significant role assigned to it in Dearing's Interim Report. But the extent and character of such moderation was not a matter addressed in the Final Report. Instead, Dearing rehearsed the broad issues of principle and promised further work before the system could have a clearly understood and effective set of moderation procedures:

> An effective system of moderated teacher assessment at the end of each key stage is needed to underpin the criteria. But great care must be taken to assess the 'opportunity costs' of any moderation system.

> We must balance the need for objective scrutiny of the marking standards in individual schools against the very considerable costs in teachers' time that such a system inevitably involves. (para. 7.7)

When it came to the recording, reporting and publication end of the system, Dearing also had little specific to offer beyond the guidance on simplification in appendix 6. Those who had hoped that the retreat from publishing school performance tables at Key Stages 1 and 3, announced by the Government in August, would be followed by a firm commitment to the performance data which remained being published on a 'value added' basis were to be disappointed. This too was a decision for the future after the group appointed by the SCAA to advise on the value-added approach had reported.

On the central question posed in relation to assessment during the second phase of the review — the future of the ten-level scale — the longest chapter in the Final Report discussed at some length the various options (para. 7.12):

(i)   retain the ten-level scale for all foundation subjects;
(ii) modify the scale 'to minimize its imperfections';
(iii) abandon it and replace it with key stage grading scales;
(iv) use a modified ten-level scale for some subjects and key stage gradings for others.

Teacher opinion on the merits of the ten-level scale was split and there was evidently no consensus on what should replace it. The majority of specialist bodies consulted, including schools' inspectors (to whose 'clear recommendation' to retain the scale Dearing gives particular weight), favoured retention of the TGAT scale in modified form. The Report concluded that for a variety of reasons, not least the lack of a clearly superior alternative, 'we should devote our energies to an improved version of the ten-level scale' (para. 7.60).

But, although the decision to retain the ten-level scale was clear enough, perhaps the most critical area of continuing uncertainty lay in what was to happen to the statements of attainment set out at each of the ten levels in the assessment model which had emerged post-TGAT. The declared intention was to achieve:

> a substantial reduction in the number of statements of attainment to provide a definition of what is expected at each level, which is sufficiently clear and rigorous to be of use to teachers but which avoids the excessive detail of the present approach. (para. 2.33)

It was recognized, however, that simply reducing the number of statements of attainment might not do much to solve the problems being encountered. Tentatively, a more radical redefinition of this central component of the model was suggested:

> The opportunity might, rather, be taken to gather the main statements of attainment into clusters to create a more integrated description of what a pupil must know, understand and be able to do at each

level. The challenge in producing such 'level descriptors' would be to produce a statement which concentrates attention on the pupil's performance as a whole but which is nevertheless sufficiently sharp and meaningful to help secure reliable assessment across different schools. (para. 7.29)

Thus, in two sentences of an eighty-page Report, the possibility emerged of the criterial statements at the heart of the system — what TGAT had referred to as 'attainment targets' and had subsequently been developed as 'statements of attainment' — being rewritten as 'level descriptors'. It was not clear from a reading of the Report if those who favoured such a change were aware of the prior experience of such descriptors in other criteria-based systems or whether they appreciated how radical a step it would be for both testing and teacher assessment to abandon specific statements and substitute broad descriptors.

The Initial Response

It was on the main Dearing recommendations that the response of ministers and of the press would naturally concentrate. And it was the recommendations on the curriculum, as distinct from those on assessment, which were given most prominence in the press reporting of the Report and indeed by Dearing himself in an article, in *The Times* 'My start of term report' (6 January 1994).

As with the Interim Report there was no scope for the press to highlight differences between Dearing and ministers because, no doubt as a result of prior consultation before the text of the Report was finalized, the Government accepted the recommendations in their entirety. Instead, again echoing coverage of the Interim Report, some sections of the press made much of the extent to which the Dearing Review, forced upon it by teacher opposition to policy, represented an embarrassing retreat for the Government in general and for the Secretary of State for Education in particular. *The Daily Telegraph* chose 'Patten backs down on the National Curriculum' as its headline for a report of the Dearing recommendations; *Today* preferred 'Take six of the best young Patten'. *The Independent* (6 January 1994) was critical of the Government:

Seek a guiding intelligence behind the Government's education policy, and you will search in vain.

... the fact is that the ministers never planned or wanted this review; it was forced on them by teachers' boycotting last summer's tests, and its outcome represents a comprehensive capitulation to professional pressure.

but supportive of Dearing:

Item by item, Sir Ron's proposals are practical and laudable.

The majority of editorial opinion in the national press was equally sympathetic to Dearing's arguments and backed most of his recommendations. *The Times* (6 January 1994), for example, while commenting that the retention of 'the unwieldy ten-level scale' was 'disappointing', concluded that:

> Sir Ron's sensible recommendations have given John Patten, the Education Secretary, an invaluable chance to remould the National Curriculum and restore its original purpose.

The Final Report was given a noticeably lower profile in the press than its predecessor. This was partly attributable to a perception that the main issues for the Government had already been resolved in August, though the resignation the previous day of Government Minister Tim Yeo also contributed to the relegation of National Curriculum policy to the inside pages. Yet, even at this early stage of the response to what was intended to be the basis for five years of stability in policy, some of the omens were unpromising. The reactions of most of the representatives of the teacher unions were cautiously positive:

> 'Teachers should recognise a victory when they see it'. (David Hart, NAHT, quoted in *The Guardian*, 6 January 1994)
> 'It will take some time for Dearing's reforms to be felt in the classroom. It will take some time for professional confidence to be restored'. (Peter Smith, ATL, quoted in *The Guardian*, 6 January 1994)
> 'The National Curriculum as proposed today is virtually unrecognizable from the Byzantine bureaucratic monster imposed by Kenneth Baker.' (Nigel de Gruchy, NAS/UWT, quoted in *The Independent*, 6 January 1994)

But the National Union of Teachers' General Secretary, Doug McAvoy, was in a far from conciliatory mood. His response would seem to confirm the view that some elements of the teaching profession were so opposed to any form of national assessment system that they would not be satisfied until the whole edifice had been dismantled:

> The tests will continue to be used for school comparisons and league table purposes, purposes to which we are fundamentally opposed. We continue to believe that the tests and statutory assessment cause additional and unnecessary work, are not supportive of learning and are of no value to parents. (quoted in *The Independent*, 6 January 1994)

Conclusion

The purposes of national assessment were once again surfacing as the underlying source of many of the problems in developing a consensus on policy. Indeed Dearing himself had stressed 'it is particularly important that we are clear about the purposes of national tests as distinct from those of teacher assessment' (Interim Report, para. 1.12). Within a year of his appointment Dearing had repaired some of the damage caused to public and professional confidence in the national assessment system during the 1992/93 winter of educational discontent. The system had been subjected to a genuine review in the course of which all the many problems emerging from five years of experience had been identified and discussed with all of those who might have a contribution to make to reconstruction.

Yet some of the more fundamental problems encountered in developing a national system of assessment remained unresolved and, arguably, some had not even been clearly diagnosed. The national tests were still in place but only just, with no immediate prospect of the necessary participation by all schools across the country. Though the cost of it all was seldom an issue highlighted by the opponents of testing, it could clearly be argued that the £4 million spent in 1993 on the direct costs alone of producing and distributing the Key Stage 3 tests was not yet showing much of a return on investment.

Dearing had undoubtedly retrieved the situation politically but there remained a gulf separating a substantial section of teacher opinion from the main thrust of Government policy. That gulf was less about the practices of assessment than about the purposes which a national system should serve and about which of those purposes should have priority. The process had began of creating an alternative set of national assessment arrangements to replace the TGAT approach which remained, even after Dearing's two reports, the only fully and coherently argued attempt to devise a model for National Curriculum assessment.

8   Policies and Policy-Making

Introduction

Of the several major reforms introduced through the 1988 Education Act, the plans to assess all pupils at regular intervals throughout their schooling were among the most ambitious and the most radical. By comparison the National Curriculum itself, though a clear break with the post-war convention that the school curriculum should be determined locally, was conservative in its design. Indeed some observers, critical of the National Curriculum's definition in subject terms, made much of the similarities between the 1988 curriculum specification and the school curriculum regulations of the nineteenth and early twentieth centuries.

Much of the ambition of the policy of national assessment lay in the very idea of assessing all pupils (over 600,000 pupils in each year group) in the state-maintained schools of England and Wales. They were to be assessed across all aspects of their attainment in ten subjects (eleven in Wales) for the eleven years of compulsory schooling from the age of 5 to the age of 16. Most of the pre-existing assessment arrangements were administered either by local education authorities (for example, 11+ selection) or by the several independent examination boards (public examinations for 16-year-olds and 18-year-olds). A national system, the Assessment of Performance Unit, was in place to monitor attainment in certain areas of the curriculum but, for that purpose, it needed to test only a small sample of pupils and it had scaled down its original plans to assess a broader range of attainments.

The scale of the enterprise, inherent in the number of pupils involved and the breadth of attainment encompassed by the scope of the National Curriculum, was not the only sense in which the policy would be ambitious. Any review of that policy in its early years of design and implementation must also take note of the ways in which policy-makers in the Government and the system-designers appointed by the Government, drawn mainly from among professionals in education, turned an inherently large-scale project into one which had many radical features and was exceptionally ambitious in its aspirations.

Some of the radicalism stemmed from the thinking of politicians and their closest advisers. Since the early 1980s Government ministers had been drawn to assessment as the main vehicle for redefining curriculum priorities and, in so doing, to 'raise standards'. Sir Keith Joseph's advocacy, and carrying through, of the GCSE was the prototype for assessment-led curriculum change, a test-bed for some of the ideas which would become the basis for national assessment policy. It was Joseph who was the first Government minister, in his 1984 Sheffield speech, to propose specific attainment objectives as a vital element in any attempt to raise attainment standards. It was Joseph who argued that a wider range of assessment methods, including assessment by teachers in the classroom, was essential if attainment was to be more broadly defined. And it was Joseph who was among the most enthusiastic of converts to the idea of measuring attainment in relation to pre-specified criteria rather than on the well-established norm-referenced scales where pupils were compared only with each other.

But much of the radicalism also stemmed from the advice given to ministers by educationists who had their own views of what national assessment could achieve. Their ideas, while in conflict with those on the political Right, who were to voice frequent concerns that the Government was too ready to compromise with professional interest groups, were at least as far-reaching but often grounded in different assumptions and aspiring to different goals. The most notable example of educationists exerting substantial influence on national assessment policy was the work of the Task Group on Assessment and Testing. In the early years of national assessment, as the TGAT vision of the future was being obscured by pragmatic, piecemeal policy-making, the case for a different, professionally-oriented approach to assessment was often articulated by teachers and assessment specialists. This is not the place for a detailed analysis of the academic critique of national assessment policy but, as evidence of implementation became available, such a critique was developing in the columns of academic journals and the educational press (see the bibliography for selected references). Throughout the early years of implementation a polarization of opinion can be observed on both the aims of national assessment policy and on the practices best fitted to meeting preferred priorities.

Policy Dilemmas: Sources

The seeds of the problems which surfaced in subsequent years and which ultimately led to the bitter harvest of the crisis of 1993 were sown in 1987. It was in 1987 that the decision was taken to legislate for an assessed National Curriculum, that the Government received an electoral mandate which would give it at least five years for implementation and that the Task Group on Assessment and Testing prepared its proposals.

Against the advice of many of the Government's Right-wing supporters the then Secretary of State for Education and Science, Kenneth Baker, proposed a National Curriculum which, while conservatively expressed as a list of school subjects, was broadly conceived. That breadth was present both in the number of subjects to be made statutory and in the range of attainments to be encompassed. Such breadth was greeted with suspicion by many on the Right (including Baker's predecessor, Sir Keith Joseph), who would have preferred a minimally-defined curriculum concentrating on 'the three Rs', but was welcomed by many education professionals (see Haviland, 1988).

From the perspective of the Right, Baker compounded the error of a relatively broad statutory curriculum by proposing an assessment system which would not be confined to the core subjects but would also operate across the cumbersomely-termed 'non-core foundation subjects' (i.e. the rest). Only for art, music and physical education was it hinted that some subjects might not be given the full national assessment treatment. Even the fact that the Prime Minister, Margaret Thatcher, strongly favoured a narrowly-focused system of conventional written tests did not prevent Baker from embarking on a large-scale, wide-ranging programme of national assessment.

Into this essentially political process, of a Secretary of State shaping policy against the background of a range of opinions within his own Party, were introduced the first appointed groups largely comprising professional educationists. While non-educationist members were included in these groups — the subject working groups for mathematics and science and the Assessment Task Group — the groups' thinking on curriculum and assessment was inevitably much influenced by the specialist members with experience in those fields. The two subject groups were set up and produced interim reports ahead of the Task Group and were beginning to develop their own views on how best to define and measure attainment (see in particular the Interim Report of the Science Working Group) when the TGAT Report came on the scene as the first and, in the event, only fully developed design brief for national assessment policy.

The TGAT Legacy

It is to TGAT, rather than to ministers or their political advisers, that we can attribute many of the defining features of national assessment policy (see chapter 2). In their responses to the 1987 consultation paper many of those expressing concerns about the likely effects of national assessment had alerted the Government to questions based on experience of assessment in practice. Questions such as:

- Which of the several stated purposes of assessment would be uppermost in the minds of those designing the system and of the teachers implementing it?
- Would the methods used really be as varied and as sensitive to different individuals' attainments as was promised or would the suspected preferences of many Conservatives for simple written tests prevail?
- Would the aggregated results be handled with care or trumpeted as crude performance indicators by those whose main reason for favouring national assessment was that it would give parents the information they needed on which to base a choice of school?

In effect, TGAT's response to those questions was that there were no irreconcilable tensions in such matters. If the system was designed and implemented with care according to the Task Group's specification, all the various aims could be realized and the fears of educationists could be allayed. The details of that specification are set out in chapter 2 but it is worth drawing attention to the ways in which fundamental policy dilemmas were played down in the Task Group's recommendations. Some of these dilemmas have become more apparent as implementation has proceeded but many were noted in the period immediately following publication of the TGAT Report (see, for example, Torrance, 1988).

For TGAT, the several uses of attainment information were not incompatible with each other but could be viewed as data from a common source which would be processed and acted upon in different ways. The commonly accepted 'backwash' effect, through which the use of attainment data colours the way teachers teach and the way pupils learn, would not it seemed be a problem if, as the Group advocated, the system was designed with formative assessment as a central principle. In particular, the effects of publishing results on a school-by-school basis, argued by many as damaging to public perceptions and pupil performance, would, it was suggested, be minimized if results were available only to parents and were accompanied by written reports placing each school in its socioeconomic context.

Thus, in dealing with the use of data, the Task Group sought not wholly convincing ways of allaying professional anxieties. In respect of assessment methods, it went beyond the cautiously reassuring into the world of 'standard assessment tasks'. Challenging popular perceptions of a dualism of examination papers and coursework (in public examinations) or tests and routine classwork (in schools' own assessment procedures), the Group portrayed all assessment as a seamless web of methods from the highly formalized to the most subtle interaction between teacher and pupil. Not only would such tasks take on an almost infinite variety of forms (see para. 48 of the Report) but they would be integrated into classroom teaching, obscuring the conventional distinction between assessment and teaching. It was an exceptionally ambitious concept. For those who were suspicious of any attempt by educationists to subvert straightforward testing and even for those who were attracted to the idea of standard assessment tasks, there must have been more than a few doubts about the feasibility of using them as a starting point for national assessment.

The Consequences of Criterion-referencing

Another radical feature of the Task Group proposals, the use of criterion-referencing, can be seen more as a matter of convergence of policy ideas between educationists, interested in using assessment formatively, and the political Right, keen to ensure that educational objectives were more clearly defined and more effectively measured. Central though criterion-referencing was to the Task Group's 'principles', the Group was, in advocating this basis for measuring and reporting attainment, echoing the case for criterion-referencing already being made by some in the Conservative Party, notably Sir Keith Joseph.

Both sources of support for criterion-referenced assessment were sustained in part by a hoped-for greater clarity of curriculum definition, with the potential benefits of feedback for the learner and the teacher as well as more meaningful measures of the outcomes of schooling which were important to politicians anxious about national standards. The first TGAT principle — that assessment results should give direct information about pupils' achievement in relation to objectives — might seem at first sight to be unexceptionable. What could be more reasonable than to abandon the opaqueness of norm-referenced letters or percentages and to report instead in terms of what had been learned? The arguments in principle in support of criterion-referencing are indeed persuasive and the TGAT Report makes a compelling case for its use. However, the chequered history of criterion-referenced assessment in other educational contexts, especially in the United States, might have cautioned the Group as to its feasibility for a multipurpose national assessment system (for a recent cautionary review see Wolf, 1993).

The radicalism of TGAT did not lie only in its advocacy of assessment being related to attainment criteria; the Task Group also proposed the describing, subject by subject, of 'expected routes of educational development, giving some continuity to a pupil's assessment at different ages' (para. 5). Most pre-existing assessment systems, in the UK as elsewhere in the world, were age-related. The TGAT view of progression, again widely endorsed by educationists as right in principle, not only presented the system-designers with the challenge of defining attainment criteria. Those who were given the job of drafting the criteria would also have to write them in such a way that they could be used in describing the performance of a pupil of any age between 5 and 16. The ten-level scale they proposed was indeed a bold enterprise even for those relatively few specialists who had already laboured, with limited success, to define the nature of progression within a subject field.

By proposing the defining of attainment in terms of criterial statements which were not linked to pupils' ages, the Task Group did more than challenge the system-designers. They put in place a type of reporting scale which would not readily lend itself to reliable reporting at the end of each Key Stage. Though it was not recognized by policy-makers at the time, such a scheme for defining attainment would never be capable of fulfilling the purposes of those in the Conservative Party who wanted national assessment to yield for each of several age groups a few limited, relatively precise indicators as a basis for comparisons across the system. Educationists and schoolteachers would subsequently spend long hours trying to devise, implement and operate assessment criteria expressed as statements of attainment set out at ten levels and grouped under attainment targets. Those who had seen national assessment as a way of clarifying and improving 'standards' were left bemused and frustrated by an assessment system which seemed incapable of giving clear answers to questions such as 'How well can 7-year-olds count?' or 'What are the trends in the ability of 11-year-olds to read?'. Some critics mounted a strong attack on the suitability of the ten-level scale as a basis for calibration of national standards (see, for example, Marks, 1991 and 1993).

Honest Idealism or Deliberate Subversion?

There have been many post-mortems on TGAT's legacy to national assessment policy. Almost all those who have criticized the TGAT model have failed to acknowledge that the Task Group's Reports were a design brief, ready to be filled out, trialled and modified, and not a fully-developed blueprint for the system. TGAT *was* extraordinarily ambitious but it is important to remember that some of its proposals were not implemented (Black, 1993) and that the interpretation and implementation of those ideas which were taken up was done at a pace the Group would not have endorsed. The Group was disbanded in March 1988 after publication of its Three Supplementary Reports and before the Government had indicated its position on any of the Group's recommendations.

TGAT's critics on the Right have tended to blame the Task Group for the system's subsequent failure to achieve what they saw as national assessment's main purposes — the provision of summative information about individuals and evaluative data to be used to judge how well the system was performing. For the more conspiracy-minded among them the TGAT Report was yet another 'educational establishment' plot to subvert the aims of Government policy. Even the Secretary of State responsible for setting up the Group and also for accepting its proposals was subsequently inclined to see malicious intent in the work of the SAT developers who interpreted the TGAT model. Reflecting in 1992 on what had gone wrong, Kenneth Baker referred to standard assessment tasks 'becoming positively Byzantine, deliberately I suspect' (*The Guardian*, 24 November 1992).

The simpler truth of the matter is that the Task Group's model was an honest attempt to reconcile the irreconcilable. It was the only model on offer to Kenneth Baker in 1988 and, since it appeared to satisfy all the many demands he had set out in his briefing to TGAT, he accepted it. The signs were already there in the early warnings of academics (see, for example, Murphy, 1987) and in some of the more thoughtful responses to *The National Curriculum 5 to 16*. But what TGAT offered Baker politically was the prospect of an assessment system acceptable to most teacher opinion and thus removing the threat of immediate confrontation with the profession on the assessment and testing issue.

The educational idealism of the Task Group allied to the political radicalism of a Government committed to fundamental change in schools ensured that the TGAT model was adopted as the starting point for national assessment policy. What followed was several years of development during which some attempts were made by ministers to change parts of the system so that it better served the purposes to which they gave highest priority. But those years also saw the tensions and contradictions within the TGAT model exposed to the realities of implementation.

The Process of Design and Implementation

Following the Government's decision to accept the Task Group's recommendations on almost all matters, the TGAT Report became the central reference point for all the work, wherever undertaken, on designing and implementing national assessment. Within six months of Kenneth Baker's announcement that he had accepted most of the TGAT recommendations, the draft Statutory Orders for mathematics and for science had been published and the first contracts had been let to the agencies which would develop the testing of 7-year-olds. Three recurring characteristics of the design and implementation process can be seen with hindsight to have contributed over time to the crisis for national assessment policy which John Patten, the fourth Secretary of State for Education in the years which followed the 1988 Act, was to face in April 1993. The pace of change, the fragmentation of work on system design post-TGAT, and inconsistencies in decision-making all played their part in the decline from the hopes of Professor Black and his Task Group to the 'send for Ron Dearing' rescue exercise which John Patten instigated after five years of hectic and controversial development.

The Pace of Change

The Task Group had given considerable attention to a timetable for carrying through its proposals. Twenty-nine paragraphs of its Report are concerned with phasing, with the support structure which would be needed and with the in-service training implications. The key recommendation is unequivocal:

> We recommend that the new assessment system should be phased in over a period adequate for the preparation and trial of new assessment methods, for teacher preparation, and for pupils to benefit from extensive experience of the new curriculum. We estimate that this period needs to be at least five years from promulgation of the relevant attainment targets. (TGAT Report para. 199)

The Group's proposed sequence of events, including design, trialling, training and preparation, would have led to what it termed 'the first operational use of assessment at ages 7 and 14' at the end of the fourth year following the introduction of a statutory curriculum in the subjects being assessed (paras 190 and 196). The third of its Supplementary Reports further elaborated on 'a system of support' for implementation. On the TGAT timetable, the first use of statutory testing in mathematics and science would have occurred in the summer of 1993 with tests in other subjects and at other Key Stages to follow on a similar pattern of phasing. In fact, by that time Sir Ron Dearing was already embarked on his review and the Government policy on national assessment was in disarray.

In the event, the programme of implementation which the Government settled upon was intended to ensure that the system was up and running within a much shorter period. On the Government's preferred timetable all the preliminaries would have to be completed within three school years from the point at which curriculum implementation had begun. To take Key Stage 1 as the example, in the period from September 1989 to June 1991 the end-of-stage tests or SATs in mathematics and science (the first Curriculum Orders to be introduced) would have to be trialled and piloted. More generally, administrative arrangements would also have to be developed and put in place, as would the training the support systems required for the conduct, moderation and administration of the Key Stage tests. On top of that the most daunting timetable of all, if taken seriously, would be that for teacher assessment. With or without the relevant training and support, teachers would be expected, alongside implementing the new curriculum, to embark at short notice upon the process of assessing their students in relation to the new attainment targets.

Three main sets of effects can be attributed to what politicians referred to as 'a demanding timetable' but which teachers criticized from the outset as being unrealistic. The first was the recurring problem of decisions often being made about the next phase of development before the evidence from the previous phase had been collected, still less collated and analyzed. Test developers found themselves drafting reports for SEAC on the test cycle just completed at the same time as they were working on the test items which SEAC would have to approve for the following year. If the contract they were working to also happened to be up for renewal, some of their energies would also be going into developing a bid to meet the new specification. While the agencies awarded test development contracts were no doubt kept on their toes by the fast-moving events they were required to respond to, the frenetic atmosphere created in those circumstances did not lend itself to careful, evidence-based decision-making.

Substantial resources were in fact committed by SEAC to provide for independent evaluation of the new assessment system as it developed, with evaluation contracts being awarded separately from the in-house evaluation carried out by SEAC officials and the test development agencies themselves. But, more often than not, the reports of such evaluations came to be a source of embarrassment for the policy-makers. Typically published (or on occasions leaked) some months after the policy in question had been changed, or at least modified, they provided ready ammunition for critics of the system seeking evidence to challenge or discredit testing policy.

The second set of consequences for those at the policy-making end of the system was the inevitable prioritizing of some aspects of policy and the downgrading, conscious or unconscious, of others. The relative lack of attention to devising appropriate systems of moderation (see chapter 4) is one example of policy remaining underdeveloped in certain crucial respects while ministers, officials and the Government's advisers were preoccupied with the more obvious priority of ensuring that the tests would be in schools by the target dates set. On another aspect of policy, the deferring of decisions on how the results from testing would be reported and published (see chapter 6) can be explained in part as an illustration of the characteristically pragmatic approach of policy-makers, piecing together the components of national assessment rather than implementing a coherently designed system. But it is also true that everybody in a position to influence policy was so busy dealing with next week's deadlines that little attention was given to anything, however significant it might be in policy terms, which could be deferred until next month or next year.

The third effect of the Government's demanding/unrealistic timetable for implementing national assessment was the impact it had on the attitude of teachers to what was required of them. It was the cumulative weight of those requirements on teachers, the workload issue, which finally sparked their campaign for a fundamental review. But it was the speed at which they were expected to introduce not just a new curriculum but also the novel assessment arrangements which united all teachers, secondary and primary, in the eventual challenge to Government policy. Secondary teachers had protested in 1985 about how little time had been allowed for training and preparation before teaching to the new General Certificate of Secondary Education courses began in September 1986. But at least by Easter 1986 most of the GCSE syllabuses had been circulated, together with sample examination questions, and a national training programme was under way. National assessment implementation was on a much tighter schedule than that for GCSE with guidance often appearing many months after the process to which it related had begun.

When teachers were to ask the questions to which they required answers so that they could plan their teaching, the likely answer from those to whom they could turn at local or national level was, in effect, 'wait and see'. Ideally, teachers would have liked to know what form the end-of-stage tests would take *before* deciding on the teaching scheme for that Key Stage. In no instance was that possible; in most cases the test development process had not even begun. Given that teachers were also finding themselves in the largely unfamiliar world of criterion-referencing, the absence of any indication of the form tests would take was a real source of insecurity for many. One specific example from the many which could be quoted is the part which the shortness of notice to be given about the Key Stage 3 English tests played in discrediting those tests in the eyes of many secondary English teachers (see chapter 7). Another example, from the primary sector, was the appearance late in 1990 of the first official guidance for teachers at Key Stage 1 on teacher assessment, something which they had already been trying to interpret and implement for the previous eighteen months. While the style of testing was a major cause for concern among certain groups of teachers and the extra workload affected some more than others, the timetable for change was seen by all as being unreasonable.

Fragmentation in Policy-making

The processes through which the TGAT model was to be translated into a working system have already been outlined (chapter 2, p. 32); many of the problems which developed post-TGAT can be attributed to in-built weaknesses in those processes. In each of the groups and organizations concerned with developing national assessment, decisions were made about one component of the system without much regard for the impact of that decision on the system as a whole.

Some of the fragmentation arose from the way in which the Subject Orders were developed. Each subject working group, appointed by the Secretary of State, set about its task under the aegis of the Department for Education (with, for Welsh and for history, the Welsh Office also having a role). The brief each group was given included reference to the framework for national assessment. In the subjects tackled first the TGAT Report was the clear point of reference. The Mathematics Group, for example, was called upon to 'take account of . . . the work of the Task Group on Assessment and Testing' (*Mathematics for Ages 5 to 16*, 1988, p. 92). Two years later, the equivalent guidance to the History Group was that it should 'take account of . . . the broad framework for assessment and testing announced by the Government on 7 June 1988 and subsequent development of it in the light of advice from the School Examinations and Assessment Council' (*History for Ages 5 to 16*, 1990, p. 187). None of the working groups was encouraged to go beyond defining what the terms of reference typically referred to as 'a sound basis for assessment and testing'. The first two working groups were actually told not to concern themselves with assessment methods and procedures:

> The assessment instruments used, including tests, will be developed separately in the light of the working group's recommendations. (*Science for Ages 5 to 16*, 1988, p. 109)

This was modified in the terms of reference given to subsequent subject groups, for example:

> The attainment targets are expected to provide specific objectives so that pupils, teachers, parents and others have a clear idea of what is expected and there is a sound basis for assessment and testing. (*Modern Foreign Languages for Ages 11 to 16*, 1990, p. 120)

The message from such terms of reference was that the groups' task was one of *curriculum* definition, with assessment as a matter which they had to keep in mind but which was the concern of others who would do what was required after the working group had drafted the statutory curriculum. There were few signs in the composition of the groups that those responsible for forming the groups (ministers advised by their officials) thought assessment expertise should be available to the group from within. One can only speculate that curriculum and assessment were seen as essentially separate matters to be tackled in sequence, perhaps by so doing to deflect criticism that the National Curriculum would be 'an assessment-led curriculum'. In practice, there is no better way of ensuring that assessment drives the curriculum in inappropriate ways than to leave determination of assessment methods and procedures until after the curriculum itself has been finalized.

Given such terms of reference the subject working groups carried out their work with variable but often limited attention to assessment. Their progress towards recommendations took place behind closed doors until proposals, in the form of first Interim and then Final Reports, were revealed for comment and consultation. During that time the groups were administered and guided by DES officials. The Government's advisory bodies — NCC, SEAC and CCW — had no status or influence until the groups' proposals were made public and sent out for consultation. This meant that lessons being learned from the early development of National Curriculum and assessment (the kind of evidence which those advisory bodies were steadily accumulating) had less influence than it might have done on the thinking of the later groups. To take one example, the Geography Working Group was shown evidence by SEAC of the unworkability of the original Science Order's approach to statements of attainment — several hundred content-specific statements. The Geography Group, guided by DES officials that subject content must be specified in the attainment targets, chose to ignore that advice and proceeded to follow the Science Group's precedent.

Aside from the obvious fragmentation due to subject groups working in sequence and independently of each other (a weakness which was to some extent remedied in the way the 1993 Review was conducted) the agencies responsible for policy also contributed to the fragmented, and increasingly incoherent, process of development and implementation. At each Key Stage, test development proceeded apace, moderation arrangements were introduced, regulations for reporting to parents were drafted and the needs of the system centrally for data to be supplied by the schools were defined. Each new set of requirements impacted on the schools in its own way but no-one at the centre appeared to be considering either the cumulative effect on workload or the potential for those requirements to conflict one with another.

As discussed earlier (chapter 5) record-keeping is perhaps the best example of load being inadvertently increased and clarity of purpose being lost. Separate and conflicting demands were made on the procedures which had to link the gathering of evidence of attainment, through tests and teacher assessment, with the transmitting of information about attainment to several audiences for diverse purposes. Like teacher assessment, record-keeping seldom surfaced as an issue for the policy-makers because it was represented as being something for teachers to decide upon for themselves. But in effect it was in such contexts that teachers found themselves, with little support from the centre, working at the rough edges of the system where its separately designed components rubbed against each other, bringing discomfort and frustration for teachers experiencing the effects of developments whose inconsistencies and ambiguities had not been resolved by the policy-makers.

There were many immediate, practical questions to which teachers needed answers. How much evidence of pupils' work should be retained from teacher assessment for moderators to scrutinize? How do teacher assessment and test results relate to each other? What form should the passing on of information — to parents, LEAs, other schools, SEAC — take? But too often the answers were either not forthcoming or unclear. No-one at the centre seemed to have the time or the inclination to revisit the TGAT model and modify it in the light of experience. If the task belonged anywhere in the structures at national level it was a task for SEAC. But when newly-appointed members, such as Dr. John Marks, challenged some of the TGAT principles, there was little support for a fundamental rethink of policy. Only rarely did SEAC Council and officers engage in dialogue with those assessment specialists outside its staff whose developing critique of national assessment policy was, alongside the more practical criticisms from teachers, gradually eroding that policy's credibility in the eyes of the public as well as among education specialists.

Changes in Policy: 1988–93

Such problems were compounded by changes in policy as successive education ministers considered both the specifics and the broad character of the evolving assessment arrangements. For the first two years following the 1988 Education Act little was done which challenged or changed Kenneth Baker's June 1988 acceptance of the TGAT model. Policy decisions during that period can best be described as a modifying of the TGAT legacy rather than a more fundamental challenge to it. Beyond the gradual emergence of distinct Key Stage variants on the model, the most obvious modifications were in the scale and scope of national assessment. The decision in April 1990 by Baker's successor as Secretary of State for Education, John MacGregor, to restrict the formal testing of 7-year-olds to the core subjects was just one example of the Government adjusting policy as the potential scale (and cost) of the whole national assessment enterprise became apparent. The progressive reduction, year on year, in the time teachers were expected to give to those tests at Key Stage 1 was another example of this gradualist approach to modifying what TGAT had proposed. But until MacGregor was replaced, in November 1990, by Kenneth Clarke, most of the TGAT principles, if not all the details of the Group's proposals, were still to the fore in policy-making.

Clarke's appointment marked the start of a new phase in the evolution of national assessment policy. There was a notable change in style, with the new Minister's characteristically populist rhetoric being frequently reported in a Right-wing press which welcomed his impatience with the failure of the system to date to have the impact its advocates had hoped for. Clarke's decision to discard the TGAT neologism, 'standard assessment task', in favour of the familiar notion of 'test' epitomizes this new phase. But there was substance as well as style in Clarke's contribution to national assessment policy. The Key Stage 3 tests were soon being described as 'examinations' and conducted in a manner much closer to the familiar rituals of public examinations at 16 than the diverse test conditions envisaged by TGAT. That curiously archaic term, 'pencil-and-paper tests', was back in favour and the idea of a 'long task' carried out by pupils under classroom conditions over a period of weeks was retained only in technology and in Welsh. The pilot Key Stage 3 tests in 1991 became a 'lame duck' exercise because by that time the new Secretary of State had made known his intention to introduce a different type of test from 1992. The new tests would have a narrower focus on those attainments which the Government viewed as 'the basics' and would largely take the form of time-limited, unseen written examinations.

Policy on Key Stage 4 (see chapter 6) also felt the full force of the Government's attempt to regain the initiative on issues where many on the Right believed the 'educational establishment' to have taken control of national assessment. The speech delivered to the Centre for Policy Studies by the Prime Minister, John Major, in July 1991 is a significant landmark here, heralding not only the changes in policy on GCSE but also the changes shortly afterwards in the chairmanship of the Government's two main advisory bodies on national curriculum and assessment, NCC and SEAC. During July 1991 the chairmen of both bodies 'resigned' and were replaced by successors whose political sympathies were known to lie to the Right. The appointment of Lord Griffiths, the Centre for Policy Studies' Chairman, to be Chairman of SEAC was a very clear signal of a move to the Right in assessment policy. The interviews Griffiths gave to the press following his appointment offered abundant evidence of the type of advice ministers could expect from that source in future. Decisions on assessment policy were, of course, for the Secretary of State for Education but, from mid-1991, it was clear that Kenneth Clarke and his successor, John Patten, could expect a stronger Right-wing line both from his chief policy adviser and from the Prime Minister. John Major's own strongly-held views on education issues have been revealed both in his speeches and in correspondence (Jarvis, 1993).

A new line on national assessment having been established during 1991, it fell to John Patten, appointed Secretary of State for Education after the General Election in April 1992, to defend that line. He did so enthusiastically and vigorously right up to the point when he had to concede the need for Sir Ron Dearing to undertake a review. To a large extent he inherited the policies that led to the crisis of early 1993 but he was evidently determined not to make concessions, whether on designating the latest version of English testing at Key Stage 3 as a pilot or on the publication of league tables of schools. His predecessor, Kenneth Clarke, had emphasized that his priorities were for written tests, which he hoped would be more reliable whatever the cost might be in terms of validity, and for test results as evidence for judging the comparative performance of schools. Within a year of his appointment as Secretary of State, John Patten had gone from confident disregard of criticism of national assessment policy to the embarrassment of having to concede that there was a case for review. The groundswell of criticism had at first been met with a refusal even to meet teachers' organizations to discuss the many difficulties their members were encountering in implementing the Government's assessment policy. But ministers' tough line of no concessions to the critics actually served to feed opposition to assessment policies on a broad front so that, when Sir Ron Dearing was called in, it was the fundamentals of policy as well as the details which were on the agenda for review.

It is possible that the more conciliatory tone and content of the policy decisions taken by John MacGregor might have retained the support of enough of the teaching profession to avert a crisis. But it is also arguable that his approach too would have foundered when faced with the escalating workload of teachers, the cumulative complexity of the system and the political imperative of maintaining the momentum of change. Moreover, the retention of the policies on national assessment which were in place during MacGregor's time as Secretary of State would undoubtedly have proved unacceptable to many in the Conservative Party, not only to those on the Right of the Party who took a special interest in education policy.

The pace of change, the fragmentation of decision-making and the changes in policy, especially after 1990, all played their part in bringing national assessment to the point where the demand for review was irresistible. But there is also good reason to doubt whether, in a different political world (and in effect an unreal one), a TGAT-guided policy, coherently, consistently and cautiously implemented would have fared much better as the Task Group's ideals were tempered by the realities of implementation.

A Fresh Start in Policy-making?

The Dearing Review of 1993/94 will no doubt prove to be a landmark in the development of a national assessment system. But what kind of a landmark? A beacon guiding National Curriculum and assessment policy towards a new consensus about what was both desirable and attainable? Or a mirage which would give those engaged in designing and implementing the post-Dearing system only the appearance of a clear road ahead?

On the process of change itself, some of the lessons from the initial stages of development of the system had obviously been learned. There was now, following the 1993 Education Act, a single statutory body in England advising the Government on curriculum and assessment policy (and a parallel body for Wales). The inconsistencies resulting from separate subject groups working independently of each other were to be ironed out by a rather different procedure for reviewing the Subject Orders. Subject advisory groups would operate in parallel and be overseen by groups for each Key Stage which would be in a position to identify and deal with avoidable differences in both the style and the substance of the draft revised Subject Orders. Thus, in principle at least, the potential for fragmentation and inconsistency in this new set of 'slimmed down' Curriculum Orders would be reduced.

It was also clear that the voice of the teaching profession, on whom National Curriculum and assessment policy ultimately depended, was at last being listened to. Those invited to participate in the subject advisory groups were mainly classroom teachers and the teacher organizations were regularly consulted by SCAA as the review progressed. The continuing conflict over English and the fact that some of that advisory group's advice was not accepted by the SCAA Council did not significantly detract from the overall feeling that policy-makers were at last consulting the people who knew at first hand the realities of implementing policy decisions.

Policy-making on national assessment had been hampered from the outset by the apparent assumption among many of those closest to ministers that anyone who actually worked in the education system was part of an inherently hostile 'educational establishment'. How else can one explain the fact that only two of the fifteen members of the original *School* Examinations and Assessment Council, appointed by ministers, actually worked in schools? As time went on this climate of hostility towards any criticisms of policy from within the education system grew and the role of statutory advisory bodies as apolitical, non-partisan sources of advice was undermined. In particular, Kenneth Clarke's decisions in 1991 to appoint to the membership and chairmanship of those bodies individuals whose party political allegiances were well known ensured that the bodies they were appointed to could no longer be regarded as in any sense independent of the Government. During 1993 and 1994 some ground had been regained in that education professionals once more began to feel that their opinions mattered to those who were framing policy. But it is worth noting that such a recovery of confidence in the policy-making process was heavily dependent on the reputation of one man, Sir Ron Dearing.

Though steps had been taken to repair the damage caused by fragmentation of decision-making and inadequate consultation with those who would implement policy, another main source of problems in the early years of implementing national assessment, the pace of change, remained. The subject and Key Stage groups which had a central role in developing advice to Dearing were given only three months in which to complete their work. That was a timetable dictated by the Government's wish (shared by many teachers looking for an end to uncertainty) to bring the changes into effect at the earliest possible opportunity. If the Orders were to be in place by September 1995 — the Government's preferred deadline — and there was to be time before that for consultation on the outcomes of the Review, no more than three months could be spared for the groups to do their work. For anyone who saw 'slimming down' and 'simplifying' as being not much more sophisticated than deciding which sections of the pre-existing Orders to delete that would be a reasonable timescale. However, if the groups were to be expected to draw on the experience to date in order to develop slimmer attainment targets and slimmer programmes of study, coherent in themselves and compatible with each other, it was a very tight deadline for them to meet. And if a more radical rethink of the criterial statements was to be undertaken, allowing only three months for the drafting of an untried alternative to statements of attainment would be to ask too much of small groups of specialists meeting for only six days or so in all.

A New Model for National Assessment?

Looking more broadly at what Dearing envisaged as the new framework for national assessment policy, it is not only the risk, in respect of level descriptors, that the system would experience a further phase of experimentation that gave cause for concern. It was the failure in the course of the Review to find workable solutions to the tensions within the system under review.

The declared policy of the Government was that the National Curriculum should be broadly defined. Finding assessment arrangements which did justice to such a broad curriculum remained as problematic as when TGAT had first sought a solution. For the assessment framework itself, simply rearranging the categories, whether the broad ones of attainment targets as subsets of subjects or statements of attainment as sub-sets within the attainment targets, did nothing to resolve the problem of matching the attainments to be assessed to the curriculum as specified. Teacher assessment would not necessarily become any more manageable as a consequence of repackaging the same range of attainments into fewer categories (as teachers of mathematics and science had discovered when those Subject Orders were first reviewed). And testing which took less time and was increasingly expected to be under examination conditions could not, by definition, reflect the whole range of attainments set out in each Order. Sir Ron Dearing might recommend that SCAA should 'continue to simplify the national tests in the core subjects without sacrificing validity and reliability' but in practice such tests would inevitably sacrifice something in validity with each step towards limiting both their length and the contexts in which pupils would be able to demonstrate their attainments.

Another attempt to square the circle is evident in the decision to retain a criterion-referenced base for all elements of the assessment system, including the tests, which would be expected to be reliable enough to deliver both an accurate (if limited) summative picture of the individual's attainment and a dependable performance indicator when those results were aggregated. One paragraph in Dearing's Final Report acknowledges that some had argued that to be 'mission impossible':

> (Their) view is that a criterion-based approach to the measurement of pupil achievement is, whatever its theoretical attractions, in practice extremely difficult to deliver. Those who think this believe that it is the misguided attempt to define unambiguous criteria for the complex processes of teaching and learning which explains many of the difficulties teachers have experienced in teaching the National Curriculum, assessing pupil progress and reporting that progress to parents. They argue that the only sensible way forward is to recognize the enormous difficulty (if not impossibility) of the aim; to abandon any attempt to develop objective criteria for the different levels and, instead, to adopt an approach in which the programmes of study define what has to be taught and simple, standardised tests are used to assess pupils' progress. (para. 7.9)

But that was not to be the conclusion reached by Dearing. He was ready instead to sanction a continuing search for criterial statements which were broad enough to reflect the full curriculum specification, precise and unambiguous enough to be the basis for reliable assessments and few enough in number for them to be manageable for the teacher or test designer.

The relationship between the two sets of procedures which would continue to supply the evidence for attainment to be summarized also remained problematic. The pretence that the tests could do other than provide data for summative and evaluative purposes had been dropped. But 'teacher assessment', the part of the system which would take place day-in day-out, remained an elusive concept. It was what teachers chose to do to make their own independent judgments on their pupils' progress; a potential, though far from inevitable, contributor to the formative and diagnostic purposes of assessment. It was also to be the source of attainment evidence to be reported to parents alongside any available test results. And, beyond that, it would still be expected to fill in the gaps for those aspects of attainment in the core subjects which were not covered by the end-of-stage tests. But how could the justifiably idiosyncratic assessment practices of thousands of teachers be expected to form a reliable enough basis for reporting to parents on the ten-level scale, still less to be used as a part source of data for summative and evaluative uses?

The answer in principle, of course, lay in the moderation of teacher assessments. But no such assessments could be expected to produce reliable attainment data without moderation arrangements which controlled both the tasks set by teachers and the way teachers interpret pupils' responses to those tasks. The national assessment experience of moderation both at Key Stage 1 and Key Stage 3 provided evidence in abundance of the difficulty of achieving at a national level, and at acceptable cost, a degree of consistency across teacher-assessors which was sufficient for there to be confidence in the use of the results from teacher assessment. Perhaps moderation arrangements could exert sufficient influence on teacher assessments for the results obtained to be used as part of the feedback process to a pupil and his/her parent. But would they ensure the degree of consistency which would be expected if teacher assessments were to be aggregated into data used for comparisons between teachers and across schools?

Dearing: A Provisional Verdict

Viewed from soon after publication of the Dearing Final Report and before what it recommended had been translated into specific arrangements and then subjected to the realities of implementation, the Dearing Review appears too deeply flawed in its recommendations on assessment to be a secure basis for future policy. Whether because modification was judged to be preferable politically to more radical change or because some of the weaknesses in the original design had not been fully diagnosed, Dearing has not put forward a new model for national assessment. There are many specific proposals but there is no overview of purposes, practices and outcomes nor a vision of how the many components of the system are expected to interact with each other.

Also, in an important sense, the thinking which underpins Dearing's recommendations remains firmly in the mould of 1987 and 1988. The model which informed the first five years of national assessment can be seen as a heady cocktail produced by mixing the educational idealism of TGAT and the political radicalism of a Government which viewed National Curriculum and assessment as just one element in bringing about fundamental changes to the education system. The Dearing Review had not scaled down the ambitiousness of the enterprise; it had modified only the means by which it was hoped those ambitions will be realized. Like TGAT and Kenneth Baker, Dearing was remarkably optimistic about what a national assessment policy might achieve. Though the number of attainment targets, the time taken in testing and the amount of teacher assessment had all been scaled down, the system Dearing envisaged was as ambitious in its goals as TGAT was at a time when there was no evidence from implementation to temper that optimism.

To take perhaps the most telling example, the chapter in Dearing's Final Report which, on balance, recommended the retention of the ten-level scale begins with this statement:

The objective is to provide a framework for assessing achievement which:

- offers a clear statement of progression in each National Curriculum subject;
- encourages differentiation of work so that pupils of all abilities are fully stretched;
- provides an easily intelligible means of reporting pupil achievement to parents, teachers and pupils;
- is manageable in the classroom;
- helps to inform parents when deciding on a school for their child;
- helps teachers, parents, governors and society as a whole to assess the achievement of individual schools and the education system generally. (para. 7.1)

The most fundamental question of all, unasked and therefore unanswered in the course of the Review, remains whether *any* system of defining, measuring, recording and reporting attainment, operating at a national scale, can hope to serve all those purposes. The tensions inherent in a multipurpose system, underplayed by TGAT, had been behind so much of the conflict on specific issues which had characterized the first five years of the national assessment system. Could a single framework and one set of assessment procedures really be as useful as an aid to children's learning as they were for supplying data for published indicators with which to compare schools? Could these and other purposes really be met without the processes contributing to one type of outcome proving incompatible with those appropriate for another?

It is at this level of the purposes informing practice that serious fault can be found with the Dearing Review. In the short term it was undoubtedly a triumph politically, retrieving a situation in which the Government had seemed to have lost control over National Curriculum and assessment policy. Many more schools participated in the 1994 tests than did so in 1993 with the School Curriculum and Assessment Authority estimating that the Key Stage 3 tests were used in about half of all schools (though only 29 per cent reported their results). A year after Dearing's appointment, confidence in national assessment policy, though fragile, had been restored to an unlikely extent in the eyes of the public and even of many teachers. Education was no longer at the top of the list of the policies in which an unpopular government was seen to be failing.

But if evidence were needed that Dearing's year-long review and two reports had left many fundamental questions unresolved it was there in abundance in the period leading up to publication, in the autumn of 1994, of a new set of National Curriculum Orders. During the month of July, often favoured by ministers as the time of year to pull policy rabbits out of well-concealed hats, several Government initiatives emerged which reopened issues which most observers thought had been settled by Dearing.

The draft of proposed assessment and testing arrangements in England and Wales for 1995, released on 1 July, offered some confirmation of previously reported policy decisions. For example, regulations would require schools to publish national assessment results in their prospectuses and in governors' annual reports but, in 1995, there would be no published performance tables for Key Stages 1, 2 and 3. Only for Key Stages 2 and 4 were such tables still on the agenda and the former would be published only when the tests were 'established'.

Yet the same July 1994 consultation document also contained radical new measures. Dearing had made much of teacher assessment having 'equal status' with the tests and his Interim Report had referred to moderated teacher assessment as a 'central part of any system of assessment' (para. 5.20). The Government, twelve months later, now proposed abandoning all statutory moderation ('external audit') of teacher assessments at Key Stage 1 and discontinuing the central funding for the associated training of teachers and moderators. The Secretaries of State (for Education and Wales) rather lamely expressed the hope that local moderation arrangements would still continue. What price the supposed equal status of teacher assessment when even less central support than before would be given to ensuring that it played its part in the national system?

The second radical change now proposed was the return of the idea of external marking of tests, something many observers thought Dearing had looked at and rejected, though in fact his Interim Report had been more equivocal:

> Given . . . the divided views among teachers on the merits of external marking and the resource considerations, I hesitate to make a recommendation other than to advise against attempting external marking for both Key Stage 2 and Key Stage 3 in 1994. (Dearing, 1993a, para. 5.43)

In the July 1994 proposals ministers were now recommending that 'in 1995 and subsequent years, tests for 11 and 14-year-olds should be marked by agencies working under contract'. Ever since TGAT had established assessment by teachers as a defining principle of its model, the benefits to the teacher and to the learner of the work a pupil had done being marked by his/

her own teacher had remained a central feature of national assessment. Even when standard assessment tasks had become tests and had changed their character, they were still marked in the schools by teachers. Now it seemed, in the face of a continuing dispute with some teacher unions about teacher workload and the political necessity of finding a way of ending the teacher boycott of testing, there would no longer be any official pretence that the tests could reveal something of value to the teacher. In the increasingly bizarre politics of national assessment, some of the teachers whose excessive workload in assessing their own pupils had precipitated the 1993 boycott would, in 1995, be paid to mark the work of pupils of other teachers in their spare time.

This new detour along the already tortuous route towards implementing national assessment proved to be one of the last policy decisions of the by-now beleaguered Secretary of State for Education John Patten. Deciding where to go next would be for his successor, appointed in a Cabinet reshuffle in July 1994, Gillian Shephard.

Conclusion

In 1987 and 1988, Secretary of State Kenneth Baker had needed all his political skills to steer the early course of National Curriculum and assessment policy from the consultation paper of July 1987 through the Education Reform Bill to the 1988 Act and all that followed. He had faced strong opposition, in particular on the policy for assessment, from influential elements in the Conservative Party, from the overwhelming majority of teacher opinion and even from his own Prime Minister.

It is salutary to look back at the kind of national assessment system Baker had portrayed in April 1987 when making the formal announcement of the Government's intention to legislate (see page 13). 'We do not want teachers to teach only what is testable'; 'it will be essential to assess work done in the class'; the tests and assessments 'would fall to teachers but each would be externally moderated'. What had happened to what at the time had appeared to be carefully created common ground between the Government and the teaching profession, a common ground which TGAT was to turn into a design brief for the system?

Seven years later, in the wake of the Dearing Review, opposition to the modified policy on national assessment was, if anything, more firmly entrenched and the system itself was only in the early stages of recuperating from its near collapse in 1993. The fact that more schools were now using the tests must have encouraged ministers but the idea of 'national tests' could have little meaning if, even in a better year, only 29 per cent of schools (Key Stage 3) were reporting the results. Criticisms of the system were still being voiced from all sides and the critics were now able to justify their case with evidence from the system in operation. While the National Union of Teachers confirmed its hostility to testing and to league tables, critics on the Right (for example: Lawlor 1993; Marenbom 1993; Marks, 1993) were far from satisfied with Dearing and argued for a system focused on testing and school performance tables.

That so many essential features of national assessment had still to be defined in a way which was both clearly understood and practicable was a sad reflection on the national assessment policies of successive governments and on the process of policy-making. What form should national tests take and which attainments should they attempt to measure? Where does the assessing done day-in day-out by teachers fit into the national picture, if at all? How much effort and resources should be put in to training for, and moderating of, teacher assessments? To what use or uses should the evidence, obtained from teacher assessment and/or the tests, be put? The Secondary Examinations Council had commented in response to the 1987 consultation document: 'it is not clear who is to act on the information generated'. Was the answer any clearer in 1994 after seven years of development? Was national assessment policy to provide the information about individuals on which pupil, parent and teacher could act, so that the learning of those individual pupils was enhanced? Or was it, as it seemed to have become in a world of league tables and parents choosing schools, more a source of aggregate performance data in the move towards a particular form of accountability for state-maintained schools? That it could not expect to be equally successful in meeting both sets of objectives had become obvious even to those who had not pointed out at the beginning that one system could not be expected to serve several distinct purposes.

The Task Group on Assessment and Testing had been the first to propose a coherent model for national assessment. Since Christmas Eve 1987, when the Group presented its report, four Secretaries of State for Education had received advice from statutory bodies, from National Curriculum Working Groups, from civil servants and from their own political advisers. Latterly they had been forced to take fuller account of the experience of the teachers who were trying to implement policy decisions. And yet at no time did the policy-makers or their advisers lift their sights from short-term pragmatic decisions about the particular issues of the moment and consider taking a fresh look at the whole picture of purposes as well as practices. Even the man charged with reviewing the system, Sir Ron Dearing, stayed with the second-level questions of how to improve the system's administration, how to 'simplify' testing and whether to retain the ten-level scale.

As the post-Dearing system moved off the drawing board and into the early stages of implementation, the Government faced the difficult prospect of finding both a clear enough model for national assessment and a broad enough base politically on which to build the foundations of a viable national assessment system.

References

BALL, S. (1990) *Politics and Policy Making in Education*, London, Routledge.

BASH, L. and COULBY, D. (Eds) (1989) *The Education Reform Act: Competition and Control*, London, Cassell.

BLACK, P. *et al.* (1992) *Education: Putting the Record Straight*, Stafford, Network Educational Press.

BLACK, P. (1993) 'The shifting scenery of the National Curriculum', in O'HEAR, P. and WHITE, J. (Eds) *Assessing the National Curriculum*, London, Paul Chapman, pp. 57–69.

BROADFOOT, P. *et al.* (1992) *Policy Issues in National Assessment*, Clevedon, Multilingual Matters.

BROWN, M. (1991) 'Problematic issues in national assessment', *Cambridge Journal of Education*, **21**, 2, pp. 215–29.

BROWN, S. (1981) *What Do They Know? A Review of Criterion-referenced Assessment*, Edinburgh, HMSO.

CAMPBELL, J. and NEILL, S. (1994) *Curriculum Reform at Key Stage 1: Teacher Commitment and Policy Failure*, Harlow, Longman.

CURRICULUM COUNCIL FOR WALES (1993a) *The National Curriculum and Assessment Framework in Wales: Interim Report*, Cardiff, CCW.

CURRICULUM COUNCIL FOR WALES (1993b) *The National Curriculum and Assessment Framework in Wales: Final Report*, Cardiff, CCW.

DEARING, R. (1993a) *The National Curriculum and its Assessment: Interim Report*, London, National Curriculum Council/School Examinations and Assessment Council.

DEARING, R. (1993b) *The National Curriculum and its Assessment: Final Report*. London, School Curriculum and Assessment Authority.

DEPARTMENT OF EDUCATION AND SCIENCE (1977) *Education in Schools: A Consultative Document*, London, HMSO.

DEPARTMENT OF EDUCATION AND SCIENCE/WELSH OFFICE (1980) *A Framework for the School Curriculum*, London, DES/WO.

DEPARTMENT OF EDUCATION AND SCIENCE/WELSH OFFICE (1984) *Records of Achievement: A Statement of Policy*, London, DES/WO.

DEPARTMENT OF EDUCATION AND SCIENCE/WELSH OFFICE (1985a) *General Certificate of Secondary Education: The National Criteria*, London, DES/WO.

DEPARTMENT OF EDUCATION AND SCIENCE/WELSH OFFICE (1985b) *Better Schools*, London, HMSO.

DEPARTMENT OF EDUCATION AND SCIENCE/WELSH OFFICE (1987) *The National Curriculum 5–16: A Consultation Document*, London, DES/WO.

DEPARTMENT OF EDUCATION AND SCIENCE/WELSH OFFICE (1988a) *National Curriculum Task Group on Assessment and Testing: A Report*, London, DES/WO.

DEPARTMENT OF EDUCATION AND SCIENCE/WELSH OFFICE (1988b) *National Curriculum Task Group on Assessment and Testing: Three Supplementary Reports*, London, DES/WO.

DEPARTMENT OF EDUCATION AND SCIENCE/WELSH OFFICE (1989) *Report of the Records of Achievement National Steering Committee*, London, DES/WO.

DEPARTMENT OF EDUCATION AND SCIENCE (1991) *Education: A Charter for Parents*, London, DES.

DEPARTMENT FOR EDUCATION/WELSH OFFICE (1992) *Choice and Diversity: A New Framework for Schools*, London, HMSO.

FLUDE, M. and HAMMER, M. (Eds) (1989) *The Education Reform Act 1988: Its Origins and Implications*, London, Falmer Press.

GIPPS, C. (Ed) (1986) *The GCSE: An Uncommon Examination*, London, Institute of Education.

GIPPS, C. (1988) 'The TGAT Report: Trick or treat', *Forum*, **31**, 1, pp. 4–6.

GIPPS, C. (Ed) (1992a) *Developing Assessment for the National Curriculum*, London, Kogan Page.

GIPPS, C. (1992b) 'National Curriculum assessment: A research agenda', *British Educational Research Journal*, **18**, 3, pp. 277–86.

GIPPS, C. (1994) *Beyond Testing: Towards a Theory of Educational Assessment*, London, Falmer Press.

GIPPS, C. and STOBART, G. (1993) *Assessment: A Teacher's Guide to the Issues*, London, Falmer Press.

GRAHAM, D. (1992) *A Lesson for Us All: The Making of the National Curriculum*, London, Routledge.

HARLEN, W. *et al.* (1992) 'Assessment and the improvement of education', *The Curriculum Journal*, **3**, 3, pp. 215–30.

HARLEN, W. (Ed) (1994) *Enhancing Quality in Assessment*, London, Paul Chapman.

HARLEN, W. and QUALTER, A. (1991) 'Issues in SAT development and the practice of teacher assessment', *Cambridge Journal of Education*, **21**, 2, pp. 141–51.

HAVILAND, J. (1988) *Take Care, Mr. Baker!*, London, Fourth Estate.

HMI (1977) *Curriculum 11–16*, London, HMSO.

HMI (1980) *A View of the Curriculum*, London, HMSO.

HMI (1985) *The Curriculum from 5 to 16*, London, HMSO.

HMI (1988) *The Introduction of the General Certificate of Secondary Education in Schools, 1986–88*, London, DES.

HMI (1992) *Assessment, Recording and Reporting: A Report by HMI on the Second Year, 1990–91*, London, HMSO.

HMI (1994) *Assessment, Recording and Reporting at Key Stages 1, 2 and 3: Fourth Year 1992–93*, London, OFSTED.

HILLGATE GROUP (1987) *The Reform of British Education*, London, Claridge Press.

HORTON, T. (Ed) (1986) *GCSE: Examining the New System*, London, Harper and Row.

JAMES, M. (1993) 'Evaluation for policy: Rationality and political reality: The Paradigm Case of PRAISE', in BURGESS, R. (Ed) *Educational Research and Evaluation: for Policy and Practice?*, London, Falmer Press.

JAMES, M. and CONNER, C. (1993) 'Are reliability and validity achievable in National Curriculum assessment? Some observations on moderation at Key Stage 1 in 1992', *The Curriculum Journal*, **4**, 1, pp. 5–19.

JARVIS, F. (1993) *Education and Mr. Major*, London, Tufnell Press.

JONES, G. (1994) 'Which nation's curriculum? — The case of Wales', *The Curriculum Journal*, **5**, 1, pp. 5–16.

KELLY, A. (1989) *The National Curriculum: A Critical Review*, London, Paul Chapman.

KINGDON, M. and STOBART, G. (1988) *GCSE Examined*, Lewes, Falmer Press.

KNIGHT, C. (1990) *The Making of Tory Education Policy in Post-War Britain*, London, Falmer Press.

LAWLOR, S. (Ed) (1993) *The Dearing Debate: Assessment and the National Curriculum*, London, Centre for Policy Studies.

LAWTON, D. (Ed) (1989) *The Education Reform Act: Choice and Control*, Sevenoaks, Hodder and Stoughton.

LAWTON, D. (1992) *Education and Politics in the 1990s: Conflict or Consensus?*, London, Falmer Press.

McCALLUM, B. *et al.* (1983) 'Teacher assessment at Key Stage One', *Research Papers in Education*, **8**, 3, pp. 305–26.

MACLURE, S. (1989) *Education Re-formed: A Guide to the Education Reform Act 1988*, Sevenoaks, Hodder and Stoughton.

MARENBON, J. (1993) *Testing Time: The Dearing Review and the Future of the National Curriculum*, London, Centre for Policy Studies.

MARKS, J. (1991) *Standards in Schools: Assessment, Accountability and the Purposes of Education*, London, The Social Market Foundation.

MARKS, J. (1993) *Why There is No Time to Teach: What is Wrong with the National Curriculum 10-level Scale*, London, The Social Market Foundation.

MOON, B. and MORTIMORE, P. (1989) *The National Curriculum: Straightjadcet or Safety Net?*, London, Educational Reform Group.

MOON, B. *et al.* (1989) *Policies for the Curriculum*, Sevenoaks, Hodder and Stoughton.

MURPHY, P. (1989) 'TGAT: A conflict of purpose', *Curriculum*, **9**, 3, pp. 152–8.

MURPHY, R. (1986) 'The emperor has no clothes: Grade criteria and the GCSE', in GIPPS, C. (Ed) *The GCSE: An Uncommon Examination*, London, Institute of Education, pp. 43–54.

MURPHY, R. (1987) 'Assessing a national curriculum', *Journal of Education Policy*, **2**, 4, pp. 317–23.

MURPHY, R. (1989) 'National assessment proposals: Analyzing the debate', in FLUDE, M. and HAMMER, M. (Eds) *The Education Reform Act 1988: Its Origins and Implications*, London, Falmer Press, pp. 37–49.

NORTH, J. (Ed) (1987) *The GCSE: An Examination*, London, Claridge Press.

O'HEAR, P. and WHITE, J. (Eds) (1993) *Assessing the National Curriculum*, London, Paul Chapman.

ORR, L. and NUTTALL, D. (1983) *Determining Standards in the Proposed System of Examining at 16+, Comparability in Examinations: Occasional Paper 2*, London, Schools Council.

POLLARD, A. *et al.* (1994) *Changing English Primary Schools: The Impact of the Education Reform Act at Key Stage 1*, London, Cassell.

PRING, R. (1989) *The New Curriculum*, London, Cassell.

SCHOOL EXAMINATIONS AND ASSESSMENT COUNCIL (1990a) *National Curriculum Assessment (Key Stage 1): Responsibilities of LEAs in 1990/91*, London, SEAC.

SCHOOL EXAMINATIONS AND ASSESSMENT COUNCIL (1990b) *A Guide to Teacher Assessment: Packs A, B and C*, London, SEAC.

SCHOOL EXAMINATIONS AND ASSESSMENT COUNCIL (1991a) *A Report on Teacher Assessment by the NFER/BGC Consortium*, London, SEAC.

SCHOOL EXAMINATIONS AND ASSESSMENT COUNCIL (1991b) *National Curriculum Assessment (Key Stage 1): A Moderator's Handbook 1991/92*, London, SEAC.

SCHOOL EXAMINATIONS AND ASSESSMENT COUNCIL (1992) *Teacher Assessment in Mathematics and Science at Key Stage 3*, London, SEAC.

SEXTON, S. (1987) *Our Schools — A Radical Policy*, London, Institute for Economic Affairs.

SHORROCKS, D. *et al.* (1993) *Implementing National Assessment in the Primary School*, London, Falmer Press.

SIMON, B. (1988) *Bending the Rules: The Baker 'Reform' of Education*, London, Lawrence and Wishart.

STOBART, G. (1991) 'GCSE meets Key Stage 4: Something had to give', *Cambridge Journal of Education*, **21**, 2, pp. 177–88.

TORRANCE, H. (1988) *National Assessment and Testing: A Research Response*, London, British Educational Research Association.

TROMAN, G. (1989) 'Testing tensions: The politics of educational assessment', *British Educational Research Journal*, **15**, 3, pp. 279–95.

WILIAM, D. (1993) 'Validity, dependability and reliability in National Curriculum assessment', *The Curriculum Journal*, **4**, 3, pp. 335–50.

WILIAM, D. (1994) 'Creating matched National Curriculum assessments in English and Welsh: Test translation and parallel development', *The Curriculum Journal*, **5**, 3, pp. 17–29.

WILLIAMS, I. *et al.* (1994) *Evaluation of the National Curriculum Assessment of Welsh and Welsh as a Second Language*, London, School Curriculum and Assessment Authority.

WOLF, A. (1993) *Assessment Issues and Problems in a Criterion-based System*, London, Further Education Unit.

Index